Memory, Oblivion, and Jewish Culture in Latin America

Memory, Oblivion, and Jewish Culture in Latin America

EDITED BY MARJORIE AGOSÍN

University of Texas Press   AUSTIN

Requests for permission to reproduce material from this work should
be sent to Permissions, University of Texas Press, P.O. Box 7819,
Austin, TX 78713-7819.

∞ The paper used in this book meets the minimum requirements of
ANSI/NISO z39.48-1992 (R1997) (Permanence of Paper).

LIBRARY OF CONGRESS CATALOGING-IN-PUBLICATION DATA

Memory, oblivion, and Jewish culture in Latin America / edited by
Marjorie Agosín— 1st ed.
    p.   cm.
Includes bibliographical references and index.
ISBN 0-292-70643-x (cloth : alk. paper) —
ISBN 0-292-70667-7 (pbk. : alk. paper)
1. Jews—Latin America—History.   2. Sephardim—Latin America—
History.   3. Jews—Latin America—Social life and customs.   4. Jews—
Latin America—Personal narratives.   5. Jews—Latin America—Social
conditions.   6. Latin America—Ethnic relations.   I. Agosín, Marjorie.
F1419.J4M46   2005
980'.004924—dc22

                                                    2004025995

*To the memory of the Jewish-Spanish communities
that were exiled from Spain and traveled to the
New World with their hopes and their songs.*

*To my grandmother, Josefina Agosín Halpern,
who always wondered if life was good or bad for the Jews.*

*And to Luisa Smirnoff, who
believed in hope.*

Contents

Acknowledgments

During the past two decades, an extensive corpus of literature and visual expression devoted to Jewish life in the Americas has been an essential component of research and reflection. The Jews in Latin America are no longer an "invisible minority" thanks to the courage and commitment of scholars, writers, and artists who have incorporated Jewish life into their work as well as their private lives. I thank each of them for inspiring me to follow in their footsteps. This collection encompasses the discoveries and revelations of others as we venture together in this important and too often neglected history of the Americas.

I am particularly grateful to my colleagues who are also friends and people of great integrity. In these politically charged times that have provoked increased intolerance to otherness and in the face of the resurgence of anti-Semitism in Europe and the United States, the willingness of my dear friends to listen and support me is especially gratifying. It is impossible to thank them all, but I would like to name a few: Adina Cimet, Betty Jean Craige, Celeste K. Cooperman, Bapsi Sidwa, Paul Roth, Silvia Berger, Rabbi Donald Weiss, Laura and Paul Nakazawa, Ruth Behar, Isabel Borland, Emma Sepúlveda, Barbara Mujica, and Rebecca Leavitt.

I also thank my family for the love and support that they have always given me: my two children, Joseph and Sonia, whose joy and hope allow me to believe in the world; my husband, who has always provided calmness and love; my parents, who are the tree of my life that sustains me and gives me roots. I am grateful for their presence in my life.

I thank Theresa May for her constant belief in my work, and Lynne Chapman and Sheila Berg for helping me through the final stages of this project. My former student, Monica Bruno, who is now a translator and editor extraordinaire, deserves more than an acknowledgment. Her superb work reflects her commitment to excellence and sensitivity of spirit. I am deeply grateful to her.

Introduction

I grew up in Valparaíso, Chile, the port city to which most of my family emigrated from eastern Europe and Russia and where my family has lived for four generations; they married, had children, and helped build the first Jewish community there, beginning with a school and a burial society. But most of all, they created a sense of home and permanence in this very impermanent world, especially for Jews.

It was in my earliest years that I developed a passion to tell stories and to listen to others weave their tales. We used to gather at the table, and the after-dinner conversation would revolve around magnificent and fantastic journeys, some historically accurate and others wildly imaginative. The delicate balance between truth and imagination was rarely maintained, but what really mattered were the stories and the gatherings at which they were heard.

It started first in the 1920s with a benevolent patriarch, Joseph Halpern, who fell in love with a cabaret dancer in Vienna. This dangerous alliance, according to my great-grandmother Helena, allowed Joseph to undertake perhaps the most important and adventurous journey of his life, which would lead him to the safety of Chile. After looking at an old map, Joseph decided to disembark at the end of the world—Valparaíso, Chile.

My maternal great-grandmother, Helena, and her handsome son, Mauricio, arrived in Chile from Vienna in 1939. Mauricio grew up to be a magnate and married into the Chilean aristocracy, the Montecinos, converts who continue to hide their Jewish roots. My paternal grandparents came from Odessa, walked to Istanbul, and set sail from Marseilles to the port of Valparaíso. My great-grandmother Sonia truly understood the meaning of impermanence and uncertain journeys. But all of my grandparents used to have suitcases packed and ready, and when news came, they would ask themselves if this was good or bad for the Jews. I have come to believe that some things are good and some are bad for the Jews as well as for everyone else.

These stories, told around the dinner table throughout my childhood, adolescence, and adulthood, became symbolic of our identity. The gene-alogies of our voyages and the passion to tell them in a way made all of us sophisticated storytellers who told stories to save our memories and to reaffirm the power of our shared humanity through words.

Judaism meant not only belonging to a religion but also to an intense culture of vibrant voices, despite the countless times these voices were silenced, sometimes forever, because they were Jewish. At home, many people visited us: Russian Jews who taught us how to make borscht; ele-gant eastern Europeans who made blue cabbage, which they told me was a magical food. I was taught the culture of the Sephardim, from their *burre-kas,* songs brought from ancient Sepharad, modern-day Spain, that spoke of nostalgic love and a fervent longing to return.

I remember whistling the song "Adio Kerida" on my way to school. It is a melodic and nostalgic song about unrequited love and loss. I have come to realize that this song also evokes the loss of a country and the pain of displacement, like Ruth Behar's film on Cuban Jewry that is dis-cussed in this collection. Her film bears the same name as the nostalgic song that I used to whistle. In making this film, Behar returns to an almost imagined land, the land of childhood, and reclaims the losses that are also journeys symbolic of those who died in the Diaspora.

This volume bears the passion of storytelling from the diverse Jew-ish communities of the Americas. It presents both the collective history of Jewish life in the Americas and stories of personal voyages of immigra-tion and fortitude. It speaks about how a daughter of Holocaust survivors overheard in Buenos Aires that the Holocaust never took place and about a film by a Cuban American anthropologist-poet-filmmaker that records the memories of others living in Cuba and at the same time allows the filmmaker to take ownership of her own memories.

There are essays on Jewish humor in Latin America and how this hu-mor has amalgamated histories of the past and present. And there are serious concerns as well: the presence of the Nazis in southern Chile, the persecution of Jews during the military dictatorships in Argentina, and the divided Jewish community in Chile over the controversial figure of the Chilean dictator Augusto Pinochet. Many Jews left the country during the presidency of Salvador Allende and returned during the dictatorship of

Pinochet because they felt safe under his government. And yet another wave of migrations and immigrations took place when Pinochet came to power, when members of the Jewish community feared persecution under fascist rule.

It is my hope that *Memory, Oblivion, and Jewish Culture in Latin America* will enable an engagement with this Jewish Latin American culture — that it will bring understanding of its roots, its shortcomings, and its accomplishments and occasion an examination of this dual sense of belonging to the People of the Book and to society at large. But most of all, I would like to establish the understanding that from the past of this suffering people a future was and continues to be forged.

The past was a tortuous path for the Jewish communities since Christopher Columbus's arrival at Santo Domingo, and the path continues to be so in contemporary times. The contributors to this volume address the ways in which governments and individual citizens have responded to the presence of Jews in their own countries and in their own spirits. For the past decade, the Jewish presence has received attention in academic circles and has been incorporated into official historiographies. I believe this recognition, although a very tardy one, has been of extraordinary significance to the field of Latin American studies. I also believe that this book moves further in demonstrating that the Jewish experience is not isolated but encompasses the history of Jewish Spain, the expulsion and the voyage of Columbus, as well as the histories of world migrations after the first and second world wars. This is an ambitious collection that encompasses generations of people and their tenacious pursuit of survival as well as their taking roots in landscapes, languages, and religions. This undertaking has made the Jewish presence in Latin America fascinating both in its power to survive despite an often hostile Catholic church and in its ability to acculturate without losing its traditions.

This is why this collection begins with Sepharad, a place of promise, of hope, as well as the central metaphor for exile and displacement of the Jewish community since their expulsion from Spain in 1492. Though Jewish communities have existed practically throughout the world, historians consider the Spanish Diaspora one of the most fundamental and destructive moments in Jewish history. The Jews of Sepharad became the Jews of Latin America who preserved the Judeo-Spanish in many variations; they felt at home with Spanish and wrote in it. Many poets, from Rilke to Milozh, have said that the only true homeland is language. And all those who escaped persecution and landed in the New World infused Spanish with traces of Ladino; some, in Argentina, for example, continued to speak

Yiddish and created newspapers and plays in this language so that it would not disappear.

While I write these comments, on the shores of Valparaíso the lights seem to grow in the dancing hills where Joseph Halpern arrived, then Helena, then my grandmother from Buenos Aires who crossed the Andes on a mule. All these generations later, I am still listening to the after-dinner stories, now retelling my own stories for my children and taking them to the recently erected one-room Jewish museum in Valparaíso where photographs of my great-grandparents grace the entrance. These photographs inspire and accord recognition to Jewish life in Latin America, which implies always being from somewhere else or always being in transit. Theirs is a life that is even more vibrant, eloquent, and complex because it has survived. Today there are half a million Spanish- and Portuguese-speaking Jews.

The complex and multifaceted history of the Jewish people of Latin America leaves many questions to be asked, ranging from the most basic details of the Jews' first arrival in America to the ways in which they established themselves in their new societies. The synagogues of the first Jewish settlers in the Caribbean are still in use. The synagogue in Curaçao still has sand floors, representative of the times when Jews had to keep very silent when praying so as not to be discovered by the Inquisition. Today the synagogue in Recife is being reconstructed; it is a symbol of the promise and revival of Jewish life in the Americas.

Despite the very small size of most of the Jewish communities in the region, there is a resurgence of Jewish life and expression through literature, movies, food, and music. These contributions have not yet captured the liveliness of Jewish life, however, in communities where the Jewish presence is quite large, such as in Buenos Aires and Rio de Janeiro. Jewish culture and the Jewish people continue to be seen as the other, as a foreign minority, as a marginalized group exemplified by its differences from other communities of immigrants. The past few decades have witnessed an increase in discrimination against them, such as the anti-Semitism manifested during the Argentine dictatorship. This anti-Semitism survives today in laws prohibiting Jews from becoming president or from serving in the armed forces; these rights are reserved only for Catholics. The poignant testimony of the distinguished Argentine journalist Jacobo Timerman in his book *Prisoner Without a Name, Cell Without a Number,* which describes his imprisonment and mistreatment, exemplifies the conditions of the Jews, especially during the 1970s, and the impossibility of living as both Jew and Argentine. These conditions culminated in terrorist attacks on the Jewish community, the deaths of thousands, and the destruction of books, classrooms, and the heart of the communities.

In Chile in 2002, the government allowed a meeting of the Nazi Congress (it drew fewer than ten participants). The recent dictatorships of the Southern Cone have contributed to the increase in anti-Semitism manifested in the conspiracy theory propaganda linking the Jewish presence in Latin America to Zionism and the oppression of the Palestinian people.

This collection should be seen as a rehearsal and an exploration of the history of Jews in the Americas and as an introspective meditation about what it has meant to be Jewish in a Catholic society. We analyze the politics of identity and how they are forged, negotiated, and integrated. We explore history's subjectivity, its subtleties and hues. One of the key questions that the authors in this collection explore is how the immigrant's previous culture intersects with his or her immigration experience. All minority groups analyze the clues to their own identities. They must delve deeply into the gestures of absence and presence, inventing survival strategies, but at the same time, they must be able to express their own histories with their own uncertain travels, ambiguous integrations, and promising futures. Each author in this collection has a vision of Jewish culture in Latin America from a personal and collective experience, allowing both their experiences as Jewish individuals and the fact that they were Jews in history to speak.

When I began to assemble this collection, I wanted to bring forth in particular the vibrancy, passion, and multifaceted perspectives found in Jewish life in the Americas. I wanted to showcase how this ancient culture allows for the possibility of change and innovation and how we can work from a tradition that has achieved plurality and has embraced a sense of community in spite of its diverseness.

A handful of anthologies published in the past decade have explored the Jewish presence in Latin America. Many of them focus on specific Jewish communities. The Argentine community has probably received the most attention. Edna Aizenberg's *Books and Bombs in Buenos Aires*, for example, explores the history of Argentina through a meditation on Jewish writing from Gerchunoff to Borges.

The uniqueness of *Memory, Oblivion, and Jewish Culture in Latin America* resides in its communal and cohesive vision of the Jewish world as the center of a diasporic and fragmented existence that is able to transcend persecution and displacement in order to re-create a new sense of being and existing in the world. Thus, these essays must be read as if we were immersed in a passionate voyage whose inner journey begins with

Sepharad and the expulsion of the Jews in 1492. The essays by Reyes Coll-Tellechea and Angelina Muñiz Huberman are reflections on exile, language, and loss, but also on the reconstruction of what is vanished and comes alive. I believe that the Jewish Diaspora is a new phenomenon in Latin American history unlike any other, especially from the point of view of language and the preservation of Ladino and Spanish cultures through all these journeys.

The Jewish presence in Latin America must be seen as an evolutionary process that encompasses the historical, political, and cultural. By the end of the twentieth century, it emerged with its own autonomous and original voice. In the 1990s, when Spain established relations with Israel that had been abruptly halted during the Franco regime and when the first few synagogues in Madrid and Barcelona reopened, writers such as Carmen Reiría and Angelina Muñiz Huberman began to write about Jewish characters. Muñiz Huberman, in particular, is a Spanish-Mexican Jew who writes about the marvelous and mysterious Merchant of Tudela as well as the life of the Spanish conversos living in Mexico. Thus, history and memory are reconciled.

The nexus for this history and the essays in this volume is Spain. We assume that memory, politics, and the way in which politics have arbitrarily tried to silence certain parts of national histories are inseparable. There has been a continuous and systematic history of oppression, punishment, and secrecy. I say "secrecy" because it is not until recently that we have begun to discuss more openly the complex relationship between the Spanish Jews and the Spanish government, as well as the fact that Spain did not recognize the state of Israel until 1986.

These challenging essays ask overall what the Jewish identity in Latin America is, how it changes through time, how Jews exist or do not exist in the hyphens. And they leave a lingering question: Does being Jewish speak to a transitory history or a more permanent one in the Americas?

This anthology begins at an essential historical moment — the exile of the Jewish community from Sepharad to the New World. Reyes Coll-Tellechea's essay provides the framework for the volume. It is a meditation on the historical silence of Spain regarding the Jewish expulsion five hundred years ago, a historical expulsion that is beginning to be studied with great interest. Coll-Tellechea wonders whether the expulsion was exclusively anti-Jewish or a way to seek political unity and poses necessary questions: Why the silence? Why the delay in recognizing the Israeli state? Why the tenacity of the Sepharad Jews and the new Sephardic Jews who write in Spanish and try to keep alive their musical traditions so they can always belong to the Sepharad? She also leads us to reflect on the ways in which society deals with and understands the past and how other Spanish writers are reclaiming it through fictional stories that reach into the historical past.

A possible answer to the various questions raised by Coll-Tellechea can be found in the essay by the Mexican writer Angelina Muñiz Huberman, whose ancestry is Spanish and whose family became part of the history of the conversos. She picks up where Coll-Tellechea leaves off with regard to the situation of converted Jews. She questions how it was possible to eradicate a powerful and vigorous Sephardic community in Spain that had lasted for more than fourteen centuries and which was silenced by the Inquisition and the collective humiliation of the autos-da-fe. She postulates a fundamental idea that appears throughout these essays: the tenacious desire to keep the Sephardic tongue alive. For Muñiz Huberman, the perseverance of the Sephardic language—from the Middle Ages to the writings of Maimonedes to the texts of de Leon, Baruch Spinoza, and Elias Canetti—is tied to a legacy that goes beyond language; it assumes an identity, a way of life that accepts faith and the surrounding world. According to Muñiz Huberman, Sephardic also found refuge in colonial Mexico as a living language that explores the Jewish feelings of the Diaspora through modern-day literature, including her own work. She suggests that although the Jews were expelled from Spain, the Sephardic language has had continuous rebirths and has found living legacies.

Because the Diaspora and constant voyages to uncertain territories are part of Jewish history, one must consider the points of arrival, entry ports, which were often difficult and unsafe to enter, as well as the points of departure. These stories of arrival represent a living history of people in perpetual search of a home. The essays by David Brailovsky and Murray Baumgarten conjure a serene aspect that speaks of an origin that is then reconstructed and transformed into presence. Their arrivals conjure up two different ports, Valparaíso and Colón, and two different points of departure, Shanghai and Berlin. What is important is that the arrivals are points of contact between a somber past that annihilates the possibility of human life and the present—a constant stream of changing memories. Baumgarten's essay can be seen as an inconclusive geography of moments in the past, of uncertain presents where memory reigns, where the Caribbean Sea is confused with Europe and Israel. For both Brailovsky and Baumgarten, the promised land is Latin America, which offers refuge but, more important, allows them to recover their memories.

The historian Sandra McGee Deutsch takes us on a personal journey regarding what motivated her to think and write about the Judeo–Latin American culture. Her experience of a complex and powerful anti-Semitism led her to reevaluate how Argentina's prejudice against all things Jewish is still part of the national culture and legacy.

One of the great migratory waves to Latin America took place in the years before and after the Holocaust, 1938, 1939, and 1945. Jewish immigrants had to take refuge in any country that would accept them, since new visas were being denied in the United States and Canada. That "other America," the Southern one, became a possible place for refuge and shelter, but there was a paradox: Nazis also sought refuge and shelter there. Perhaps the most well-known examples are Adolf Eichmann in Argentina, Joseph Mengele in Bolivia, and Walter Rauff in Chile. Gustavo Farias's *La ruta de los Nazis* (*The Path of the Nazis*) is the most thorough examination of this important and often overlooked area of Latin American historiography.

These two forces—the Holocaust and Latin American dictatorships—epitomize the loss and pain of displacement. For example, Argentina's Juan Perón, a notorious anti-Semite, used to say: "Be a Patriot, Kill a Jew." The Canadian historian Graeme Mount's essay clearly documents the historical relationship between Nazism and fascism that is only now beginning to be revealed. He presents an in-depth analysis of the Nazi presence in Chile from its beginning during World War II and its relationship with the Allies. He also explores the complex relationship between Chile and the United States: the former's desire to remain independent from the latter while harboring a deep-rooted connection with the German immigrations to southern Chile and the later immigration of Nazis to the same region. This essay is of particular relevance since Pinochet's government had strong connections with the Nazi enclave. Evidence of the relationship between General Pinochet and the Nazi legacy becomes clear as more and more information is unveiled concerning Colonia Dignidad, a Nazi enclave in southern Chile where many political prisoners were held and subjected to torture.

Two essays present intimate portraits of the Jewish community in Mexico today. Diana Anhalt examines and reflects on the history of the Beth Israel community, which was founded in 1953. Although there was controversy initially, it continues to exist, albeit in a weakened state due to leadership problems. Anhalt explains the weakening of this community as in part related to the disintegration of minority communities throughout Latin America. The essay by Adina Cimet, written from a sociological perspective, deals with the Mexican Jewish community from its inception in 1958 through its decline as a result of factions vying for leadership and finally its fragmentation and dislocation. Cimet observes how the democratic spirit of a community begins to erode and how it then becomes a community dominated by an authoritarian force rather than by an inspired leadership. Cimet's insightful analysis demonstrates how a power struggle arising from different visions can occur among a religious and cultural minority.

These essays are a clear affirmation of the Jewish community in Latin America in all of its cultural manifestations as well as its migratory projects. Each essay explores the particular experience of Jews in particular countries as well as the different cultural manifestations through which the Jewish culture has incorporated its history, traditions, and legacy. Both the past and the future, ancient myths and fables, are gathered here to draw a portrait of the migration experience and the search for an identity through the unique vision of new cultures in a new world. One of the key aspects that developed in the past decades in the field of Jewish studies is the vindication of Jewish figures in the cultural life of their respective countries. The literary section discusses new writers whose contributions to Jewish literature in Latin America have been of extraordinary importance.

Naomi Lindstrom focuses on the Mexican writer Margo Glantz, whose book *Genealogies* is a pathbreaking combination of autobiography and memoirs and began an important autobiographical tradition that many female writers in Latin America followed: Sabina Berman in *La Bobe,* Marjorie Agosín in *A Cross and a Star,* and Teresa Porzecansky in *Perfumes of Carthage.* Glantz exhibits a marked sense of humor mixed with the traditional Jewish humor that can be found in eastern European writers such as Shalom Aleichem, but she also exhibits a unique postmodernity that allows her to explore ethnic and religious identity from an audacious perspective, and she accepts her history with its fatalities and dreams.

Rhonda Dahl Buchanan's essay on Perla Suez's *Letargo* presents, with delicacy and kindness, the complex life of a Jewish girl in the province of Entre Ríos who is subjected to a history of secrets and silences. The secret life of the main character in *Letargo* has many parallels to the collective history of the Jewish people and their particular historical coordinates due to the Holocaust.

Stephen A. Sadow's essay begins the section on culture history, and representation. Sadow explores the ramifications for the Argentine Jewish community of the bombing of the headquarters of the Asociación Mutual

Israelita Argentina (AMIA). His reflections point to the peculiar and difficult relationship between Jews and non-Jews. The evident complicity and silence of the Argentine community and especially of its government with regard to investigating this terrorist attack has not been resolved. Despite the damage to the moral fiber of this community and the destruction of important documents, books, and plans for future projects, an astonishing number of literary works were produced by members of that Jewish community. These works included books of poetry by the victims' relatives as well as novels and stories about the experience at the AMIA. Sadow's essay evidences the vitality of this community. However, as Edna Aizenberg suggests, the bombing of the AMIA headquarters, which left broken bodies amid the rubble, also left a powerful gap in the Argentine imagination.

Certain aspects of Jewish culture in Latin America have not been studied in depth previously; these aspects of Jewish existence speak to the delicate balance that Jews must maintain in a predominantly non-Jewish society. The article by Raanan Rein deals precisely with this issue. On the one hand, he explores the laws postulated by the Catholic church wherein the Catholic religion is mandated by law to be taught in all state-funded schools, creating a very difficult situation for the Jewish communities. With the arrival of Pinochet's regime, according to Rein, these laws were relaxed, demonstrating more tolerance for the existence of democracy and religious plurality in Argentina. This essay presents a historical revision with regard to the issue of Jews and identity.

Darrell B. Lockhart's essay complements the one by Naomi Lindstrom. It inaugurates a new vision of popular Jewish culture in Argentina and the ways in which popular culture can be inserted into the search for identity. Lockhart explores the ways in which literature, film, and theater have helped to create the popular and everyday spaces vis-à-vis the mythical search for one's identity. For example, Lockhart points out that Alberto Gerchunoff's *Los gauchos judíos,* a utopian vision of a Jewish gaucho who adapts to Argentine reality, and later a movie dedicated to this topic, has managed to insert itself in a popular culture that is both Argentine and Jewish and both accepted and denied.

Two visual artists, Gabriel Valansi from Argentina and Ruth Behar from Cuba and the United States, propose an alternative vision of the issue of memory. David William Foster analyzes the work of Valansi, one of the most well known contemporary Argentine photographers whose work has strong symbolic associations with post-Holocaust European and Latin American culture. Valansi's photography presents an alternate way of speaking about the unimaginable, that which cannot be expressed, that which is left unsaid, and creates certain parallels with postwar Europe and present-day Argentina. Both are looted, without a future, annihilated by economic corruption and the exploitation of minorities, in this case, the poorest.

If Valansi's work lacks human figures and shows absence as a possible continuity between the wars and the worlds, in Ruth Behar's cinematography memories exist through the presence of a voice, of human figures that she reconstitutes. In order for it to speak, the human voice is presence and memory, the past and the future united by the dimension of the present that the camera lovingly shields through nostalgia. The filmmaker is able to reconstruct the elements of memory slowly, because she is the initiator, the carrier of memories and remembrances. The audacious lens of the camera allows her to write, reconstruct, and reassemble her memories. Valansi understands that the Holocaust emptied out memories and that is why his landscapes are nighttime episodes and dark galleries that only leave traces. Behar takes these traces and weaves histories with them.

I wrote part of this introduction on the first night of Passover. The nostalgia we experience during all religious celebration allows us to re-think the landscape of our human geography that is, above all, a historical and emotional geography. Each of the essays collected here has a complex, ambiguous, yet victorious history—but, most important, a history that creates and re-creates itself. It is a history built of remnants, and it is constantly being formed in the same way that our ancestors found a way to leave Egypt. To a certain degree, this anthology coincides metaphorically with the public "debut" of Jewish Latin American culture.

I am writing these concluding words in Valparaíso, a port city that for me is a window onto the world, a privileged horizon to which immigrants, among them Jews, arrive. This is where my great-grandparents landed and where my grandparents found their faith and hope. Stories tell us that since there were no synagogues at the time, my grandparents were married in a church but still kept their traditions and history.

Let us begin our travels of imagination and hope. We start out in the land of Sepharad, a land of promise, and end in Latin America, the template Caribbean lands, the remote communities in the south of Chile and at the Panamanian border. During our travels, we will explore the mystery of those who share the collective memories of World War II survivors and their children as well as those who survived the AMIA. Past and present must coexist not only in one voice but also in a never-ending dialogue of voices and history.

I have assembled this collection as part of the constant pursuit of justice, truth, and hope that I found in Latin America. This collection affirms and evidences the life and cultural vibrancy of Latin American Jewry. It is a sign of the possibilities for a new world and the hope for one in Latin America, particularly, that, regardless of its traumas and difficulties, accepts the idea of coexisting and gives refuge to those histories and voices that today have become a reality. These essays converse with the past and illuminate our future.

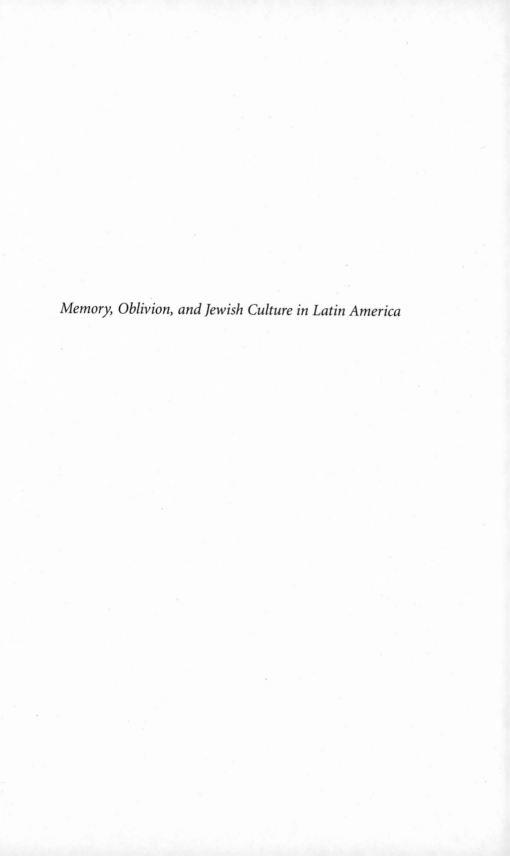

Memory, Oblivion, and Jewish Culture in Latin America

SECTION I

Sephardim in Our Memory

Remembering Sepharad

Accompanying Christopher Columbus on board the *Santa María* as it left the Iberian Peninsula on August 3, 1492, was Luis de Torres. De Torres, a polyglot, was the expedition's interpreter. Like many other Iberian Jews, de Torres had recently converted to Christianity in an attempt to preserve his right to live in Sepharad, the land Iberian Jews had inhabited for twelve hundred years. The Edict of Expulsion, dated March 31, 1492, deprived Jews of all their rights and gave them three months to put their affairs in order and go into exile. Implicit in the edict was exemption if Jews converted to Christianity. It was only implicit, of course, because neither the laws of the land nor the laws of the Catholic church provided for forced conversion. Although conversos would be granted full rights of citizenship, the Inquisition, in turn, had the right to investigate and persecute the "new" Christians in order to prevent deviations from church doctrine. Those who did not accept conversion would be expelled from the land forever. The fate of Sepharad was irreversible. Now we can only remember Sepharad.

Remembrance cannot restore that which has been lost, but it is essential to recognize the limitless power of human action to create as well as to destroy. Memory is not a matter of the past but a fundamental tool for analyzing the present and marching into the future with knowledge and conscience. Warnings about previous catastrophes caused by human actions are not enough to ensure a safe future. Remembrance should not be limited to the destructive chapters in the past, as it often is. The historiography of Sepharad has been overshadowed by the historiography of the Inquisition. That is to say, many know about the end of Sepharad, but far fewer know about its creation, its development, and the conditions that made her very existence possible. Certainly, knowledge of the past can provide us with many lessons about the irreversibility of human actions. Moreover, it can provide the means to recognize the irreversibility and unpredictability of our actions in the present. This is why I believe that the remembrance of Sepharad should not be limited to her death but should also embrace her life.

Jews had inhabited the Iberian Peninsula since at least, the third century and lived continuously in it for at least twelve hundred years—longer than they had lived in any other area of the world. During the Middle Ages, the Iberian community became the most important Jewish community in the world. It was larger than all the other Jewish communities of Europe combined. To refer to the peninsula they inhabited, Jews used the Hebrew word *Sepharad,* from verse 20 of the Book of Obadiah. To refer to their culture, tradition and their own kind, they used the term *Sephardim,* meaning "from Sepharad."

For centuries, the Iberian Peninsula was occupied and successively controlled by Romans, Visigoths, Muslims, and Christians. The Sephardim, therefore, always lived under the rule of non-Jewish peoples. The Sephardic contribution to Jewish and Western civilization at large remains unparalleled to this day.

Nevertheless, Sepharad was crushed on March 31, 1492. Although generations of historians have studied evidence left behind, more than five hundred years after the end of Sepharad they are still attempting to find answers to fundamental questions. Why did it happen? How did it happen? There is no agreement among experts on these or on many other issues regarding Sepharad, and great confusion reigns in the realm of popular knowledge.[1] Confusion, in turn, facilitates the manipulation of public opinion and knowledge. Remembrance is at stake. More academic scholarship is required, as is in-depth revision of popular versions of its history. It is a matter of transmission of knowledge. Knowledge is essential if we wish to anticipate and avoid catastrophes such as that of Sepharad.

Furthermore, we must seek answers to other fundamental questions regarding Sepharad. For not only is it her end that is of great importance. Of critical relevance to us, and to future generations, is the knowledge of her very existence, of the social conditions and actions that gave birth and nurtured that civilization. How did Jews, Muslims, and Christians coexist in the Iberian Peninsula? What conditions and actions made coexistence possible? What conditions and actions were necessary to produce the sophisticated advances in all areas of knowledge, culture, and art that characterized Jewish, Muslim, and Christian Iberia? How were those life conditions reached? How did the leaders of those communities interact? How did the common men and women interact?

What Iberian Jews called Sepharad in the Middle Ages was not, and is not, the equivalent of Spain, for the nation we call Spain had not yet been born. Spain as we know it today was not yet an official entity in 1492.

Sepharad was an imagined community that was contemporary with many kingdoms.[2] Sepharad lived within those kingdoms and across them. At one time or another, Sepharad encompassed Hispanic Jews (from Roman Hispania), Andalusian Jews (those from Muslim al-Andalus), Castilian Jews, Aragonese Jews, Portuguese Jews, and Navarre Jews. They shared traditions and ways of thinking. They recognized each other as members of the Sephardic community, even if they were subjects of different kings, inhabitants of different lands, and spoke different languages.

Christianity came to the Iberian Peninsula with the Romans, who called the region Hispania. By the fourth century Christianity had become the official religion of the Roman Empire, which included Hispania. In the fifth century the Roman Empire fell, and Hispania was occupied by non-Christian Visigoth tribes. But in 586 Recaredo, king of the Visigoths, converted to Christianity. Soon after, in 613, King Sisebuto ordered forced conversions in all of his dominions. This was the first official persecution suffered by the Iberian Jews.

In 711 Arab colonizers began conquering Christian Hispania and soon occupied most of the peninsula. For almost eight hundred years, from 711 to 1492, the lands of the Iberian Peninsula changed hands numerous times, and Iberian Jews, Christians, and Muslims lived together in cities, towns, and villages. All peoples needed to adapt rapidly to each new circumstance — a new ruler, new laws, a new war with new allies and new enemies, a new language, and often a new religion. Only pluralistic societies produce citizens able to survive this kind of living conditions. Only rulers who understand plurality can effectively rule over such societies. And, in the end, only the daily and conscientious actions of average citizens can provide the context for coexistence.

Against all odds, medieval Iberians maintained long-lasting friendships and alliances and bought and borrowed from each other. Jews, Muslims, and Christians lived together, worked together, and fought together. There is ample historical evidence of this daily coexistence.[3]

Most Jews lived in small villages farming and sheep breeding. Some Jews lived in towns, where they were often shopkeepers, grocers, dyers, and weavers. Daily cooperation enabled collaboration on a different level. On the Iberian Peninsula, Muslims, Jews, and Christians shared their knowledge and actively sought to complement each other's knowledge of the world and of humankind. In the great cities of medieval Iberia, such as Córdoba, Granada, Toledo, Barcelona, and Salamanca, interethnic groups of scholars worked incessantly on the transmission of knowledge old and new. Their patrons were Muslim caliphs, Christian kings, rabbis, and rich men of all kinds. Muslim artisans built Jewish temples, and Jewish temples were dedicated to Christian kings. Some Jewish scholars, such as Maimonides, wrote in Arabic. Christian leaders employed rabbis to translate the Bible as well as Arabic manuscripts of enormous scientific and philosophic importance.

Of course, mistrust and envy were also present in medieval Iberia, as in all human affairs at all times. But it can be said that in the Middle Ages Iberia was home to several pluralistic, multicultural societies. Moreover, the end of plural and multicultural Iberia historically coincides with the age of intolerance, the manipulation of inherited knowledge and collective memory, religious fanaticism, and greed and imperialism in the name of one god and of one (Christian) nation.

Two hundred years after first entering the peninsula, an Arab ruler began the process of independence of the Islamic Iberian state, al-Andalus, from Baghdad, which was then the center of the Islamic world. In the tenth century, 'Abd al-Rahman III founded an independent caliphate whose capital was Córdoba. Under his rule, Jews and Christians were considered *dhimmis* (People of the Book) who were to be protected. They were granted freedom to worship and to practice traditions in exchange for obedience to Islamic rule and payment of special taxes. And they were granted access to education. The interaction with Andalusi Muslims provided the Sephardim with access to vast areas of Eastern and Western knowledge: astronomy, astrology, medicine, philosophy, art, commerce, literature, geography, algebra, and history. In fact, for a long period, the Jews of al-Andalus used the Arabic language even when writing on religious subjects. But it was also in that Muslim land that Hebrew secular poetry was born, and it was in that land that biblical Hebrew was reborn and chosen as the classical language for all Jews.

Biblical Hebrew came to life again, in part, because 'Abd al-Rahman III pursued pluralistic policies that enabled the production, distribution, and sharing of all kinds of knowledge among his subjects. 'Abd al-Rahman chose Hasdai ibn Shaprut (b. Jaén, 910), one of the greatest Sephardim of all times, to be the representative of the Jewish community at the royal court. With the support of the caliph, Hasdai brought foreign Jewish philosophers, scientists, grammarians, poets, and talmudic scholars to Córdoba. Their mission was to enter into intellectual dialogue with the native Jews and to contribute to Andalusi culture. And, together with the Sephardim, the newly arrived *dhimmis* set the stage for the Jewish religious renaissance in Muslim territory.

Among those who chose to move to al-Andalus was Dunash ibn Labrat, born in Fez and trained in Baghdad. Dunash's greatest accomplishment was the writing of Hebrew verse that followed, not Hebrew meter, but the meter employed by Muslims in Arabic poetry. Soon Jewish poets began adopting the forms and genres of Arabic poetry. But they wrote in Hebrew, thus creating a new type of Hebrew literature. Then the Jews of al-Andalus developed a new type of synagogue poetry. Instead of using the language of rabbinic literature, they chose to adopt biblical Hebrew as their classical language, and this, in turn, produced the renaissance of the language of the Hebrew Bible. Among the most important Hebrew poets of Sepharad are Samuel Nagid (933–1055), Salomon ibn Gabirol (ca. 1020–ca. 1057), and Moses ibn Ezra (ca. 1055–ca. 1135).

Hasdai ibn Shaprut must also be credited for the initiation of the great scientific corpus produced in Hebrew in al-Andalus. Under his patronage, translations of fundamental Arabic works into the Hebrew language were produced. In addition, Hebrew astrolabes were constructed and Hebrew astronomical tables developed.

The Córdoba caliphate split in the eleventh century and Muslim Iberia was fragmented into twenty small kingdoms, with the cultural center in Granada. For some time, favorable circumstances for the distribution, production, and sharing of knowledge among Jews and Muslims remained in place.

The Aristotelian worldview that permeated medieval Arabic civilization deeply influenced Jewish thought. The best example is of course the great Moshe Ben Maimon (b. Córdoba, 1135), known to Christians as Maimonides and to Muslims as Abu Imram Musa ben Maimun ibn Abdalá. Arguably the most accomplished of the Sephardim, Maimonides wrote a systematic code of Jewish Law (Mishne Torah), a commentary on the Mishnah, several treatises on medicine, and *The Guide to the Perplexed*, a masterpiece of Judaic philosophy.

Despite all these cultural, social, and scientific advances, there were constant wars between the Iberian Muslim kingdoms. Two new contingents of Arabs, the Almohads and Almoravids, arrived in al-Andalus. With them, a fundamentalist interpretation of Islamic rule was imposed, and a policy of persecution and forced conversion was initiated. Daily life became unbearable for Christians and Jews alike. Many left the land, among them Maimonides.[4] Some converted to Islam. Religious fundamentalism and the inability to live in a pluralistic society marked the beginning of the end for al-Andalus.[5]

As pluralism disappeared from al-Andalus, the cultural center of Iberia moved to the north, to the kingdoms ruled by Christians: Castile, Navarre, Aragon, and Portugal. Andalusi Jews, fluent in Arabic and with ample knowledge of Muslim customs, laws, and thought, now began serving the Christian courts as translators, administrators, and diplomatic advisers. Jewish refugees from al-Andalus settled in Christian territories. At the same time, sensing the weakening of Muslim al-Andalus, Christian kings began to increase their incursions into Muslim territory. Once again Christians, Muslims, and Jews lived together in villages, towns, and cities. Once again they had to adapt to constantly changing circumstances.

Arabic science and thought reached Christianity through the translation into Latin of Arabic texts.[6] Many of the translators were Jewish. The Sephardim now used Hebrew instead of Arabic as their language for writing. But in Toledo (Castile's capital), under the rule of King Alfonso X (1252–1284), all kinds of texts were now being translated into Latin as well as into the vernacular Castilian language. Again, interethnic groups of scholars and translators were formed. Thus Iberian Jews, Muslims, and Christians *together* were responsible for the transmission of knowledge into Latin and Castilian. The first great figures of Iberian Jewish science were the Aragonese Abraham bar Hiyya and Abraham ibn Ezra in the twelfth century. Two Castilian Jews, Isaac ibn Sid and Jehuda ibn Mosca, the astronomers who produced the famous Castilian astronomical tables for King Alfonso X, followed them. Soon Jews began to contribute to Castilian literature as well. Such was the case of Shem Tob ben Ardutiel (Don Sen Tob de Carrion), author of *Proverbios morales*.[7]

As Christians gained in the ongoing territorial wars with Muslims, anti-Jewish and anti-Muslim legislation spread. Christian fundamentalism began to take center stage. In some instances, the Christian kings protected Jews. In fact, in most of the Christian territories, Jews were legally under the direct jurisdiction of the kings.

During the early fourteenth century, conversion to Christianity spread among the Sephardim living in the kingdoms of Castile and Aragon. Some rabbis and other important leaders, such as Rabbi Abner of Burgos (Alfonso de Valladolid) and Rabbi Salomon ha-Levi[8] (Pablo de Santa María), converted publicly.

Despite the deteriorating situation, Hebrew poetry continued to flourish. Among the most important Hebrew poets of the period are Salomon Bonafed and the conversos Salomon Piera and Vidal Benveniste.[9] In the kingdom of Aragon the art of Hebrew manuscript illumination reached its apogee. The majority of the codices produced were, of course, Bibles commissioned by Christians. However, the production of Hebrew prayer books and medical and scientific treatises also continued. In 1348, for example, we find Levi ben Isaac Hiyo copying Maimonides's *Guide to the Perplexed* for a Jewish patron, Menahem Bezalel.[10]

How could this be achieved? Daily life, as well as intellectual life, was still possible for the Sephardim. They were still legal subjects under the direct jurisdiction of the kings. Their communities were still vibrant. Their religious practices and traditions were legal. Jews served the kings in official capacities. They were part of the land. Between 1336 and 1357 Samuel Halevi, treasurer of Peter I, king of Castile, financed the construction of a new synagogue in Toledo. Samuel dedicated it to the Christian king and employed Muslim artisans (*mudejars*) in its construction.[11] The dedication, which was written in Hebrew, uses Arabic meter. Although Halevi and his family were later imprisoned, tortured, and executed on orders from the same king, the Jewish temple built and decorated by Muslims and dedicated to a Christian king has managed to survive to the present time.[12]

Jews were still free to worship and to practice their traditions. They bought and sold and freely practiced their professions. Friendships were still being made and alliances kept. Pluralistic relations still prevailed,[13] which enraged the fanatics. Thus this was a time when synagogues were being built and at the same time destroyed. Fanatic Christian preachers traveled the lands inciting Jews to convert and Christians to violence.[14] The Christian kings intervened numerous times, but the situation only worsened.

On March 15, 1391, the infamous anti-Jewish Father Ferrán Martínez, preached in Seville.[15] Following his sermon, anti-Jewish violence exploded in the city. Seville's Jewish quarters were sacked on June 6. Then the violence spread to the Jewish neighborhoods of all Christian kingdoms. Mass conversions to Christianity followed. These conversions would dramatically complicate matters for the Iberian Jews who remained Jews as well as for those who converted.

Because of the mass conversions, by the fifteenth century the ranks of Iberian Christians had expanded considerably. The conversos, or "new" Christians, acquired the same social and political rights that the "old" Christians enjoyed and, therefore, could avoid all the restrictions that were being imposed on Iberian Jews.[16] However, religious fanaticism did not stop with conversion; it only increased, fueled by envy, bad faith, ignorance, political strategy, fear, and hate. We do not know yet in which proportions.

In 1413 a public dispute between Christian and Jewish scholars took place in Tortosa. The goal was to determine which was the superior and true faith. Representing the Christian side was Jerónimo de Santa Fé, a first-generation converso whose Jewish name had been Joshua Halorquí. This formal dispute among scholars ended with thousands of conversions to Christianity.

As the Sephardic communities were dwindling dramatically as a result of conversion, Jewish mysticism and Kabbalah were replacing traditional Jewish learning. There is evidence of an increase of messianic speculation among the Sephardim as well.[17] Perhaps this was an attempt to imagine a future free of unpredictability. However, biblical and talmudic scholarship did not cease.

In 1433 Rabbi Moses Arragel completed a translation and commentary of the Jewish Bible for a Christian patron, Luis González de Guzmán. Arragel worked under the supervision of two friars. Even later, in 1473, Abraham Zacut (1452–1515?) wrote a set of Hebrew astronomical tables for the University of Salamanca.[18] Amid the chaos and the fear, perhaps there were some pockets of plurality. Perhaps some judged the end of Sepharad impossible. Perhaps some were determined to resist. We need to know more.

By the end of the fifteenth century, the "new" Christians were as much the target of the Christian zealots as were those Jews who resisted conversion. Some conversos might have thought of conversion as a tool to avoid what they considered irreversible circumstances. But, again, the future proved unpredictable. Conversos and their descendants were accused by Christian fanatics of being heretics who were still practicing their old religion in whole or in part. Christian heretics were under the jurisdiction of the Roman Inquisition while Jews were not. It was only a matter of time until prominent Christian voices rose to demand the establishment of an Inquisition in Castile.[19] Recent conversos as well as those born Christian but of converso descent were now trapped by the very same accusation: heresy.

By this time, Christians controlled much of the Iberian Peninsula. Furthermore, the strategic marriage between Isabel, queen of Castile, and Fernando, king of Aragon, had united their separate kingdoms. Muslim Iberia was reduced to a single kingdom, Granada. And the relations between Jews and conversos were openly hostile.[20]

Leaders of religious orders received permission from the monarchs and the pope to create an Inquisition in Castile. With it, they claimed, it would be possible to eliminate rampant religious deviation. In 1480 the Castilian Inquisition was established, against the opposition of the Castilian conversos. Evidence shows that its methods of operation were organized terror and fabricated accusations against conversos.[21]

As the Inquisition organized the persecution of the "newest heretics," the conversos, Inquisitors also sought to convince the monarchs of the need to expel the Jews. There was too much interaction between Jews and former Jews. The Inquisition had no jurisdiction over Jews,[22] and it was the Jews, said the Inquisitors, who were preventing conversos from being true Christians. Isabel and Fernando granted the Inquisitors' wishes.

First, the Sephardim were expelled from Christian Andalusia (then part of the kingdom of Castile) in 1482; then they were expelled from the kingdom of Aragon in 1486. But expulsions were not enough for the Inquisitors. And, again, they got from Isabel and Fernando what they wanted. In 1492 all Sephardim were expelled from all of Castile and Aragon, as well as from all other territories under the control of the monarchs.[23] Only if they converted to Christianity would they be allowed to remain in their lands. There is evidence that the Jewish community had not anticipated the expulsion.[24]

Immediately, some Sephardim opted for exile, some for conversion. Of those who chose exile, most left, by land or sea, for Portugal, Navarre, or North Africa. Some never made it to safety. Some were unable to reach exile and returned to convert and save their lives. Others reached what they thought was safety in Portugal and Navarre.[25]

But just six years later, in 1497, as a condition of the marriage between King Manoel of Portugal and Isabel (daughter of Isabel and Fernando), all Jews who wished to remain so were expelled from the kingdom of Portugal. A year later Jews who were not willing to convert were expelled from Navarre. Sepharad was irreversibly gone.

Too many fundamental questions remain unanswered. We do not know enough about the life of Sepharad and, in spite of the wealth of writing, we do not know enough about her death. In my opinion, an accurate remembrance of Sepharad's construction and destruction will materialize, in the present or in the future, only when and if interethnic teams of students seek the necessary knowledge together. The historiography of Sepharad requires such collaboration. Our current political circumstances might seem contrary to this collaboration, but at the same time it is this

lack of collaboration that fuels the political circumstances.[26] The production and distribution of knowledge is at stake. Remembrance, and our
present and future, is at stake.

America, January 2003. José Alperovich, an Argentinean federal sena-
tor, is running for the governorship of the province of Tucumán. The elections are set to take place in March or April 2003. While most electoral
polls are on his side, Alperovich is facing an old new challenge. In spite
of popular support, some leaders are questioning his qualifications. Their
opposition stems from the fact that Alperovich is Jewish and, thus, they
say, cannot comply with Article 80 of the provincial constitution, which
requires the governor to take a Christian oath. For Alperovich's chal-
lengers—whose leader is Tucumán's Roman Catholic archbishop, Mon-
signor Luis Villalba—this means that the governor must be Catholic.
Article 80 was written in 1990.[27]

NOTES

1. For differing and sometimes opposite interpretations, see Roth 1937; Baer
1961–1966; Netanyahu 1995; Roth 1995; Gitlitz 1996; Kamen 1997.
2. In 1492 Queen Isabel and King Fernando, known as the Catholic Monarchs, had jurisdiction over most parts of the Iberian Peninsula. The Christian
territories of Portugal and Navarre were not under their control, and Muslim Granada was conquered only in 1492. In other words, Fernando and Isabel were not
sovereigns of "Spain." Immediately before their marriage (1469), the situation
was even more fragmented. Castile and Aragon were independent Christian kingdoms, with different laws and customs. Even earlier, in the twelfth, eleventh, and
tenth centuries, the fragmentation was more pronounced.
3. See Mann, Glick, and Dodds 1992; Roth 1995.
4. Maimonides left in 1148 and settled in Egypt, where he died in 1204.
5. The end would come in 1492 with the conquest of the last surviving Muslim
kingdom, Granada.
6. Some of these translators were Petrus Alfonsi (b. 1062, convert), Mair Abu-
lafia (d. 1244), Abraham ibn al-Fahkhar (d. 1240), Meshulam Piera, and Abraham
bar Hiyya.
7. See Sen Tob [1345] 1974.
8. See Roth 1995.
9. See Scheindlin 1992.
10. See Sed-Rajna 1992.
11. See Dodds 1992.
12. See Estow 1995.

13. S .e Roth 1995.

14. See Netanyahu 1995; Roth 1995; Kamen 1997.

15. See Roth 1937.

16. On the restrictions imposed on the Sephardim, see Roth 1995; Kamen 1997. On the social success of conversos, see Roth 1995.

17. See Roth 1995.

18. Zacuto's tables were to accompany Columbus on his 1492 expedition.

19. A Catalan Inquisition had been active since the twelfth century. In 1483 the infamous Tomás de Torquemada was appointed General Inquisitor for Aragón-Catalonia. See Roth 1995.

20. On this issue, see Roth 1937; Roth 1995; Netanyahu 1995; Kamen 1997.

21. See Roth 1995.

22. The Inquisition only had jurisdiction over the Christians, "old" and "new." Jews, as long as they remained within their faith, could not be persecuted. Once converted, however, they fell strictly under the Inquisition's control.

23. See the Edict of Expulsion in Raphael 1992, pp. 189–193.

24. See Roth 1995.

25. There is no agreement among historians about the number of Jews who left the peninsula in 1492 and after.

26. My gratitude to Shaari Neretin, Donna Penn, and Susan Krause for their help with this work.

27. As reported by the *Boston Globe,* January 14, 2003, p. A14.

SELECTED BIBLIOGRAPHY

Arendt, Hannah. 1958. *The Human Condition.* Chicago: University of Chicago Press [paperback edition, 1989].

Baer, Yizhak. 1961–1966. *A History of the Jews in Christian Spain.* Philadelphia: Jewish Publication Society of America.

Castro, Américo. 1983. *España en su historia: Cristianos, moros y judíos.* Barcelona: Grijalbo Mondadori.

Dodds, Jerrilynn. 1992. "Mudejar Tradition and the Synagogues of Medieval Spain: Cultural Identity and Cultural Hegemony." In *Convivencia: Jews, Muslims and Christians in Medieval Spain,* ed. Vivian Mann, Thomas Glick, and Jerrilynn Dodds, 113–132. New York: George Braziller in association with the Jewish Museum.

Eimeric, Nicolau. 1973. *El Manual de los Inquisidores.* Ed. Luis Sala-Molins. Barcelona: Muchnik.

Estow, Clara. 1955. *Pedro the Cruel of Castile, 1350–1369.* Leiden: E. J. Brill.

Gampel, Benjamin. 1992. "Jews, Christians, and Muslims in Medieval Iberia: Convivencia through the Eyes of Sephardic Jews." In *Convivencia: Jews, Muslims and Christians in Medieval Spain,* ed. Vivian Mann, Thomas Glick, and Jerrilynn Dodds, 2–38. New York: George Braziller in association with the Jewish Museum.

Gitlitz, David. 1966. *Secrecy and Deceit: The Religion of the Crypto-Jews*. Philadelphia: Jewish Publication Society.

Glick, Thomas. 1992. "Science in Medieval Spain: The Jewish Contribution in the Context of Convivencia." In *Convivencia: Jews, Muslims and Christians in Medieval Spain*, ed. Vivian Mann, Thomas Glick, and Jerrilyn Dodds, 83–112. New York: George Braziller in association with the Jewish Museum.

Kamen, Henry. 1997. *The Spanish Inquisition: A Historical Revision*. New Haven: Yale University Press.

Mann, Vivian, Thomas Glick, and Jerrilynn Dodds, eds. 1992. *Convivencia: Jews, Muslims and Christians in Medieval Spain*. New York: George Braziller in association with the Jewish Museum.

Netanyahu, Benzion. 1955. *The Origins of the Inquisition in Fifteenth-Century Spain*. New York: Random House.

Raphael, David, ed. 1992. *The Expulsion 1492 Chronicles*. North Hollywood, Calif.: Carmi House Press.

Roth, Cecil. 1937. *The Spanish Inquisition*. New York: Norton.

Roth, Norman. 1995. *Conversos, Inquisition and the Expulsion of the Jews from Spain*. Madison: University of Wisconsin Press.

Scheindlin, Raymond. 1992. "Hebrew Poetry in Medieval Iberia." In *Convivencia: Jews, Muslims and Christians in Medieval Spain*, ed. Vivian Mann, Thomas Glick, and Jerrilyn Dodds, 39–60. New York: George Braziller in association with the Jewish Museum.

Sed-Rajna, Gabrielle. 1992. "Hebrew Illuminated Manuscripts from the Iberian Peninsula." In *Convivencia: Jews, Muslims and Christians in Medieval Spain*, ed. Vivian Mann, Thomas Glick, and Jerrilyn Dodds, 133–156. New York: George Braziller in association with the Jewish Museum.

Sen Tob de Carrion. *Glosas de sabiduría o Proverbios morales y otras rimas*, ed. Agustin García Calvo. Madrid: Alianza, [1345] 1974.

Vernet, Juan. 1999. *Lo que Europa debe al islam de España*. Barcelona: El Acantilado.

ANGELINA MUÑIZ HUBERMAN

Translated by Miriam Huberman

The Sephardic Legacy

In chapter 54 of the second part of *The Adventures of Don Quixote,* it is written:

Thou knowest well, neighbour and friend Sancho Panza, how the proc-lamation or edict his Majesty commanded to be issued against those of my nation filled us all with terror and dismay; me at least it did, inso-much that I think before the time granted us for quitting Spain was out, the full force of the penalty had already fallen upon me and upon my children. I decided, then, and I think wisely (just like one who knows that at a certain date the house he lives in will be taken from him, and looks out beforehand for another to change into), I decided, I say, to leave the town myself, alone and without my family, and go to seek out some place to remove them to comfortably and not in the hurried way in which the others took their departure; for I saw very plainly, and so did all the older men among us, that the proclamations were not mere threats, as some said, but positive enactments which would be enforced at the appointed time; and what made me believe this was what I knew of the base and extravagant designs which our people harboured, de-signs of such a nature that I think it was a divine inspiration that moved his Majesty to carry out a resolution so spirited; not that we were all guilty, for some there were true and steadfast Christians; but they were so few that they could make no head against those who were not; and it was not prudent to cherish a viper in the bosom by having enemies in the house. In short it was with just cause that we were visited with the penalty of banishment, a mild and lenient one in the eyes of some, but to us the most terrible that could be inflicted upon us. Wherever we are we weep for Spain; for after all we were born there and it is our natural fatherland. Nowhere do we find the reception our unhappy condition needs; and in Barbary and all the parts of Africa where we counted upon being received, succoured, and welcomed, it is there they insult and ill-treat us most. We knew not our good fortune until we lost it; and such is the longing we almost all of us have to return to Spain, that most of those who like myself know the language, and there are many who do, come back to it and leave their wives and children forsaken yonder, so great is their love for it; and now I know by experience the meaning of the saying, sweet is the love of one's country.[1]

These words, spoken by Ricote, who pretends to be a *morisco* (a Spanish Moor), could well be used to describe the situation of the Sephardic Jews who were expelled from Spain in 1492. Never before had a historic event affected a people in such a way. Almost fourteen centuries of life in Spain were cut at the root, and those of the Spanish people who considered themselves as Hispanic as the Christians were banished without knowing why. Thus if Maimonides used to sign his writings "The Sephardi," if the entire Jewish population of Spain called itself—even today—Sephardim, if their tongue is called *judeoespañol,* how was it that their fatherland would no longer be Spain? In a tolerant period this conflict would not have existed and their identity would have been that of Spaniards of Jewish religion. Earlier, a Spanish king had boasted of ruling over three religions. But, as history is not guided by logic, nor do justice and tolerance characterize it, things did not happen in a fair way. The expelled Jews experienced a new exile and carried with them the best of the land: the language. This language, which I call *florida* (flowered) was considered as holy as Hebrew. Therefore, it is a language suitable for talking with God and about God.

The preservation of the Spanish language by the Sephardic Jews is a unique phenomenon. It is an identity; it is the way to be recognized and to establish a home anywhere in the world: the home of the language that in a foreign country provides the warmth of sharing a profound way of being, of existing, of living. Chants, poems, literature, and colloquial speech are all expressed in the same manner—and ritual, dress, rhythm, and gait. Everything responds to the sounds of the mother tongue, a tongue that in exile is a unique comfort.

A ti lengua santa,
a ti te adoro,

más que a toda plata,
más que a todo oro.
Tú sos la más linda
de todo lenguaje;
a ti dan las ciencias
todo el avantage.[2]

You, Holy Language
I thee adore,
More than all silver,
More than gold.
You are the most beautiful
Of all language;
To you all sciences gives
All the advantage.

For the Sephardic Jew, the Spanish language is a holy language. It is more valuable than wealth, it is beautiful, it is beloved. It expresses science, poetry, and religion. In the first place there is love for the language, this same language that is spoken today in Spain and in Latin America. Almost 500 million people have inherited the *lengua florida*.

First, love. Then, memory. To start speaking is to recover history. For him who begins to live, magic is nothing else but words. What amazes a child is the evidence that each thing is a word, just as it amazed God in his nominalism and Adam in his babbling.

Language gives life and preserves it, from the oldest manifestations to the most recent. Language is time's artificer, from the *jarchas* to contemporary literature, from Yehudá ha-Lev to modern publications in Ladino. It is a flow of words as an ornament of expression. Language is heritage, and as heritage it is tradition. The tradition of kabbalism is transmitted orally rather than by means of the written word. Kabbalism, with its ciphered language, metaphoric world, allegory and symbolism, flourished in medieval Spain.

The lengua florida lives in everyday speech, as well as in proverbs, wedding songs, mourning songs, *romances,* stories, tales, novels, and plays. It has produced five thousand texts, and it was still remembered by León Hebreo and Baruch Spinoza and by Elias Canetti.

This same language arrived in the New World. Some Jews, barely escaping persecution in Spain, sought shelter in colonial Mexico in vain, because the Inquisition found them there too. But not before they wrote poems, memories, diaries: the testimony of lives that struggle to leave a record of their sufferings, their tenacity, and their living language.

For the Jews who settled in Spain, exodus was a biblical theme, and, even if it was possible to consider an eventual return to the Holy Land, Spain was also regarded as a promised land. That is why, when they experienced the new Diaspora in their own flesh, spirituality and mysticism proliferated. The kabbalistic tradition that had its origins in the thirteenth century found new ways of explaining and interpreting a historical event of such magnitude. It turned to the idea of God's inner dwelling, or Shekhinah, as an aspect of the divinity that detaches itself from divinity in order to accompany the people of Israel in their exile. Without being a hypostasis, it is almost an independent element of the divinity. It recovers the mythical aspect of the Jewish religion and incarnates the feminine principle: the mother, the wife, and the daughter. The reason for its popularity was its connection to the historic exile. However, for the rabbinical orthodoxy, it became a controversial issue. Nevertheless, for the people, the idea that a part of God separated itself from God and was accompanying them in exile offered relief and consolation.[3]

Shekhinah is closely related to feminine symbolism and to the soul. Being a metaphor for the moon, it is subject to changes, phases, and opposites. It may be a source of light or the origin of darkness, mercy, or inclemency. In its most dramatic and extreme form it is the Tree of Death. While its primordial manifestation is that of First Mother, its contradictory aspects originate a symbolism full of mythical elements. In some kabbalistic versions, the Shekhinah has its corresponding opposite in the figure of Lilith, mother of the profane people and queen of the impure. Thus the Shekhinah structure is highly complex and difficult to grasp in all its meanings.

Kabbalist tales, under the influence of chivalric literature, dwell on the image of the Shekhinah who accompanies the people of Israel as the queen or the princess who has been banished by the king. As female figure, the Shekhinah has the following manifestations: mother, daughter, bride, queen, and princess. It represents wisdom, and it is ready to guide the people in their wanderings. As bride, or *kalah,* it appears in the welcoming ceremony of the Sabbath. In the sacred matrimony of the king and queen, it is the one who blesses the union. The Shekhinah, or holy presence, is part of every event that takes place in community life. According to Moses de Leon (d. 1305), author and compiler of the *Zohar,* or *Book of Splendor,* in the cosmic jubilee it will be responsible for the soul transcending its earthly wrappings and communing with the celestial world by reintegrating itself into the divine mind.[4] In other tales in the same book, sins are the cause of the separation between the king and the queen. The banishment of the latter is the metaphysical consequence of those sins. All of which may be related to what Cervantes has Ricote say about sin and exile.

Given that sin and exile march side by side, Kabbalism hopes to redeem sin by returning to Paradise or the Holy Land, or even to Sepharad. The ultimate purpose is to reunite the Shekhinah with God. That may be why Ricote returns to Spain, in an attempt to redeem sin: "con justa fuerza fuimos castigados con la pena del destierro" (with powerful justice we were punished with the ordeal of banishment).

The concept of Shekhinah is part of the Sabbath prayer ceremony welcoming the advent of the seventh day, the day that gives light for the rest of the week. The symbolic image of the marriage between the king and the queen is the way in which the kabbalist relates to the Shekhinah during the Sabbath. The Sabbath is the bride to whom special psalms are sung. These psalms must be sung with eyes closed, because the Shekhinah is described in the *Zohar* as follows: "A beautiful maiden who has no eyes and whose body is concealed and yet revealed—revealed in the morning and concealed during the day—and who is adorned with ornaments which do no exist."[5] The beautiful maiden has no eyes because she has cried so much in exile that she has lost them. While reading the Torah on the Sabbath, the Shekhinah may be identified both with it and with the metaphorical tradition of the Song of Songs.

Among the best-known Sabbath hymns that allude to the cryptic image of the Shekhinah is "Leja dodi" (Come, My Beloved). Although it appears late in Safed, around the sixteenth century, its basis is the medieval tradition of the Sephardic Kabbalists, reinforced by the 1492 expulsion of the Spanish Jews. Thus the Castilian language retains a chant that uses the metaphor of the bride for the seventh day and God's inner dwelling (Shekhinah) to describe the nostalgia for the lost country.

Ven, amado mío
Ven amado mío, al encuentro de tu novia;
el *shabat* aparece, salgamos a recibirlo.[6]

Come, my beloved
Come my beloved, to meet your bride;
the Sabbath comes, we will receive her.

Because of the suffering of exile, Hispanic Jews preserved their tongue as a ritual manifestation and as a proof of loyalty. The expulsion from Spain became a memorial date in the Hebrew calendar that cannot be forgotten because it coincides with the destruction of the Temple of Jerusalem. The Sephardic people sought comfort in mysticism and messianism. That is why the holy day acquired an even more complex meaning. In poems such as the one quoted above, the Sabbath expresses the idea of reunion, of the reintegration of the Shekhinah with God, of divine matrimony. But mainly, and this is the Sephardic tradition's contribution, it erases for a few hours the idea of exile and once again humankind becomes a part of the divinity. For a few hours, meditating and reading the Torah and the Kabbalah will be the blessing, the return to the lost Paradise, the bridge that unites humankind with the divine essence, so that they may forget the loss of land and home. As Ricote says, "We knew not our good fortune until we lost it. . . . [S]weet is the love of one's country." Furthermore, for the Sephardic Jew, the Sabbath is a day exiled from the rest of the week, for which humankind has to wait six days. It contains the promise of a renewed pact: the return to Spain is possible. And this promise has been fulfilled in our time, five hundred years later.

The image of the horror of exile produced another doctrine that became very popular after the expulsion of 1492: metempsychosis (*gilgul*). According to this, the exiled soul went through several stages, like proscription or nakedness, incarnating all the comings and goings of the banished people. Gershom Scholem writes: "Absolute homelessness was the sinister symbol of absolute Godlessness, of utter moral and spiritual degradation. Union with God or utter banishment were the two poles between which a system had to be devised in which the Jews could live under the domination of Law, which seeks to destroy the forces of exile."[7]

The idea of the transmigration of the soul is one of the most important themes in Isaac Luria's kabbalistic theories. The reality of exile, along with the movement of the body, led to the idea that the soul also moves. Thus the exiled soul, seeking its elevation, has to start from the banishment from Paradise. If Adam incarnates all the human souls, he also incarnates the possibility of transmigration or metempsychosis. However, he who has lived a sinless life does not follow this path and awaits for the moment in which his soul be part of Adam's soul. In any case, what this is about is applying the idea of exile to the soul's journeys.[8]

Antonio Enríquez Gómez, also known as Enrique Enríquez Paz, uses the themes of exile and metempsychosis, probably inspired by earlier kabbalistic sources. The Inquisition persecutes Antonio Enríquez, born in

Segovia to a Portuguese converso family, for his relation to *judaizantes* (people who practice Judaism). He flees from Spain and reaches France, where he obtains a position in King Louis XIII's court. Afterward he seeks shelter in Amsterdam, where the Sephardic community protects him. When he learns that he has been burned in effigy in Seville, he exclaims with a great dose of humor: "Ahí me las den todas" (May everything so happen to me). His ironic style leads him to mock Scholasticism and to condemn the Inquisition. In the style of the picaresque novel, he criticizes, among other things, the doctrine of *limpieza de sangre,* or purity of blood, and the sense of honor. In *Vida de don Gregorio Guadaña,* which forms part of his book, *El siglo pitagórico,* Enríquez Gómez refers to metempsychosis, which he took from hermetic and Neoplatonic theories and probably from kabbalistic texts: "Basándose en la fábula de la trasmigración, refiere las trasformaciones de un alma que encarna sucesivamente en diferentes cuerpos pertenecientes a distintos estados sociales" (Based on the fable of transmigration, it refers to the transformation of a soul that successively reincarnated in different bodies belonging to distinct social statuses).[9] The exile theme is prominent in Enríquez Gómez's poetry and narratives. In one of his poems about his escape from Spain, he is the mirror that reflects the same sorrow and same subjects that Sephardic poetry deals with even today:

Dejé mi albergue, tierno y regalado,
y dejé con mi alma mi albedrío,
pues todo en tierra ajena me ha faltado.

I left my dwellings, tender with gifts,
and I left with my soul my free will,
so everything on alien lands has been missing.[10]

Messianism is another phenomenon that is profoundly connected to the idea of exile. When the millenarian feelings reappeared, it was thought that the Messiah was the intermediary who propitiates redemption. In the face of the loss of both stability and territory that the Spanish Jews had enjoyed for centuries, the mystics and the enlightened assumed messianic roles and offered the people a renewal in faith and the possibility of filling that vacuum. The apocalyptic concept is seen as a cosmological process that recovers space for the divine soul as well as for the individual soul. Once again, the individual who has been separated from his or her homeland may hope for a union of essences and a reintegration of past and future, even though the present is uncertain and dangerous. At the same time, the individual recovers and defines a sense of responsibility and of dignity, obliterating the ignominious sign of exile.

Thus conceived, exile is part of the process of creation, and this is the original contribution of the Sephardic philosophy. If exile goes beyond being considered trial or punishment, then it becomes a mission to be carried out. The purpose of this mission is to liberate the human soul from earthly bondage and elevate it toward the search for the divine light and its reintegration in the cosmic whole. Exile, in this conception, also includes the idea of redemption, because the people who were banished and sent in all directions aspired to perfect the soul of all beings. This is the same motivation of Jacobo Kulli when he gathered in the *Me-am-loez* in 1690 the history of the Hebrew culture in Ladino in order to teach "el comportamiento de la vida del hombre y todo lo que pasa en el mundo" (the behavior of a man's life and all that takes place in his world).[11]

Messianism, strengthened by the expulsion of 1492, drew on the anxiety of the Spanish Jews who believed that the end of times was approaching and that redemption would soon occur. Exile was seen as the first sign that the Messiah's arrival was near and that such a catastrophe could only be of apocalyptic proportions and would consequently bring redemption. That the expulsion from Spain had taken place on the same date as the destruction of the Temple of Jerusalem, the ninth of *av* (*tishá be-av*), made the sense of catastrophe even more evident.[12] This is why messianic movements among the Sephardic communities multiplied between 1492 and 1540.

The messianic ideal, one generation after the expulsion from Spain, is represented by the kabbalist Abraham ben Eliezer ha-Levi. According to his studies and based on the Hebrew tradition, redemption began in 1492 and was due to end in 1531. Years later, in colonial Mexico, the Carvajal family thought in the same terms. Luis de Carvajal the Young can be described as a visionary or a prophet, "drunk of God," as Seymour B. Liebman says,[13] or as a kind of Messiah that dreamed of celestial beings. Isaac Luria (1534–1572), also obsessed by the expulsion from Spain, developed new theories in which exile belonged not only to the people of Israel but also to the universe in its totality and even to God himself.

The experience of exile is manifested first in language. The mother tongue, among alien languages in foreign countries, suffers a displacement. It is preserved in forms that evolve slowly and that are idealized in a reserved manner. This is what happened to the Spanish language that Sephardic Jews took with them into exile. (Something similar had happened previously to the Hebrew language.) And it is what continues to happen in any contemporary exile. Language becomes the essence of the universe, as it had been in Genesis thanks to its nominative quality.

The Sephardic Jew turns to certain kabbalistic techniques of linguistic interpretation to analyze his situation. He begins with one of the main reasons for studying the Kabbalah: the search for the true name of God and the exegesis of the Tetragrammaton (the four Hebrew letters of the divine root). Then he explains that the Tetragrammaton was also torn apart by exile and that God's name has been divided into its four letters. The exile will end only when the four consonants are reunited in the correct order. That is when linguistic unity will be recovered and the language will return to its country.

Thus the culture of the Ladino language is influenced by the sacred character of Hebrew (Ladino is written with Hebrew rather than Latin letters) and has mystical aspirations. This is the only way in which the preservation of certain *romances* may be understood—as a process of symbolizing the divine love. This explains why Sabbatai Zevi incorporates the *romance* of "La linda Melisenda" into the kabbalistic ritual. Ramón Menéndez Pidal first mentioned this *romance* in 1948:

> Los romances al servicio del fervor religioso nos dan una nota interesante. Se trata de los cantos religiosos del judío español Sabbatai Ceví [*sic*], falso Mesías, cuya acción proselitista comenzada en Esmirna, su patria, el año de 1648, y propagada desde 1651 a Salónica, Constantinopla, El Cairo y Jerusalén, conmovió a todo el pueblo judaico. Sabbatai solía alternar con el canto de los salmos las canciones profanas vueltas a lo divino, ejerciendo fuerte impresión sobre sus oyentes, al favor siempre de su hermosa voz y de su hermosa presencia. Un pastor protestante holandés, que se hallaba en Esmirna en 1667, refiere que aquel Mesías entonaba, con alusiones místicas al Cantar de los Cantares, cierta canción amorosa española, de la cual da, traducida al holandés doce versos:

> Subiendo a un monte,
> bajando por un valle,
> me encontré a Melisenda,
> la hija del emperador,
> que venía del baño
> de lavar sus cabellos.
> Su rostro era resplandeciente

como una espada,
sus pestañas como un arco de acero,
sus labios como corales,
su carne como leche.[14]

For the followers of Sabbatai Zevi, Melisenda may be compared to the Shekhinah and the emperor to the divinity. The rest of the mystical interpretation follows the metaphoric code of the Song of Songs, in which an amorous dialogue between God and the people of Israel is established.

Including the Melisenda *romance* in the Sephardic ritual is characteristic of Judaism's exegetic technique, whereby the symbolic representations of language are revealed. Maimonides had already mentioned the need for making this distinction to understand biblical meanings. Erich Auerbach also insisted on the fundamental difference between, on one hand, Hellenism and Christianity and, on the other, Judaism, with regard to textual interpretation. Whereas the first two preferred the literal sense, the latter turned to the figurative or metaphorical one, that is, emphasizing the unsaid, the background, and the need for interpretation.[15] In this way, language exiles itself from its strict formal content and offers new variations and combinations, which may be intertwined in the strict and figurative senses of language.

Memory, a distinctive trait of Jewish culture, does not allow tradition to be lost. Wherever they went, the Sephardim took their language with them. Even famous conversos, such as Juan Luis Vives and Juan de Valdés, who barely escaped from Spain and the Inquisition, dedicated their years in exile to the study and preservation of the Spanish language. Juan de Valdés, in his Neapolitan refuge, wrote the *Diálogo de la lengua*. For him, the bases are the "punticos y primorcicos de la lengua vulgar" (details of everyday language). He studied the origins of the Castilian language and its etymology; he explained the orthographic and syntactic rules; he defended spontaneity and brevity of expression; and he drew from popular expressions and proverbs. He seemed to anticipate the experience of Sephardim after centuries of using the language. Kulli and authors of *Meam loez* employed the same critera.

The lengua florida never stopped traveling. It came to America and to the Philippine Islands. A contemporary Sephardic Jew whose family was from Turkey, the French writer Marcel Cohen, expressed his nostalgia for a language that was as sweet as honey but was condemned in our time to slowly disappear:

Se akodran de los trentycinkos kales[16] en los kuales, por syécolos, se ivan en funksyón de su provincia de orizen: al kal de Kastilia y el kal de Aragón, el kal de Mayor y el kal de Pertukal. Se akodran de las yaves de sus kazas de Toledo, Kórdova o Granada, ke los padres guardavan para ke los ijos no se olvidan el pasado, y también, sin dizirlo, enkauzo ke les suviryan mazal[17] de retornar. Se akodran de los doblones, patakones,[18] maravedís y eskudos ke salvaron a la salida de España, aziéndoles preciosas yadranes[19] ke, de madre a ija, mujeres se metyan kon fostanes[20] de shabat. *Se akodran ke, fin al siglo veynte, los exilados de España no tuvieron ni el gusto de aprender realmente al grego o al turko, seguros ke stavan de avlar la más preciosa lingua del mundo, una lingua jalis[21] sakrada, dulse como la myel.* Se akodran k'al siglo dyez y syete los merkaderes del orguyozo Luis el katorse se devyan de aprender djudyo[22] para azer sus etchos en Grecia y Turkya, ke los primeros livros imprimidos en los Balkanes y Turkya lo fueron en ladino, ke los sultanes, los pachás y los vizires tenyan doktores por matasanos, azyando konfyansa sólo a los médikos djudyos desendyentes de los médikos de Salamanca. Se akodran de los primeros sionystos ke les toparon kumiendo lokumikos,[23] travando kyef[24] y kantando las kantikas viejas. "Estos no se irán nunka a la Palestina, dichyan. Retornar a España, esto es lo ke kyeren.[25]

Although the history of the Sephardim in Mexico has been the subject of considerable research, the abundant material in the General Archive of the Nation has not been studied in depth. Some of the most important sources are *History of the Tribunal of the Inquisition in Mexico* by José Toribio Medina; *Unpublished or Very Rare Documents for the History of Mexico* by Genaro García; *Heretics and Superstitions in New Spain* by Julio Jiménez Rueda; *The Red Book* by Vicente Riva Palacio; *The Jew in New Spain* by Alfonso Toro; *Jews in Mexico* by Rafael Heliodoro Valle; "Our Sephardic Legacy" by Gonzalo Báez Camargo; *The Jews in Mexico and Central America* by Seymour B. Liebman; "The Jews in Mexican History and Literature" by José de J. Núñez y Domínguez; *The Martyr: Luis de Carvajal, a Secret Jew in Sixteenth-Century Mexico* by Martin A. Cohen; and *La vida entre el judaísmo y el cristianismo en la Nueva España* by Eva Alexandra Uchmany.

The Sephardim arrived in America on board Christopher Columbus's caravels as cartographers, pilots, and crew members. Rodrigo de Triana, the first man to spot land, was a converso. Among the captains who accompanied Hernán Cortés and who were new Christians, were Diego de Ocaña and the brothers Gonzalo and Diego de Morales and Hernando Alonso. The latter three men died in the auto-da-fé of 1528; however, the first decree against Judaizers was issued as early as 1523, which proves that an important part of the Spanish population in New Spain was of Jewish origin.

It is common knowledge that the archbishop Francisco de Victoria and the historians fray Bernardino de Sahagún and fray Diego de Durán were new Christians, as was fray Bartolomé de las Casas. Crypto-Judaism was supposed to have been eliminated in 1596 with the unfortunate but well-known trial and death of the Carvajal family. Nevertheless, in 1649, when Tomás Treviño de Sobremonte was burned alive, the Inquisition was still proceeding with its trials and executions.

There were some enigmatic cases, such as that of the hermit Gregorio López, a friend of Carvajal el Mozo, who was about to be beatified but, as far as we can tell, did not pass the purity of blood test. He was both attacked and defended by his contemporaries, and he dedicated himself to practicing medicine among poor people, thus acquiring the sobriquet "the Venerable." In his work, *Saint John's Apocalypsis,* he insists on the arrival of a second Messiah. For these reasons, he was considered a Judaizer.

The student of Judaism who wished to continue his studies in New Spain would have found it difficult to do so. The possession of books in Hebrew, even the Old Testament, was reason enough to be denounced to the tribunal of the Inquisition. The Sephardim had no choice but to turn to the Latin texts or their Spanish versions. Very few had Jewish prayer books, which meant that the tradition was barely kept alive. One source of information was travelers from Brazil or Amsterdam. The colonial Inquisition was stricter than the Spanish one, and its vigilance over forbidden books was even harsher. Nonetheless, Jews managed to find meeting places where they could exchange their ideas.

The synagogue, the center of community life, was a room in a private house or a secluded space in a store or warehouse, with no object or ornament—no candelabra or Torah—that would betray its purpose. The number of places of worship varied in time. It is estimated that in the mid-seventeenth century there were some fifteen congregations in Mexico City and its surroundings, three in Puebla, two in Guadalajara and in Veracruz, one in Zacatecas and in Campeche, one or more in Monterrey and in Mérida. It is probable that there were also congregations in Guatemala, Nicaragua and Honduras.[26]

In New Spain Jews were able to live in various urban or rural areas, in contrast to European Jews, who were forced to live in specific neigh-borhoods. Thus Jews in New Spain avoided massive persecution and were able to keep their faith alive.

The Inquisition accused many Jews of being rabbis, but we do not know whether they were actually rabbis or whether they were simply more knowledgeable about Judaism than the rest of the people. There is also no information as to the existence of a *bet din,* or tribunal for civil cases, dis-putes, and religious matters. Among those men considered rabbis were Juan Cardoso, also called Gariel Peregrino; Simón Montero, who had studied Judaism in France and Italy; and Francisco Rodríguez de Matos y Manuel de Morales. Sometimes a "great rabbi" was mentioned in docu-ments but not identified by name.

Although Jews in New Spain avoided mass persecutions, they faced many of the same dangers they had known in Sepharad. They lived a double life, continuing to be Jews but pretending to be Christians. How-ever, there were those who did not manage to lead such a life and ended up in the cells of the Inquisition. Their stories cover the pages of numerous trials and contain glimpses of perseverance and courage and of ingenuity and subtle stratagems cultivated in order to survive.

With Mexico's independence, the tribunal of the Inquisition was abol-ished in 1821. The last Jew remaining in prison, Gil Rodríguez, was set free; he had been brought to trial in 1788 in Guatemala.

Today, there are many families both in Spain and in Latin America that acknowledge their Jewish origin. They know that they are the descen-dants of those first Sephardim who migrated to the new lands to preserve themselves and their religion. Despite the passage of time, the memory of them and their tenacity has not been erased.

NOTES

1. Miguel de Cervantes Saavedra, *Don Quijote de la Mancha,* translated by John Ormsby, from the Cervantes Digital Library.

2. Angelina Muñiz-Huberman, *La lengua florida: Antología sefardí,* Lengua y Estudios Literarios (México, D.F.: Universidad Nacional Autónoma de México y Fondo de Cultura Económica, 1992), 8.

3. Angelina Muñiz-Huberman, "La idea del exilio en la Cábala," in *Casa del tiempo,* Universidad Autónoma Metropolitana, México, abril de 1989, 2–6.

4. Gershom Scholem, *Kabbalah,* Library of Jewish Knowledge, (Jerusalem: Keter, 1988), 161.

5. *Zohar,* III, 95a.

6. Fragment from the prayer book *Majzor shaaré rajamim le Iom Kippur* (México, D.F.: Imprensa Venecia, 1984), 34–35. Cf. Angelina Muñiz-Huberman, *Tierra adentro*, Serie del Volador, México, D.F.: Mortiz, 1977), 168–169.

7. Gershom Scholem, *Major Trends in Jewish Mysticism* (New York: Schocken, 1974), 250.

8. Ibid., 280–284.

9. Cited in Juan Luis Alborg, *Historia de la literatura española: Epoca barroca*, 2d ed., con índice de nombre y obras, t. 2 (Madrid: Gredos, 1974), 491–492.

10. *La novela picaresca*, 2d ed., estudio prel., selec. y notas por Angel Valbuena Prat (Madrid: Aguilar, 1946), 1680.

11. Cited in Muñiz-Huberman, *La lengua florida*, 136.

12. According to an old Jewish legend, the Messiah will be born on the 9th of av, the same date of the destruction of the Temple in Jerusalem.

13. Seymour B. Liebman, *Los judíos en México y América Central: Fe, llamas, Inquisición* (México, D.F.: Siglo Veintiuno, 1971), 192.

14. Ramón Menéndez Pidal, *De primitiva lírica española y antigua épica*, 2d ed. (Madrid: Espasa-Calpe, 1968) (Col. Austral, 1051), 93. Menéndez Pidal includes some of the modern versions of this *romance*, recollected from Salonika, Constantinople, Sophia, and Jerusalem. In *La lengua florida*, I include another version (94):

Esta noche, mis compañeros,
durmí con una doncella,
que en los días de los días
no topí otra como ella.
Melisenda tiene oir nombre,
Melisenda galana y bella.
A la bajada de un río
y a la subida de un varo,
encontrí con Melisenda,
la hija del emperante,
que venía de los baños,
de los baños de la mare,
de lavarse y entrenzarse,
y de mudarse una camisa.
Ansí traía su cuerpo
como la nieve sin pisare;
la su cara corelada
como la leche y la sangre.

15. Erich Auerbach, *Mimesis: La representación de la realidad en la literatura occidental*, trans. J. Villanueva y E. Imaz, Lengua y Estudios Literarios (México, D.F.: Fondo de Cultura Económica, 1950), 29.

16. *Kal* (Hebrew): synagogue.

17. *Mazal* (Hebrew): good luck, happiness.

18. *Pataka* (Turkish): old Turkish coin.

19. *Yadrán* (Turkish): necklace.

20. *Fostán* (Turkish): woman's dress.

21. *Jalis* (Turkish): certainly.

22. *Djudyo* (Jewish): synonym for the Spanish language.

23. *Lojum* (Turkish): sweet made of jelly dough, covered with almonds.

24. *Travar kyef* (Turkish): to be euphoric.

25. Marcel Cohen, *Letras a un pintor ke kreya azer retratos imaginarios por un sefardí de Turkya ke se akodra perfektamente de kada uno de sus modelos,* illus. Antonio Saura (Madrid: Almarabú, 1985), 24. My emphasis.

26. Liebman, *Los judíos en México y América Central.*

SECTION II
Journeys

DAVID BRAILOVSKY

Tuesday Is a Good Day

"Tuesday is a good day!" The sentence keeps echoing in my head. "Tuesday is a good day!"

I am standing alone in the middle of my room. I barely recognize it. A chair and a bed are all that is left. The room has a monastic appearance. I look around. The walls are bare; several holes, like scars after a case of smallpox, break up their smooth, monotonous surface. This is where, throughout my adolescence, I hung various meaningful mementos. Now, everything has been removed. Gone are the maps of China and Europe where, assiduously, for the last six years, I followed the ebb and flow of wars, moving daily, the little flags of the contenders. Gone are the framed pictures of the Lubavicher Rebbe, my religious leader, as well as that of Jabotinsky, the fiery uncompromising energetic Zionist whose policies I admired. A sultry picture of Rita Hayworth, in a revealing negligee, kneeling on a bed, her hair loose and cascading to her shoulders, no longer stares at me provocatively. Gone is my favorite painting, *The Tahitians*, a Gauguin, whose representation of two women smiling gracefully, yet somewhat sensually, has always been a source of great pleasure. I look again at the walls and feel uneasy, as if I am staring at a naked, defenseless, and vulnerable woman. A calendar thrown carelessly on the chair is marked with a big red capital *D*. "D" stands for "departure," the day I leave Shanghai.

Father walks in, Mother follows. I sense the emotion and the tenderness of the moment. We try to act naturally. It is not working. Mother sits on the edge of the bed and pulls out a handkerchief; Father approaches me and gently places his hands on my head as he pronounces the priestly blessing, "May the Lord bless thee, and keep thee: may the Lord make his face to shine upon thee, and be gracious unto thee: may the Lord turn his face unto thee, and give thee peace." Father's baritone voice becomes louder and louder, as he tries to drown out Mother's sobbing. Suddenly, the full blow of the moment crushes me. In a few minutes I will be leaving them. After twenty-two years I will no longer feel their proximity. Their presence will from now on be only a memory. The sound of their voices only a recollection. For the first time in my life I will be alone, alone and far away. Some last-minute words of maternal advice follow quickly. Father interrupts: "Remember, Tuesday is a good day. It is the third day of the Creation, when God ordered the earth to blossom, and it is the only day in which the Creator says 'and it was good' twice."

Appropriately we part in my room, a room filled with sweet and bitter memories. A public display of such deep emotions would make us all very uncomfortable. The blessing, that mystical, magical moment, would be impossible in front of a rowdy crowd.

I walk alone to the threshold of our apartment, a suitcase in each hand. I feel that the last chapter of a book has just been finished and the book slammed shut. A new book opens and the first page is still blank. What will its first sentence be?

I stop at the threshold. I am frightened. I am alone. A taxi pulls up in front of the house and honks its horn. My feet are bolted to the ground. I cannot move. Although my body is motionless, my vivid imagination pushes my mind into overdrive. What will my new life be like? Several scenarios emerge, not all pleasant. The taxi driver continues to honk his horn. I look at my watch. It is 11:35 A.M. I wonder how many people on this planet are, at this very instant, experiencing, like me, a crucial moment in their lives.

I look back, I see Father standing straight as a rod. I see his lips move, but I hear no sound. I am sure that he is praying. Mother's face is covered with a handkerchief. They dare not speak so as not to betray their emotions. They simply wave. I nod my head and hastily cross the threshold. The umbilical cord has been severed. The first step in my long journey to Chile is taken. There is no turning back.

The taxi driver is annoyed because of the wait. He drums the steering wheel with all his fingers. A small stub is all that remains of a cigarette that dangles from the corner of his mouth. He uses it as proof of the time he has been waiting.

The car lurches forward, the tires screech, like the sound of a crying baby. It is the same sound I feel deep inside me. We turn a corner and the house disappears. Will I ever see it again? The taxi heads for the Bund, Shanghai's waterfront. As we drive at breakneck speed, I try to engrave in my mind all the familiar sights, sounds, and smells of a city where I spent my childhood, my adolescence, and my early manhood. I am surprised that the city I so desperately wanted to leave now, as I am leaving, starts to fill me with sadness and nostalgia.

Unceremoniously, the taxi drops me off at the curb. Deftly, I navigate between numerous peddlers displaying their wares on small tables placed on the sidewalk. Spaced between them are prostitutes, young and old, pimps, and beggars with gaping wounds covered with flies. It is an effort to make my way to the pier. The acrid, foul smell of uncollected garbage adds to the squalor that surrounds me. I look at the row of buildings that line Shanghai's proud hallmark. For the first time I see these once-imposing structures, the symbol of the city's wealth and power, as what they really are today: shabby and run-down. It is as if by some sort of miracle my vision is suddenly restored, and I become aware of reality: the potholes, the peeling paint, the rusty ironwork, and the grime. The war has taken its toll. I no longer harbor any ambivalence about my departure. I am eager to leave. The city I love no longer exists.

I board the tender and wait patiently, my two suitcases close to me. Nothing seems to happen. After a while, a wailing siren announces the tender's departure. Slowly, it bobs its way toward *Sweet Victory*. The ship is to take me to Panama, the first stop in my long and circuitous journey from China to Chile. As the tender approaches the vessel, my illusions are crushed. My fantasies of traveling on a beautiful cruise ship, with elegant, witty, charming, and intelligent passengers, are shattered. *Sweet Victory* is a far cry from what I expect. It is a "liberty ship," a ship that was produced at the height of World War II, at the frantic rate of one ship every six hours. It was a race between the United States and Nazi Germany. Could the United States build ships faster than the German submarines could sink them? The prize was victory or defeat. These ten-thousand-ton ships were a tribute to superior American technology and organization. Once the war was over, *Sweet Victory*, like so many other ships of her kind, was transformed into a cargo ship; some, to increase their profitability, made room for passengers.

As the Communist troops rapidly approached Shanghai, foreigners, fearing being caught in their net, booked passage on anything that was able to float. People considered themselves fortunate to obtain tickets on ships like the *Sweet Victory*. Father bribed and paid an extra "surcharge" to obtain my passage. I was one of the fortunate few.

Sweet Victory is decrepit, rusty, and filthy, the crew a microcosm of humanity's flotsam, a motley bunch from all over the seafaring world. I study them, and they all seem to have a common denominator: brawny, tall, three-day stubble, tattoos on their arms and chests, and oil-stained dingy clothes. Somehow many of them reminded me of Bluto, Popeye's rival for Olive Oyl's heart. They all look menacing to me, and I would not want to be caught alone with any one of them in a dark alley.

The captain, Lars Anfersen, a Norwegian in his early fifties, is 6 feet 2 inches, stocky, with a ruddy, stern face, a big aquiline nose, deep-set eyes overhung by thick eyebrows, and closely cropped blond hair. A three-inch scar on his left cheek makes him look even more menacing. His thick lips curl around a pipe. The passengers on the ship are a necessary evil that he has to tolerate for the company's sake.

He sees me boarding the ship and thunders from the bridge, "You there boy, cabin 4!" A sailor points me in the right direction. My cabin is minute—a bunk, a small night table, a closet, and a bathroom with a shower. A ray of sunlight filters through the porthole and falls on the small night table. It is a comforting sight. I am emotionally drained. I do not bother to undress. I collapse on the bunk. I close my eyes and think of my parents. They promised to follow me as soon as Father was able to tie up some loose ends in his business. I pray that it should be soon. For the first time in my life I am alone. I do not dare explore the future. If this, the first day, is a harbinger of things to come, the future looks bleak. A loud, thumping, low-pitched metallic sound wakes me from my daydream. The anchor is lifted, and shortly after, I feel the ship moving. I go on deck. I want to catch the last glimpses of Shanghai. Slowly the buildings became smaller and smaller, and before long the city sinks beyond the horizon. A cool ocean breeze caresses my face, and I am unable to stop the flow of tears down my cheeks. I suddenly remember something somebody said a long time ago: "Be careful for what you wish, because your wish might be granted." If leaving Shanghai was my wish, then why am I crying?

The bell rings for dinner, and I find my way to the officers' dining room. For the first time I catch a glimpse of the other passengers: three couples, all in their mid-sixties. Each couple sits at a separate table. They speak in whispers. There are no introductions. Each couple lives in their own world. I sit by myself. I am uneasy. I do not know what to expect. The captain sits alone at a table right in front of mine. A long table placed against a wall is reserved for the officers. They are a rowdy bunch. I look at them from the corner of my eye. I see the lewd gestures and the suggestive expressions on their faces that in all probability describe their adventures in the bars and brothels of the city.

On the second evening, after dinner, I see the captain sit in front of a chessboard trying to solve a problem. I come up and silently watch him. After a while, I clear my throat and sheepishly make a suggestion.

"What do you know!" he barks at me.

"I play some chess," I reply modestly.

"Sit down!" It sounds more like an order than an invitation.

"You are black," he decides, and with that he opens his gambit.

We play in silence. The captain takes his time moving his pieces but becomes impatient with me at my slightest delay. I recall with nostalgia the games I played with Dobrinsky, the old Russian night watchman. I cannot avoid the contrasts between the two men. For Dobrinsky, chess was a social affair, an opportunity to tell me stories of his life, of his experiences on the Russian-German front during World War I. For the captain, chess is war, and during a war you do not talk to the enemy. During the game, Dobrinsky drank huge amount of kvass, whereas the captain gulps whiskey from a bottle. Dobrinsky smoked cigarettes; the captain silently puffs on his pipe. Dobrinsky warned me of my mistakes and taught me how to avoid them; the captain is only too happy to pounce on my every error. Nevertheless, I enjoy having him as an opponent. It is a battle. However, in spite of my best efforts, he always wins.

The crew notices my chess games with the captain. I sense that in a subtle way they show me more respect. The dining room steward serves me immediately after the captain and the officers, and ahead of the other passengers. I also notice that my portions are bigger.

The days seem endless. The view—sea, waves, sky, clouds—is monotonous. The routine is boring. There is no entertainment. The crew is too busy for conversation. The other passengers avoid socializing. I can study Spanish for only so many hours a day. The rest of the time I sit on the deck, close my eyes, and daydream about my uncertain future.

Then, suddenly, in the middle of our ninth night, it hits us. A powerful hurricane toys with *Sweet Victory*. Howling, gusting winds add their frightening sounds to the crashing of loud thunder. Through my porthole I see lightning illuminate the dark skies, and its tentacles, like deft fingers, open myriad heavenly spigots that pour a curtain of rain on us. Enormous waves toss *Sweet Victory*. The ship groans and moans as it plows along. Terrified, I hold on with all my strength to my bunk. Queasiness very soon turns into a full-blown case of seasickness. The storm lasts for two days. During all this time, I do not dare to leave my cabin. Fortunately, the Filipino steward is kind enough to bring my meals. I barely touch the food. The storm abates, and I decide to venture on deck. I lean against a railing; the fresh sea air invigorates me. A sailor passes by. He stops long enough to look at me. "You look like shit!" is his only comment. "This place," he says, pointing at the ocean, "is known for its storms." Before I can answer he is gone. "Calling this huge body of water the Pacific Ocean is definitely an oxymoron," I say to myself.

After crossing practically the full length of the Pacific Ocean, I am happy to land in Panama and feel the safety of firm ground under my feet. However, this period of security does not last long. I am scheduled to fly to Chile the following day. I have always associated flying with movie actors, actresses, and other important people, and have always considered it an extremely glamorous and sophisticated way of traveling. However, in spite of all my efforts, I cannot adjust to this elegant and cosmopolitan atmosphere, and it is with great trepidation that I board the Panagra flight to Santiago de Chile. It does not take long for the stewardess to notice that I am a frightened novice, and it is thanks to her comforting words and attention that I overcome my initial fear and actually enjoy the trip.

I deplane at Cerillos Airport in Santiago and follow the passengers to the arrival gate. I hand my passport to the Immigration officer. He looks at it and then at me, and reexamines the passport. "Chinese?" he says dubiously, not quite believing what he is seeing. In my broken Spanish, I explain my background, as briefly as I can. There is a long period of silence. All sorts of wild thoughts cross my mind as I try to second-guess his reasoning. I become apprehensive as I consider the possibility of being denied entry into the country. I smile sheepishly, as I anxiously await his decision. Still bewildered, he nods his head, smiles, and wishes me good luck. I run out of the airport, trying to put the greatest distance in the least amount of time between the inspector and me. I hail a taxi and give him the address of a small downtown medium-priced hotel that I obtained at the Chilean Embassy in Shanghai. It is only then that I feel somewhat relaxed and I am able to afford the luxury of sinking into the soft seat of the cab. My hotel room is small but adequate. A strong smell of tobacco permeates everything. Exhausted by the events of the day, I sit at the edge of the bed and, in a dreamlike state, stare at the many stains on the furniture and the carpet. For a long while I try to find meanings in their various shapes and sizes. The game amuses and refreshes me. I unpack hastily and rush to get acquainted with the city that is now my home. I walk along the streets and carefully examine the people and the buildings. Automatically and unconsciously, I compare all these impressions with Shanghai. The difference could not be greater. The mass of humanity that blankets the streets of Shanghai and makes every step an adventure and a challenge does not exist. By Shanghai's standards, the streets of Santiago are deserted, and I am able to stroll comfortably without bumping into anybody. The familiar cacophony of loud, strident sounds created by shouting street vendors, screaming rickshaws, the ringing of thousands of bicycle bells, and the honking of hundred of cars is unknown to this city. Here the traffic is light and orderly, and there is no hustle and bustle. The buildings in the center of town are the typical concrete gray uniform structures that one finds in the business centers of any town. What impresses me most are the imposing snow-covered mountains around the city. Their majestic white peaks stand out and glitter against a perfect blue summer sky. After walking for several hours, I return to my room, tired but happy. I like my new home. With that comforting thought, I peacefully fall asleep on my first night in Santiago.

The following morning I put on my best suit, make sure that my shoes are well shined, my tie straight, and my hair well combed, and, with my letter of acceptance to the medical school in my jacket pocket, I make my way to the Faculty of Medicine, located in the Casa Central of the Universidad de Chile, a big French-style fin-de-siècle building. An uneasiness and a series of doubts assail me as I approach the building. Could they have lost my application? Is it possible for them to have changed their minds? These possibilities are unlikely, but, nevertheless, in the realm of bureaucracy everything is possible. All my fears quickly fade away after the first few words exchanged with the Faculty's secretary, a very pleasant middle-aged woman. Her genuine warm welcome makes me feel immediately at ease. The paperwork completed, I thank her profusely and leave the building.

Walking the streets of Santiago, I am overjoyed that I am able to communicate with anybody I choose to. This is not China; here I speak the language, and I am able to read everything that I see. Only a person who has lived in a foreign land, unable to read or write the language of that country, only such a person can understand the frustration and alienation that I experienced in China, and the joy, the feeling of freedom, of integration, that I now feel.

Nevertheless, sometime during the first few weeks of my stay in Chile, I discover something that I had never noticed before, something that up to now I have always taken for granted: my sense of Jewishness. I cannot call myself an Orthodox Jew, although in Shanghai my family prayed in an Orthodox synagogue, nor can I call myself a Zionist, since I left Shanghai for Chile, instead of Palestine, yet, during these days, wandering alone in the city, I come to recognize that I am missing something, and that something is contact with my fellow Jews. I become acutely aware of this subconscious bond that unites the Jewish people. While in Shanghai, I had made up my mind that in my new home my main priority would be to become an integrated member of my new society and no longer live the life of a marginalized foreigner. However, I had never given a moment of thought to the important role my Jewishness would play in this new scenario.

Luckily, through some Jewish friends in Shanghai whose relatives live in Santiago, I find a room in a private home that belongs to a German Jewish family. This is my first contact with Jewish life in Santiago, and to my great satisfaction, an important void in my life is filled.

Several days after my arrival, Hans, my landlord, invites a group of friends for dinner. The conversation centers on the building of a synagogue.

"Why do we need a new synagogue?" I inquire innocently. "Don't we already have one on Serrano Street?" I refer to a big synagogue located on a street in downtown Santiago. Silence follows my question, and all eyes turn toward me.

"The synagogue you refer to," Hans phrases his answer as diplomatically as possible, "is for Russian and other eastern European Jews. They are Orthodox and pray in Hebrew. We follow the Conservative rite and pray in German and Hebrew, and therefore we need a synagogue of our own."

I notice that the rest of the group nods approvingly. This is my introduction to the fact that although a feeling of solidarity exists among all Jews, there are clear distinctions in the Jewish community, distinctions that are based on country of origin: Russia, Poland, Hungary, and so on. All these groups are not only organized into independent communities but also pray in separate synagogues.

"But doesn't all this split our community?" I ask in all earnestness.

"You are right, but only up to a point." One of the guests, the one sitting in front of me, replies to my question, as he shakes his index finger to stress his point. "You have to understand that we would be uncomfortable in an environment we are not accustomed to, and that is why we formed our own community."

"Take for instance our next-door neighbors," Hans, my landlord, interjects. He waits for my reaction before continuing. The truth is that I have never paid any attention to them. The nameplate on the front door of their house boasts a common Spanish surname, and my contact is limited to daily greetings and the usual neighborly small talk.

"They are Sephardic Jews," Hans proceeds to explain. "They descend from Jews who left Spain during the Inquisition. They have customs and rites that are very different from ours. They faithfully cling to their centuries-old and magnificent Jewish heritage and traditions, just as we adhere to our German central European culture, or the eastern Europeans to what they are used to." The comment is greeted with unanimous approval, and the conversation comes to an abrupt end, as dessert is served.

Although my parents came from Russia, because of my close association with the family I am staying with, I join them for services. At the time of my arrival in Chile, 1949, the German Jewish community does not have a synagogue. Services are held in a big rented movie house. Prayers are in Hebrew and German, and sermons are delivered in German. Because I do not understand either language, I am unable to participate fully. This provides me with the great opportunity to spend a considerable amount of time outside the prayer area, without feeling guilty. Destiny, however, has a strange way of playing itself out. It was during one of these many long interludes that I met the woman who would eventually become my wife. But that in itself is another story. Suffice it to say that since she was German Jewish and I was Russian Jewish, it was jokingly considered a "mixed marriage."

The summer months fly by, and with great anticipation and expectation, I await the first day of my third year of medical school. I enter the hospital's auditorium, where I find a number of my classmates. Nobody pays any attention to me. I hear them joke and laugh as they tell the stories of their vacations. Suddenly, the image of my first day at Aurora Medical School in Shanghai flashes through my mind. I can clearly see the Chinese students standing in one group speaking in Mandarin and the small number of foreign students in another, speaking in Russian, English, or French. Two parallel worlds that will never meet. I quickly erase the image from my mind. It is different here. There is only one language, Spanish, and the groups are gathered not along racial lines but rather according to hobbies and interests. I study my classmates and try to follow the expressions on their faces as they enthusiastically describe their adventures. Just as I decide to join the group closest to me, one of my classmates comes up to me. He introduces himself. "I am Isaac!" he says, as he extends his hand. "You must be new. Where are you from?" In a few sentences I tell him my story. "Are you Jewish?" is his next question. The unexpected probe into my personal life takes me aback. Surprised, I hesitate for a moment, then reply emphatically, "Yes!" At this point Isaac turns to face the whole auditorium and shouts: "We have a Chinese student!" All conversation in the auditorium stops. Dead silence. I see all faces turn in my direction. A circle forms around me and rapidly closes in. My classmates greet and welcome me, shaking my hand enthusiastically. Their warmth melts my feeling of awkwardness. "¡El Chino!" "¡El Chino!" "¡El Chino!" These two words brand me forever and become my moniker from this time on.

Isaac introduces me to my other Jewish classmates and to several Jewish organizations. I discover an active secular Jewish community geared more to the Zionist movement than to religious affiliation. It is at that moment that, like all immigrants, I am caught in a psychological tug-of-war. I want to be accepted and identify myself completely with my new environment, to be Chilean, but at the same time I am afraid of suffering the humiliation of rejecting or losing my identity, my Jewishness. My efforts to become part of Chilean society are for the most part successful, and I find that I am much more integrated in Chile than I ever was in Shanghai. However, I am careful in my choice of words. I say that my process of "chilenization" is "for the most part successful" because with time, I discover several obstacles along this road. My Jewishness is the main stumbling block. Although the Jewish community has its share of prominent professionals, politicians, and businessmen and although at no time did I ever feel any overt anti-Semitism, a subtle, covert antagonism toward Jews exists in many quarters. I notice that surnames play an exceedingly important role in placing people in pigeonholes. An eastern European surname would make its owner suspect of being Jewish, and if coupled with a biblical first name, all doubt would be erased. Nevertheless, in spite of occasional degrading anti-Semitic remarks, I continue my efforts to painstakingly blend my Jewishness with my desire to fully belong to my adopted country.

One day, approximately eighteen years after my arrival, one sentence, uttered in total innocence, like a powerful earthquake shatters the building I so carefully erected. That day, as usual, I greet the secretary of our medical department with the usual common niceties.

"Today must be a very happy day for you," she replies.

"Why?" I am surprised. I think to myself that perhaps she knows something that I am unaware of.

"The president of your country is visiting Chile!" she says in all earnestness, referring to the visit to Chile of the president of Israel, His Excellency Zalman Shazar.

"My president is the president of Chile," is my immediate reply.

"You know what I mean!" She smiles, winks knowingly, stands up from behind her desk, and leaves.

This brief episode is sufficient to utterly destroy my dream of combining the two worlds I cherish: to be a Chilean and to be a Jew. I come to realize that in spite of all my efforts, I can never be completely integrated. How far I can go on the road of integration will always depend, not on me, but on the willingness of others to let me travel along it.

The creation of the state of Israel galvanizes the Jewish community and its institutions. Many an assimilated Jew finds pride in the achievements of this newborn country and decides to take his place as an active member of the Santiago Jewish community. Open support for the state of Israel, however, comes with a price. A question of dual loyalty, to Chile or to Israel, is immediately brought out by some non-Jewish Chileans. In spite of all repudiations and denials, the suspicion lingers and adds to the arguments that a Jew can never have only the best interests of Chile in his heart.

With time, an unsuspected set of problems arises in the Jewish community. I notice it in my children. As they get older, I become aware that they, like many others, feel that the ties that bind them to the congregations that are based on the countries of origin of their grandparents and parents are beginning to loosen. To this young generation of Jews, born in Chile, this balkanization of the Ashkenazi community is meaningless. The majority no longer speaks or understands the languages of the "old country." Besides, the increasing number of so-called mixed marriages, namely, marriages of these second-generation Jews to other second-generation Jews, but of different European origins, make this separation even more irrelevant. A common denominator must be found to unite them, instead of separating them into these artificial microcosms.

The building of the Estadio Israelita, a sports facility, is a crucial step in the right direction. It provides a secular forum where Jewish youth congregate and enjoy a healthy environment, regardless of their backgrounds. In the same spirit of union, but on a religious level, I was instrumental, together with a group of friends, in the foundation of Beth El, a congregation in which prayers are mainly in Spanish, with some interspersed Hebrew text. Beth El grows steadily, but unfortunately it is dissolved when, in the early seventies, many of its members leave Chile. However, it leaves a legacy for future similar efforts.

With time, I become quite an expert at juggling the two separate worlds I live in: my religious universe and my secular universe. Deftly, I learn to give unto Caesar what is Caesar's and to God what is God's. Is it easy? Is it easy to be schizophrenic? With time, I cease to notice the great divide and learn to live comfortably in both.

Years inexorably roll by, filling countless hourglasses with the sands of innumerable deserts. The world is shaken by a series of momentous events: wars in Korea, Vietnam, the Gulf; Neil Armstrong takes "a small step for man"; Kennedy is assassinated; the Berlin Wall falls; the Soviet Union collapses. I am now an established physician in Santiago, married, and the father of three daughters.

Shanghai is now a vague memory, exiled to a deep recess of my subconscious. However, occasionally the city surfaces and comes to life, triggered by a casual remark, passing scenery, or a fleeting fragrance. These transient moments make me keenly aware that it is still very much part of my being, and that, like the mark of Cain, I will always carry it with me.

One day I receive a letter with the logo of my Shanghai medical school. It announces the celebration of the fiftieth class reunion. As I hold the letter in my hand, innumerable images project themselves haphazardly on the screen of my mind. Some are blurry, others are vivid, but all carry great emotional content. The decision to return to China is not an easy one. I debate the issue for a long time. I am afraid of the nostalgia, of the pain of returning home. I am frightened that too many closed doors will reopen, leading into rooms I would rather not enter. I am terrified by the inevitable confrontation of my mature age with the years of my youth. Would it not have been better to have left the dead alone? Finally the decision is made. As General MacArthur said, "I shall return." So, after fifty years, I am back.

It is late at night. A pouring rain greets me and my wife. A limousine with driver and a young pretty female interpreter is waiting. During the long drive into the city, I desperately try to identify some familiar sights, but to no avail. The dense rain and the darkness make it impossible.

A pewter sky marks my first day in Shanghai. Anxiously, I jump into the car. My wife shares my enthusiasm and follows me. I show the interpreter a map of Shanghai with the name of the old streets scribbled next to their new designations. I tell her that I would like to visit my former apartment house, if it still exits. She translates my request to the driver, who smiles and nods his head knowingly. As we drive slowly along the former International Settlement and into what was the French Concession, I am able to recognize several landmarks, which I proudly point out to my wife and the interpreter. I notice that my voice has suddenly acquired a slight vibrato quality, as I explain to them the purpose of these buildings in my day. The interpreter tells us what they are being used for now. The driver smiles as the interpreter translates my comments. There is no doubt that, architecturally, the city has changed, an indiscriminate mixture of old and new. The combination is not exactly aesthetically pleasant. I feel that the old buildings speak to me; like me, they are gray, stiff, somewhat staid, many requiring significant repair.

Suddenly, I shout, "There!" as I raise my right hand and point my finger, Christopher Columbus–like, at my former apartment building. I direct the car into the courtyard. As I look at the building, sadness engulfs me. The beautiful princess has become an old hag. The once-manicured central lawn is now subdivided into several small vegetable gardens. The spacious verandahs, the pride of their owners in days gone by and the site of many elegant sundowner parties, now have clotheslines stretched from one end to the other, with cheap clothing flapping in the wind. They seem like hands waving and greeting me.

The car stops abruptly. Without waiting for my wife and the inter-preter, I walk up to the door of my apartment. The number 15 is still on the center of the door. It is crooked and rusted. I knock impetuously, and my heart pounds as I beat harder and faster. Finally, slowly, the door opens, but just so slightly. Through the crack I see a pair of teary red eyes and a wrinkled face, bracketed by white hair. A flood of Chinese words fol-lows. By now, the interpreter is by my side. A lengthy conversation ensues. The door finally opens, and a shriveled old lady, toothless and smiling, dressed in padded dark blue cotton three-quarter-length coat and pants, greets me. Patiently, I listen to the interpreter translate the conversation. "I told the old lady that you used to live here and that you only want to look at it again. In the beginning she was afraid that you came back to take the apartment away from them. Three families live here now. All are at work, and she is alone." She beckons us to follow her. As she opens the door onto what was my room, a wave of conflicting emotions overwhelms me: joy, excitement, sadness, but mainly wariness at being swept by events over which I have no control. I look at what was my room. Three beds are placed one against each wall. In the center, a nondescript stove. The walls are covered with standard Communist propaganda posters: a muscular, determined young man in a military uniform, a rifle in his upraised arm; a serious and pretty young woman in a white lab coat holding a test tube; a muscular farmer driving a tractor, his eyes fixed on the horizon; a group of pink-cheeked, well-fed children singing and waving small red flags. I look around. The room is the same, the walls have not changed, but all traces of my having ever lived here have been obliterated. Desperately, I try to peel off the layers of time and look into the past. Behind the propa-ganda posters I find the pictures that I cherished: the Gauguin behind the farmer, the Rita Hayworth behind the lab-coated woman, and my Lubavicher Rebbe behind the group of children. My eyes do not see them, but my mind perceives them as vividly as the last time I stood in this room. I close my eyes, and I can feel the presence of my parents; my father's hands on my head. I can hear his blessings as well as my mother sobbing. The old woman goes toward a bed, and from under it she pulls out a cardboard box. She places it on her knees and opens it very carefully. Painstakingly, she unwraps an old newspaper and shows me a battered small toy car. I recognize it immediately. It was my favorite toy as a child. She turns to the interpreter and conversation follows. The interpreter takes the toy car and gives it to me. "Grandmother says that when they moved into this room, she found this car in the far corner of the closet. She assumed that it belonged to the former owner of the room, and she kept it all these years hoping that one day he might return and ask for it." A prolonged silence follows. I hold the car in my hand and stroke it lovingly. A time machine instantly carries me back to my childhood. I shudder as the soul of a child fleetingly enters the body of an old man. Through the fog of time, I see a little boy sitting on the floor playing with his toy. I want to touch him, talk to him. My lips move, but no sound comes out. My arms are motionless at my side. The old woman pats me on my back and wakes me from my reverie. I thank her profusely. I put my hand in the inner pocket of my jacket looking for my wallet. However, instantly, I reject the thought of giving her money. It would soil a precious thoughtful moment. I have to give her something that is mine, something personal. That is when I feel my gold Parker fountain pen. I give it to her. At first she refuses, shaking her head vigorously. No words are spoken. I press the pen into her hand. She finally accepts it. I can see her face beam. She bends forward several times, smiling and mumbling something under her breath. The debt is paid. We part.

I follow my wife and the interpreter as we leave the apartment. I reach the threshold. I stop and reflect. Half a century ago, I stood at exactly the same place on my way to start a new life, in a place far away. I embarked on an adventure that I knew not where it would lead me. Today, I am three score and ten, my hair has turned to white, my gait is slower and measured, my eyes are weaker, and my memory is not as good as it once was. I have worked hard, traveled far and wide, and seen many wonderful things. I have a loving family. My life is full and sweet, and every day I thank God for his many blessings.

Before crossing the threshold, I look up at the beautiful cloudless blue sky, and I cannot help but whisper, "Tuesday is a good day!"

MURRAY BAUMGARTEN

My Panama

Not that it was any of my doing: running from the Nazis, we were penniless, frightened, wearing out. In the terror of flight and confusion I came early from my mother's womb, popping out on the ship that was taking us to Panama. Was it a premonition that mine was not to be the ease of a citizen relaxed in the amniotic fluid of home? And it was a while after I emerged before I caught even a glimpse of the sea-green Caribbean on whose shores in Colón we lived for the first ten years of my life.

Now the town map spread before me, I am in Panama once more. Here is the Avenida Roosevelt: turn left and go west at the open-air market with its smell of penned-up chickens and bruised fruit. Two more blocks, left at the Cine RKO, and you reach our New York Store, with the late afternoon sun cutting in below the awning. If he had named his place in New York the Panama Shop, would my father have prospered as he did in Colón? Continue on Bolívar, cross Centenario, a five-minute walk, and there is the synagogue. Go north to the water, follow the curve of the land. and at the bulge into the dreamy Caribbean the school stands, next to the Washington Hotel. Then follow the railroad tracks to the entry into the Zone.

Panama and Suez—why did de Lesseps succeed in the East and fail in the New World? Do you always pass through canals en route from one home to another? Can Columbus's voyage be reversed? Take the car back down the Paseo, past the Colegio, right on Santa Isabel, and when you smell the plátanos frying and can taste the sugarcane growing in the field near the stadium, you are at the house we used to live in.

On our side of the street the rain obscures everything. On the Ostroviaks' side the sun is shining. I am Noah and the flood is beginning; the gutter overflows and the water rushes over the pavement. Next door, the

Cantina, at sidewalk level, has five inches of water cleaning it out. We watch the ominous waves lap up to our front step, but God relents and spares the family store, which specializes in ladies' fashions and souvenirs of Panama made in Brooklyn. The next day, rain stories are told everywhere—who was saved and who went under, how the Americans rescued hundreds in small boats. That's why we live on the third floor.

At the doorway, Uncle Eli stops a customer. She hasn't bought anything. He lifts her skirt and takes out the three dresses tied around her waist. Without a word she hitches up her clothes and plunges into the streaming water. He stands with the dresses in his hands, peering into the mist after her as she disappears, a Camel dangling from the corner of his mouth, the ash growing longer and grayer till it drifts onto the taffeta and satins.

The sun comes out and the water rushes off. On the corner a one-armed woman with a caved-in face sells lottery tickets by waving the stump in time to her sales pitch. She isn't so hard to look at, which must be why the police haven't moved her to the waterfront, where lottery tickets are usually hawked. I imitate my tall, handsome father's gait as we walk hand in hand through the throng of buyers and sellers on Front Street and wave to the passersby as he does. (Is it to acknowledge them or to ward them off?) Nestling into his broad side, I don't get more than a glimpse of what becomes a composite image of beggars without noses or ears, some with wounded faces and humped backs. The legless ones have surprising strength in their arms, maneuvering their wheeled carts across streets and through crowds, pushing down hard with blocks of wood, which they use like oars.

After the canaries and the pigeons, the macaws and the parrots. On Sundays, the bird market bulges with the flood of humans, tourists, Indians, Chinese, Arabs, Jews, priests. "Compre pa hablar" (Buy one! He'll talk to you), the handlers call, displaying beak and wingspan. The bamboo cages are open; the parrots perch outside.

Canaries sing as brightly as their vivid yellow feathers. I covet a parrot with its riot of tropical colors, but we are there to look, not to buy. It is an occasion, a birthday perhaps, and we go to Feldman's for ice cream. The chairs are filigree wicker, the elegant tables glass, the floor tiled, the customers subdued and European.

Why are there so many palm trees here and even more cockroaches? Once a snake gets into our house and we wait downstairs till Maria finds her friend Juan, who knows about such things, to catch it. It has silver and green markings and hisses so viciously that we instinctively fall back even though Juan has it secured in a net.

In the morning the noises come from within as the household stirs. Awakening movements of sweaty, squeaking beds, rattling of pots and pans, the bathroom door opening and closing, squealing springs and faucets make a river of sound that is dissipated in the outside quiet before it can disturb the Wachtels across the street.

From the balcony I can see their movements. Soon breakfast is served in both households, after the men have folded up their enveloping *taleysim* (prayer shawls), rewrapped the strong tefillin. Their morning chants have answered each to each. While we prepare for school, the men walk into town together, going to work in the lengthening rays of the sun.

We often go to see the *shokhet* (Kosher butcher) kill the chickens my mother takes to him, and we pluck the feathers on the balcony. On Fridays everyone helps make noodles, kneading and rolling out the dough. I punch the challah; my sisters braid and decorate it. Every day we have coconuts, bananas, mangoes, and avocados. Always peel the vegetables and fruits, my mother repeats over and over.

The sight of my father turning an orange skin into a twirling snake is a delight that, alas, emphasizes my own inadequacies. Would I grow up and amount to anything? I wonder, as I watch my father thread the gold chain of his pocket watch through his belt loops. Proudly he displays the glittering *magen david* (Star of David) the congregation gave him, letting it dangle outside his watch pocket.

Uncle Phoebus, my mother's brother (whose name utterly confounds me), lives with us. I watch him rise red-faced from his bed, adjusting the wire-rimmed glasses bent from being slept in. He has the most trouble breathing in the heat, and his sheets are more rumpled than any of ours. He sleeps in his undershirt, and the blond hairs of his chest stick through its weave like wire mesh. Though he does not pray like my father, everyone calls him the doctor and the scholar. He gets up late, long after my father has gone to work. Some mornings he is still asleep when we go off to school.

At night, as everyone gathers after supper for tea and fruit and recounts the day's events, Uncle Phoebus lies on his bed reading large, heavy books and is spoken of less respectfully. My father calls out to him: "Why do you want to go to Haifa?" voicing the thought we all have. He would be a fool not to go north like Harry and Marcus, the other uncles, but he persists.

When he finally leaves for Israel, my pale mother cries, shaking her reddish blond hair from side to side, and asks who will take care of him in that difficult land. Yet she knows he is only following the other Rosenbergs — Emanuel and Fanka, Misha and Annie, Leo and Sophie, Pinchas and Gertie, Rutie and Zvi, who made aliyah in 1938. Their father, Maier-Yosef, whose name I bear, had been a rabbi in Vizhnitz. He and his twin brother were rebels: they were learned scholars, honored in their community, and yet they advocated Zionism and life in Israel as the future of the European Jews. Every year, during the month of Elul, as she prepares for Rosh Hashanah and my father thinks about *kapoyrus,* the atonement ritual, and who will swing the chicken over our heads in preparation for atonement, my mother puts a twenty-dollar bill inside a purse and sends it to Rutie, Phoebus's sister, in Haifa.

When he leaves in 1947, Phoebus's round face and blond hair, sparkling blue eyes and stooped shoulders, vanish for us. We never know what gauntlets he ran, how he got there. We never hear stories about him in Israel, like the stories from New York where the Baumgarten boys — Harry, Marcus, and Eli — merge into our vision of the successful businessman. Phoebus was the only one in the family who lived with us who went to a place we knew rather than all-promising America.

One day we get a letter from him, with a photograph: he is standing next to a motorcycle framed by the Carmel and the whitewashed houses marching down the hills of Haifa. He has found work as a doctor. My mother gasps, my father tells us the story once more: to take his last exam at the University of Vienna and receive his medical degree, the Nazis made him walk on his knees to the lecture room.

When Israel declared its independence in 1948 my father joined the Wachtels, Angels, and Ostroviaks, friends dancing the hora in the street in front of the synagogue. Three years later, when I was Bar Mitzvah in New York, Phoebus sent me a khumash — the Torah — from Haifa with an inscription in fine black lettering. I think of him because my glasses too are wire-rimmed, and I have seen pictures of the German Jews of the second aliyah that like Phoebus's echo my own features. A year later we get a letter from Rutie: Phoebus has killed himself.

Some days when my father came home, we knew he had been with *them* by the queer look his eyes had, as if something terribly cold had been placed there. He went every day for a month. We always wanted to see them too, for we were told that they were also Jews, but Dad never consented to take us along. We helped to make potato salad and cook chicken for them. My mother went once and came back pale and shaken. Her hands patting our cheeks were very cold. She'd never looked like that before, nor did she ever again until she was dying in the hospital in New York. "Living skeletons," my father called them, but after a while he said they were beginning to recover from the ghastly things they'd been through in Europe. They were going through the canal on old troop ships, to start new lives.

Glistening Colón, Columbus's city: a city of refuge not mentioned in the Bible that yet gave us shelter, and gathered in the survivors and then passed them on to other countries. They passed through, and we remained; without knowing them, they became part of us. We had survived too, escaping from Eichmann after Anschluss in such haste that I was born on the ship.

The day before I married Sheila—Tziril Esther—I asked my father what he said to them. For a moment his eyes sank into his head, remembering, and resenting my question. Finally, shrugging his shoulders, he explained that he was the official representative of the Jewish community: "I brought schnapps and we drank *lechayim* and said a *shekheyanu.*" Knowing I didn't have the right to speak, I queried him with my eyes. "I told them how I had learned Spanish and English by reading the papers," he said, passing his fingers through his silvering hair. "The news is always the same anyway. And that way I could make a living."

After the refugees moved on, or perhaps when someone else was delegated to visit them, my parents stopped talking German. Since we kids were all in school by then, learning both English and Spanish, my father decided we would speak English at home in preparation for the hoped-for move to the United States. For mother it was a struggle, and she often lapsed into Yiddish. My father's accent didn't improve for some time, but his decision stuck, as we neglected the Yiddish and the Viennese German that had been our mother tongues.

When Hitler's soldiers marched into Vienna, my father tasted the bad time to come. One spring afternoon he left work early, stopped at the bank for some travelers' checks, making sure to leave some money in the account so as not to arouse suspicion, bought bread, cheese, and mineral water, and hurried home. There he put some things into an overnight bag. At the railroad station he showed the soldier his passport, keeping my mother's, which had expired, under his arm. The soldier chucked my sister Theadora under the chin. As a baby she had blond hair and blue eyes. "What a beautiful Aryan child," he said, waving them through. "Have a good vacation at the seashore."

The family stories say that the train got us to Rotterdam; the ship took us to Curaçao. Then the *Simon Bolívar* ferried us to Panama. As we left the dock, my mother went into labor. She gave birth on that ship that dodged the U-boats. Later on in the war, one of them fired a torpedo into her and she went down with all hands. In Curaçao the doctor had told my mother she had weeks to go. No one expected me so early.

Three days later the family arrived in Colón, Panama. They watched young boys scamper up the trees to pick coconuts. They ate sticky papayas, sweet mangoes, guavas, and avocados. The peddler told us you could pick them from the tree and eat them. It wasn't stealing. As long as you peeled them, like bananas, you could eat Panamanian fruit and vegetables and not catch tropical diseases. My parents found an apartment near the Washington saltwater pool, built by Americans at the end of the blue-green Caribbean.

They circumcised me at eight weeks, in Panama, when I was finally out of danger and home from the hospital. My parents thought of naming me Simon Bolívar for the ship that had brought us to the new world, and constantly watched me for signs of sickness. No matter what they fed me I stayed skinny.

In Panama the powerful American soldiers ate spinach. They drank milk and devoured steak and potatoes. At night the voices of their planes never stopped telling us we were safe. "Democracy," my uncle Eli, who lived with us, said over and over, looking into the distance. Perhaps he was thinking of his future in New York, where he would precede us by four years. Or meditated on how he had escaped from Vienna: a friend at work told him not to go home on Kristallnacht and gave him some money and a fake ID. And he started running and hiding.

People helped him while others hunted this Viennese Jew. Somehow he made his way to Colón, where he found us. Tall and thin, Eli, my father's youngest brother, took a special interest in me. He insisted I eat my soup and once dunked my face in it to make his point. He used to read to me, and he taught us the words of the Panamanian popular song. "La cucaracha, la cucaracha," we three children chanted over and over. It was easy to learn. We liked talking our broken Spanish with our friends.

In the store, Eli and my father sold women's clothing, souvenirs of Panama, watches, underwear. Business was good, but you had to keep your eyes open and watch the customers even if they liked the salesman's style. My father told them jokes. After school we came to the store for a snack and then went to the synagogue to study.

Fridays they closed early. My mother held her hands over the candles and swayed back and forth, her eyes shut. "Gut shabbos," she sang. She wiped her eyes and kissed each of us. And my father blessed us so that we would grow up like our biblical namesakes, Sarah, Rebecca, Leah, and Rachel, Ephraim and Menashe.

When he returned from a Zionist meeting in Baltimore in 1941 my father brought us American silver dollars; they are about the size of biblical shekels, he said. Can we go through the canal to get to the United States? my sisters ask. Are they thinking of the PX? I wondered.

Because the killing machinery of the Third Reich was not yet geared up in 1938, we were able to slip out and journey across a green ocean. Syrian Jewish merchants in Colón staked my father to shirts, handkerchiefs, and socks; the proud businessman with a degree in commerce from a fabled Viennese vocational school started commercial life in Panama as a peddler.

When I think of those Aleppo Jews who had escaped the riots of the Arab uprising in 1929, and preceded us to Panama, I am drawn to my bookshelf. I take down the Keter Yerushalayim, also known as the Aleppo Codex—the Jerusalem Crown Bible published by the Hebrew University last year—which a friend has just sent me. The Keter Aram Zova, as the manuscript of the Aleppo Codex is known in Hebrew, is the oldest masoretic text of the Bible, newly printed in a magnificent edition in Jerusalem. These Aleppo Jews saved the manuscript through centuries of turmoil and homelessness till it could find renewed life as this handsome book. One copy now resides in the house of a Jew born of refugees from the shtetl of Sborov near Lvov and the city of Czernowitz, a haven of Jewish life, to whom they gave aid and succor when they arrived in Panama. Is this too not a sign of redemption?

We were used to lots of people, gatherings of worrying relatives and friends, where we children went unnoticed. At night every room had someone sleeping in it. One day Grandmother and Grandfather arrived with Aunt Ina. She had gotten them out of Vienna after Kristallnacht; Uncle Marcus had sent them a visa for the United States. He had enough money for three affidavits: they were the oldest, and Ina was the youngest. Panama was their way-station en route to New York.

In the hot summer months my sisters and I took our pillows to the balcony, as the locals did, only to be chased back by our irate parents. We returned reluctantly to our sweaty beds, to be tucked into the security of the mosquito netting that draped us even in our dreams.

Out there, where the planes droned, was the war. In the mysterious interior the dreaded German sympathizers massed and the Americans hunted them. They found German documents, my father said. "They asked me to translate some of them," he told us.

To us the war meant that the relatives lived with us. We accepted their presence like natural forces, and wove around and between them in our children's games. We never thought to ask why so many of us huddled together in the four-room apartment; it had always been that way. As Grandma and Grandpa, Aunt Ina, and Uncle Eli left for the United States, they were replaced by the American Jewish soldiers who came for intermittent visits. We grew up with them.

When they came to town Chessie, Simon, and Sidney took us to the PX for chocolate, sugar, and Lucky Strike cigarettes for Dad. Lots of kids were always wandering through with their parents, and no one took any particular notice of us. I think it was the first time we ever passed, and all because father brought these three GIs home from the synagogue one Friday night. They introduced us to Campbell's soup and told stories about Brooklyn—where there are more Jews than Indians with sticks through their noses in Panama.

Chessie, my favorite, had broad shoulders, soft eyes, and thick brown hair; I promised him I would eat my spinach, and he promised I would end up with bulging muscles like his. Sidney was short and toothy, and hated to take off his khaki cap even when he played with my sisters because he was getting bald. Simon imitated clowns and made faces.

We never learned where they worked or what they did, though we begged them to tell us. When they left us, they disappeared like figures in a dream, forming our first image of the meaning of the Canal—it brought everything to us and just as readily took it all away.

Coming home after Talmud class one Shabbat afternoon in New York, my father told me I had spent my first two weeks in the hospital. I was premature and didn't get circumcised till I was more than a month old, following the talmudic discussion that coincided with the best Panamanian medical opinion. It couldn't have been much of a party, more like a loud sigh of relief, especially for my mother.

Was that why she kept crying when Mordecai and Mr. Kelber, who kept his hat on even in the house, came and gave me my first haircut? I was three and watched in amazement as my blond curls fell all around me, and the men raised glasses for a *lechayim*. My sisters found some of my curls in the drawer when they were cleaning it out after mother died.

I was saying kaddish, reading the prayers harder and harder, my knowledge of Hebrew—the first language I'd learned to read and write—leaping ahead. *Modim anachnu lach,* I said, standing and reciting the Amidah, bowing low and thanking God *al khayenu hamesurim beyadekha,* for our lives, which are all in Your Hands. Then why did my mother wake up in the middle of a humid Bronx night in June, hardly more than a year after we arrived in this promised city, screaming and holding her burning head as if it would break? Why did she need a cerebral hemorrhage to kill her and make me use all the Spanish curse words I know?

We always had company and Mordecai for *shabbos* dinner. He was our teacher. And a refugee, like us. Mordecai was a small man. His eyes never stopped moving, darting from place to place like the darker eyes of the Indians who came to town to sell white hats and many-colored serapes. He wore a dark suit of my father's that almost fit him. Except when he was teaching, he rarely spoke. At dinner he would stare at the gefilte fish on his plate for a long time before starting to eat.

My older sister was his best pupil. My younger sister always started to cry when she saw him. I was going to be my father's "kaddish" and had to study harder. The obligation of reciting the prayer for the dead, after he was gone, to honor his memory, required learning. That would prove I was a grown-up Jew. At five I was almost grown up and going to kindergarten. Next year I would be the watchman carrying the rifle in the play about the kibbutz.

Friends always dropped in on Saturday night. After bathing in the washtub, the kids were allowed into the living room. "Anu banu artza livnot ulehibanot ba," my sister and I sang the song Mordecai had taught us. "Build the land," Phoebus translated, "and Israel will rebuild us."

When we knew it perfectly he was going to take us to sing it in front of the British Consulate. Then the gray-haired Englishman would tell His Majesty to open the gates of Palestine to the Jews.

My father forbade the demonstration. Jews had to be careful how they protested. It was 1942, and refugees weren't allowed to be rowdy.

My father and Phoebus always argued in German.

My mother served coffee.

One Shabbat morning, when we lived in the Bronx, as I was leaving for the synagogue she told me that Phoebus had been a young radical. They had agreed that Stalin was a murderer but Lenin had been a good man. The Jews were caught in the class struggle, she said. Not what your father liked to talk about, she added. He was a businessman who thought the market would take care of him.

Did she know he had an eye for the ladies? He was a handsome, dark-eyed man, and I'd watch the reactions of the women he worked with when he gave a hello and a smile and launched into one of his flirtations, "Mejor trabajar ahora y bailar esta noche," work now and dance tonight, he would say, with that irony of encouraging the seamstresses and playing with them at the same time. Was he stuck in the struggle that is mine too? the argument with sexual passion?

How different were we? Two Jews launched by Enlightenment and Emancipation into the adventure of modernity who had given up the *arba kanfot,* the ritual fringes at the corners of the undergarment that recall us from the seductions of eye and heart? I laugh and tell Sheila she is my addiction, Tziril-Esther, come to my rescue.

Only Aunt Ina talked about our parents' wedding in Vienna. Her voice dropped to a whisper as she told us that Dad's latest girlfriend — or was she his mistress? was she the Shushu the family whispered about? — broke in while Mother was adjusting her wedding gown. Shushu insisted she should be the one under the Huppah with Max. Emanuel, the lawyer, my mother's brother, shut Shushu up and got her to leave by giving her the money the brothers and sisters, orphaned of both mother and father and banded together to succeed in Czernowitz and Vienna by studying at the university, had collected for the dowry. My mother had just finished the first year of law school. She never went back, devoting herself to this marriage she was hustled into by friends. Was that why my mother had sad eyes?

But I have to remember that Viennese mistresses weren't all bad. It was his non-Jewish mistress who told my Uncle Leo, the admirer of Jabotinsky, that he should leave town. Like his hero, he was a snappy dresser favoring a felt hat with a sharp brim, a political intellectual and Betar speech maker. (All this time, I imagine Mordecai at the Teachers Seminary, studying Hebrew grammar.) Leo's mistress, Ina told us, was connected to an Austrian Nazi — was he her husband? — and knew things. Listening to his mistress, Leo took Sophie, his wife, and headed for the train station. His connections had gotten them visas, which got them to Tel Aviv. I used to visit them once a week, when I was teaching there in 1969.

After a year in Colón, Mordecai got a job in Ecuador. It was a larger Jewish community and had a day school. Before he left, he showed us the book he had copied in Prague as a young Zionist waiting for his visa. "*Ahavat Zion,*" my sister read the flowery script of the title. "Love of Zion. The first Hebrew novel," he told us. "Here is Jerusalem," he said, pointing to the shining word.

Facing the curlicues of his handwriting, I stuttered.

My father's face was red.

I have no pictures of Mordecai.

We believed our skills had saved us. We practiced them night and day. Theadora-Teddie, the oldest, is an awesome pianist. She started playing at five. After dinner she would perform Schubert, Schumann, Chopin, Beethoven, Tchaikovsky, and Rachmaninoff for my father, as my younger sister, Gertie, and I would become drowsy and were led to our bedtime Shma and sleep by my mother, so exhausted from the endless household work of caring, cleaning, cooking, worrying, she fell asleep beside us.

No matter how we excelled in school, our skills were never good enough for our father. Though we were praised, the engine of history breathing down my father's throat urged us on. What skills could give us security and ease, so we could sit under our own biblical fig tree and not be afraid? Gertie, a genius with color, shape, and line, invented games from thin air, into which we escaped. I lost myself in texts. Would those be powerful enough to keep us out of the jaws of the dreadful Jewish destiny Hitler had planned for us?

Later, in college, I squeezed a Hebrew class into the chemistry requirements. In the summer between my junior and senior years when I had changed my major to European history, I wandered into a bookstore on the Lower East Side and found the novel Mordecai had copied. His version was at the bottom of my sock drawer, and I pulled it out to compare them. The parts about love sounded biblical. Mordecai had managed to copy only a third. What he had done was accurate.

I wanted to send the printed book to him, but my mother had told me Mordecai had left Ecuador the year before we moved to the United States. Like Phoebus, he too had gone to Israel in 1947 to fight in the War of Independence. He had been killed at Bab-el-Wad, trying to break through to a besieged Jerusalem.

Last summer I dreamed that I flew over the ocean. In my sleep I heard the pilot say we were passing Vienna. A while longer, and we landed on Zion's shores. I took a taxi into the Judean hills. At sunset I walked on Jerusalem's rocky ground, along the steep and narrow streets of the old city to the Western Wall. I wanted to say kaddish for him.

I open Mordecai's book. A photograph falls out.

It is autumn 1943, and the Jews have organized a protest march. Mordecai has brought word of the mass murders of the Nazis to the Jews of Colón.

Mordecai's photo shows eight dark-haired girls in white dresses carrying a white flag with two blue stripes and the Star of David down the middle of the street. A dozen solemn-faced men in suits and ties walk behind them.

People lean out of balconies to throw money, as the girls hold the flag open to catch the fluttering bills. Their skirts furl over their legs. The girls bear the flag between the palm trees that line Avenida Guerrero. I imagine the parade crosses the ocean. At the dock in Haifa, Rutie and her husband, Zvi, are waiting for Phoebus and Mordecai. They hug the dark-haired girls. In 1938 Rutie and Zvi arrived in Haifa, with the last visas for the Jews of Czechoslovakia the British issued. Each visa entitled a couple to make aliyah. When they arrived in Haifa, Rutie and Zvi divorced their spouses on the dock and promptly married each other.

Why is the parade silent?

One of the girls has lost the white flower from her hair.

Did I remember to wave at my father?

He wears a brown suit and striped tie as he marches behind my sister down the left side of the snapshot.

Five years later we immigrated to New York. We were helped to the top of the Panamanian quota by money my aunt Ina gave to a government official. The Baumgarten family was reunited in the Bronx, where we went to school and celebrated Shabbat and holidays together. And Eli and my father opened Doreen Shops, a women's clothing store, in Queens.

The isthmus turns eastward to reach for the looming mass of the southern continent. The Canal foils expectations and runs almost due north-south. It separates the land as it brings people together. Machines strain; dark loam is chewed by metal jaws; water rushes through. Ships float immobilized like painted images on a bobbing pond as locks groan and fill. Metal engines — "mules" — churn on gleaming tracks and haul the laden vessels to the next level. The process is repeated until the ships burst free into the wide ocean.

When the battleship *Missouri* came through at the end of the war, it scraped the sides of Gatun Lock. As we waved at the sailors, people were saying the days of the Canal were over.

We saw Eisenhower at the end of the war. It was a grand parade with flags and soldiers striding down the broad Paseo del Centenario, with trucks and marching soldiers and brass bands of sailors playing. The most impressive were the motorcycle policemen who roared up and down the street doing crowd control, their engines deep-voiced and full of power. When the parade was over we walked along the street and looked at the marble statue of Christopher Columbus. Tensed between majesty and humility, he guards the hope of the liberties of the Republic.

We switched schools, transferring to the Canal Zone Academy. Since we were not American citizens, we got into the school through connections and our father paid a higher tuition than the other parents. Our schoolmates lived at the other end of town in large mysterious houses and we played with them only on weekdays. My teacher told me the sun set at ten o'clock or later in the summer in Minnesota, where she had grown up. In Panama, which is just north of the equator, days were always the same length, sunset bringing its sudden darkness regularly at six o'clock in the evening. It was just one more bit of evidence convincing me that Americans were even bigger liars than the Panamanian fathers who always talked about the ruins of Spanish galleons and forts we never saw.

It was then that my father started calling me his *kaddishel* and requiring that I accompany him to shul on *shabbos*. In the long afternoons, we used to play in the store, shooting our cap guns at the Ostroviaks, who were similarly occupied across the street at their parents' place of business.

Friday evenings my father and I went to the synagogue and brought soldiers home with us for our Sabbath meal. On Saturday mornings we prayed in the Centro Israelita Cultural my father had helped build—that is, the men prayed while the children ran in and out engaged in hide-and-seek or cops and robbers, silenced occasionally by a *sha* or a *klop*. We finally learned decorum in American synagogues in Manhattan. There even on Yom Kippur my father couldn't clutch the curtains of the Ark and scream and plead, rocking on his heels and toes till his head beat against its wooden walls, as he had in Colón.

Saturdays dribbled away; we played at the store, or talked and read and slept. After sundown we bathed in the metal washtubs with water heated in the tea kettle, taking turns washing each other and being washed.

Sundays were the hardest—not because it was their *shabbos*, but because it was bullfight day. Sundays in Panama were the days that counted, when large sums of money could be realized and great emotions felt. Terrible things happened that my father would mention in a whisper to my mother—fights, knifings, shootings. Once I overheard him tell of a machete duel fought not far from our house, in which both men cut each other to shreds. The worst of all Sundays was New Year's, when garbage was thrown off the balconies and people danced in the streets. On Sundays we stayed indoors. It was lockup day for us.

Once more in Panama, I revisit my childhood, only to discover parts of it have never left me. One experience, when I was five, emerges from memory like a premonition of what I would become. I was playing on the balcony by myself with my favorite stuffed animal, a toy bear, when I slipped, and the bear toppled three stories to the ground. I was not allowed to go out on the narrow winding stairs by myself, so I tried to climb after him. My head fit through the bars of the railing, but my shoulders didn't, and suddenly I was stuck. I was suspended, almost weightless, for a time. Finally it was lunchtime and my father came home from the store and rescued me. My mother rubbed mentholatum on my ears, my sisters petted me, and he tugged until I popped loose.

When we left Panama I was ten. As I looked through the open porthole of the ship taking us to America, I felt again the giddy sensation — Mauricio, dangling in space — and knew that feeling would remain.

SANDRA MCGEE DEUTSCH

A Journey through My Life and Latin American Jewish Studies

Half drunk, the young Argentine radical rightist, or Nacionalista, looked me in the eye and claimed that Hitler hadn't killed any Jews. Well, maybe he had killed one million, but not six million. Hitler wasn't such a bad guy.

Perhaps I could excuse his remarks, given his youth and state of inebriation, but another Nacionalista, considerably older, more prominent, and sober, agreed with his young friend. He informed me that British propaganda during World War II had invented the myth of the Holocaust, which the Jews had perpetuated in order to reap reparations payments from Germany.

These remarks left me speechless. My parents were Holocaust survivors, and most of my family had perished in concentration camps. Until this conversation in 1977 I had never heard of Holocaust denial. The Nacionalistas had seemed rational and courteous, but perhaps they were insane. Given the overwhelming evidence, how could they doubt this event had occurred? I debated whether I should say something or hold my tongue. As the older of the two had given me access to valuable documentation, divulging my identity could endanger my work. It could also endanger my life, for at that moment a ruthless right-wing military dictatorship ruled Argentina, and some of the generals associated Jews with the "subversion" they were eradicating. The Nacionalistas had influenced military thought and practices and were linked to its campaign of terror.

In the end, I said nothing. When asked about my religious background, I hedged my response, which caused me to feel guilty for years to come. But the conversation had served several important purposes. I was studying Nacionalismo before 1932, and the existing literature on the movement during this period suggested it was not anti-Semitic. This encounter led me to suspect the answer was more complicated.

More important, it helped me understand why I was researching these individuals. It taught me that researching and writing history is a deeply personal endeavor. I realized that the topic I had chosen was intertwined with questions related to my identity. Indeed, this has been true for all my subsequent research quests as well. They represent journeys through the Latin American past, as well as journeys through my own history, a history infused with ethical questions, ethnicity, and gender.

When I entered graduate school, I planned to specialize in the Caribbean or Central America. During my first semester, however, I happened to pull a book off the library shelf that would help determine my future: Carlos Ibarguren's *La historia que he vivido*.[1] The author, a Nacionalista, related the political history of twentieth-century Argentina through the prism of his beliefs in an engaging and erudite manner. I wondered how someone with these extreme views could write so articulately. How could a thoughtful person freely choose such an ideology?

These naive questions led me to take courses on European fascism. Fascinated with the material, I decided to apply insights derived from the European case to the study of radical rightists and fascists in Latin America. Since the principal manifestations seemed to be in Argentina, I chose it as my country of specialization. I saw my compulsion to learn about fascism as merely an intellectual exercise.

When the two Nacionalistas denied the existence of the Holocaust, they unwittingly challenged my superficial understanding of my motives. I realized that my heart as well as my brain had helped dictate my choice of topic. I wanted to understand how ordinary, intelligent people could have hated and tortured my parents and relatives. Because I was a Latin Americanist, I would research similar individuals in that region. Latin America had not witnessed the persecution of Jews on the same scale as Nazi Europe, but it contained movements, like Nacionalismo, that sympathized with Nazism.

In 1977, a year after the coup that had installed a ruthless military dictatorship, I was in Argentina researching two groups for my dissertation on radical rightists before 1932. The first was the Liga Patriótica Argentina, an organization that arose in 1919 as a response to the Russian revolution and a local labor mobilization. Its upper- and middle-class members opposed immigrants, leftists, and worker militancy and autonomy. The Liga forcibly repressed strikes and smashed labor and leftist groups throughout the country. Its heyday was the early years after World War I, but it played an important role in the Revolution of 1930, and it continued to exist at least until 1977.[2]

The Liga arose after the Semana Trágica of January 1919, a week-long battle between strikers and employers allied with the state. Civilians of middle- and upper-class backgrounds also entered the fray on the capitalist side. As the overwhelming majority of the urban working class was foreign-born, bourgeois Argentines identified unions and leftists with immigrants. In addition, they tagged Jews, who numbered among these immigrants, as Bolsheviks and anarchists, thanks in part to the Russian origins of most Argentine Jews. During the Semana Trágica, privileged Argentines formed vigilante groups that attacked working-class and Jewish neighborhoods. These persons figured among the founding members of the Liga. Women also numbered among the founders, a point I filed away for future reference.

Considering the anti-Semitic origins of the group, I was surprised to find that it rarely criticized or assaulted Jews as such. In one incident in Entre Ríos Province in 1921, Liguistas attacked a group of strikers and Socialists that included Jews. Jewish farmers in that locality who opposed laborers' demands also belonged to the Liga, however. The number of Jews in the organization was never very large, yet the fact that the Liga accepted them indicated that the anti-Semitism of some of its members was superficial and episodic.

This was not necessarily the case for the other movement I was studying, the self-styled Nacionalistas. They began to coalesce in various intellectual and Catholic circles in the mid- to late 1920s. Influenced by different strands of European Catholic and rightist thought, Nacionalistas not only opposed leftists and immigrants, as did Liguistas, but liberal democracy and foreign imperialism as well. While the two groups allied with the military to overthrow the elected president in 1930, the fact that Nacionalistas were far more extreme in their views than Liguistas caused a split between them. One measure of their radicalism was anti-Semitism. As of 1977 the books on and by early Nacionalistas did not reveal their opinions of Jews, but I found these sentiments in their periodicals, which few scholars had read up to that time. Nacionalistas identified Jews with all their ideological foes and believed that a Jewish capitalist-communist conspiracy imperiled the nation. To this day, extreme anti-Semitism characterizes this movement. That the Liga did not share it demonstrates that not all rightists are alike in this regard. Yet one must note that anti-Semitism was not the main concern of Nacionalistas; creating an authoritarian corporatist state that would defend national interests was their priority.[3] One must carefully place Nacionalista views on Jews in context and not assign them more importance than they deserve, although this is not easy for a child of Holocaust survivors.

While I was conducting this research, the Argentine military was proceeding with its Dirty War. The two were interrelated: Liguista and Nacionalista forays against leftists and workers and Nacionalista anti-Semitism had influenced successive generations of military officers. Years later I discovered that the general who suppressed the workers during the Semana Trágica thought the government could have prevented it by having the labor leaders quietly disappear, without benefit of legal procedures.[4] This was a horrifying prediction of what would happen between 1976 and 1983. Although many Nacionalistas still active during the military dictatorship may have approved of its political policies, they disagreed with its neoliberal economic policies.

The terror that surrounded me helped me comprehend Nazi Germany. I had always wondered how Christian Germans could have ignored what was happening to their Jewish compatriots and why most did nothing to aid them. There were several instances in which I, too, witnessed frightening arbitrary acts against civilians. Late one evening as I was walking home, I saw that the military was scaling the walls of the building across the street from mine and breaking into an apartment through its windows. I averted my eyes, entered my building quickly, and was relieved to close the doors of my apartment behind me. Too paralyzed by fear to ask my neighbors about this incident, after a few weeks I heard that the military had kidnapped someone in this incursion. Another night, a friend and I were eating in a restaurant when the military entered, asked diners and employees for their papers, and finally left, dragging out a cook. My companion and I were so terrified that later we could not remember what we said to each other while the officers moved from table to table. I do not know what happened to the unfortunate persons taken by the security forces in these two episodes, nor did I do anything to find out or otherwise help them. Like many Germans in the 1930s and 1940s, all I could think of was making myself as inconspicuous as possible. I could no longer blame them for their inaction.

It was more difficult, however, for me to accept the notion that Germans had no idea what was happening to Jews and others that the Nazis identified as enemies. Again, my Argentine experiences provided some insights. After 1983 it was common to hear bourgeois Argentines insist that they had not known what was going on around them during the dictatorship. Even some Jews joined this chorus, even though this community suffered disproportionately from the terror: Jews amounted to 1 percent of the population and about 10 percent of the disappeared.[5] In the fourteen months I spent in Argentina during the Dirty War, it was possible to forget the disappearances and repression for days or even weeks. But then something would happen to jolt one into awareness, such as the kind of incident mentioned above, guarded references in newspapers, or the weekly demonstration of the Mothers of the Plaza de Mayo, who were seeking information about their missing children. I could never completely lose sight of the gruesome Dirty War, and I conjecture that those who say they did simply did not want to know about it. Knowledge promoted pain, exacerbated fear, and raised uncomfortable questions that some preferred to avoid.[6]

Although they taught me many things, my experiences in Argentina and my research on its extreme right-wing movements did not answer my original questions about how ordinary people could subscribe to brutal and irrational ideas. The peril of losing one's status during an economic crisis, political transition, or revolutionary situation and the influence of European fascist and Catholic views were partial answers, but they did not satisfy me. Perhaps it is impossible to fully grasp the depths of inhumanity. Yet my work had prompted new queries that opened up areas for investigation. If the Liga Patriótica Argentina and the Nacionalistas could differ so strikingly, what could be said about radical rightist groups in other countries? I chose Argentina, Brazil, and Chile as the subjects for comparison. What were the similarities and differences among such groups in these nations? How did extreme rightist ideology change over time and vary across borders? Why had radical rightists seemingly exercised greater influence in Argentina than in Brazil and Chile over the course of the twentieth century? While broad and sweeping, these queries were more concrete than the ones that had set me on my research path, and thus I believed that I could answer them.[7]

Comparing the movements in the three South American nations, I found that one of the differences among them was the degree of adherence to anti-Semitism. To understand this variation, it is necessary to explore the changes that took place in radical rightist ideology and practice over time. There were three distinct periods of activity during the years under study, 1890 to 1939. During the first period, which took place between 1890 and World War I, precursors criticized the liberal model of economic development for encouraging class conflict and the domination of foreigners and a greedy local ruling class. Many incipient rightists saw the immigrants and, in Chile, the Peruvian and Bolivian inhabitants in the north as the incarnations of the various dangers that undermined the nation. The Brazilian Jacobinos denounced the Portuguese, while the Chilean Ligas Patrióticas and Argentine vigilante bands not only criticized but also assaulted Peruvians and immigrant workers, respectively. While one can find anti-Semitic sentiments in all three countries, they were more pronounced in Argentina, where vigilantes in 1910 attacked a Jewish working-class neighborhood. This nation had the largest Jewish presence of the three, but demography does not completely explain the patterns of prejudice.

In the second period, from World War I and the Bolshevik Revolution to roughly the mid-1920s, radical rightists began to shift targets, from foreigners to militant laborers. In Brazil and especially in Argentina, the two categories overlapped, which added strength to far rightist forces and their claims. Groups such as Ação Social Nacionalista of Brazil, the Liga Patriótica Argentina, and the Ligas Patrióticas of Chile upheld the class hierarchy against worker mobilizations and the leftist threat — the Argentines and Chileans using violent means to do so. The Argentine vigilantes who were the precursors of the Liga Patriótica Argentina were the only rightists of the three countries to intentionally assault Jews. Here the working class appeared to present the strongest challenge to capitalists, whose response was the most far-reaching. Anti-Semitism is an indicator of the most extreme tendency among radical rightists.

During this period, Catholic study centers in Argentina and Brazil began to train a generation of intellectuals in corporatist thought, which included a large dose of anti-Semitism. These and other lay thinkers would join extreme right-wing groups, and they and their clerical mentors would help shape their ideology. Thanks in part to this Catholic participation, anti-Semitism would replace anti-Portuguese views among Brazilian radical rightists and permeate the Nacionalista movement in Argentina. In contrast, anti-Jewish and anti-immigrant prejudice had little resonance in Chile. Both the Brazilian and Chilean Jewish communities were tiny, yet in Chile foreigners in general had only a minimal presence in the general population and the working class, except in the extreme north and south. Nor was the Catholic influence on the far right, with its anti-Semitic component, as strong in Chile as it was in Brazil and Argentina. The church was tied to the still prominent Chilean Conservative party, whereas in the other countries it was isolated from the secular elite and lacked a political outlet. Since it had a voice, the Chilean church did not need to search for political allies among extremist groups.

The third period encompassed the late 1920s to 1939, the height of radical rightist movements. In the wake of the depression and the crisis of the liberal economic and political systems that it fostered, rightist Catholicism and European fascism found new adherents in the Southern Cone. The Argentine Nacionalistas, Ação Integralista Brasileira (or Integralistas), and Movimiento Nacional Socialista (MNS, or Nacistas) of Chile were among the groups to advocate such ideas and put them into practice through ruthless attacks against workers and leftists. All three movements attributed many of the ills of their countries to Jews, notions that resembled those of fascists elsewhere. Nevertheless, the Nacionalistas once more appear to have been the only ones to purposefully assault Jews before 1940.

This was not the only difference in anti-Semitic actions among groups in the three nations. While the Argentines and Brazilians consistently denounced Jews, the Chileans' anti-Semitism was intermittent. The MNS arose in 1932 but devoted little attention to the Jews during its early years. Between 1935 and mid-1937, the Nacista popular press contained many expressions of radical anti-Semitism. During this time, however, MNS platforms, books, and pamphlets written by leaders and its journal, *Acción Chilena,* only occasionally manifested such ideas. Apparently Nacistas concluded that anti-Semitism might appeal to the masses but not to the more educated readers of their weightier publications. The height of MNS anti-Jewish sentiments coincided with its main efforts to fight workers, yet attract some of them through revolutionary-sounding slogans and the cult of violence. The economic content of anti-Semitism gave Nacistas a radical and dynamic guise, although not necessarily a wide appeal. After mid-1937 the movement shifted its strategy and aligned itself with the leftist parties it had previously despised. During this uneasy alliance, the MNS (which eventually renamed itself the Vanguardia Popular Socialista) curtailed its anti-Semitism; now that it identified with the left, it criticized capitalism as a whole and not just its supposedly Jewish aspects. When the alliance ended in 1940, the Nacistas once again turned against the Jews. The history of the movement demonstrates how its anti-Semitism was opportunistic and tactical.[8]

Radical rightist groups in all three countries during the 1930s used anti-Semitism to demonstrate their opposition to international capitalism, as was the fashion overseas. Another factor promoting anti-Semitism may have been the arrival of refugees from Europe, which augmented the Jewish presence. Yet if one looked at demography alone, one would expect the Nacistas to have been more consistently anti-Semitic than the Integralistas, since the Jewish population was slightly higher in Chile than in

Brazil. As this was not the case, one may conclude that other issues had weight. Since the early twentieth century, anti-Semitism and nativism had influenced rightists in Argentina, and nationalism overlapped Catholicism. For similar reasons, Integralistas also were anti-Semitic. The distance between the church and the radical right, the weakness of anti-immigrant sentiments, and the local political context in Chile help to explain the varying degree of Nacista anti-Semitism.

By 1939 the Integralistas and Nacistas were in disarray, and they never recovered. Only the Nacionalistas survived this period intact, having achieved important inroads into the church, the military, intellectual circles, and the Conservative party. Nacionalistas retained their corporate identity and many of their beliefs until the early 1980s. This remarkable continuity and degree of influence helped shape the policies of the recent military dictatorship. Nacionalista officers controlled much of the Dirty War, as the severe persecution of Jews and use of anti-Semitic rhetoric indicated. Significantly, anti-Semitism did not pervade the dictatorship of Augusto Pinochet in Chile (1973–1990) and only rarely surfaced during that of the Brazilian generals (1964–1985). In these countries extreme rightists did not exert as much influence among military officers as they did in Argentina.

My research and travel experiences have opened up windows through which I have viewed my Jewish heritage and attitudes that have affected the lives of Jews in Latin America and other places. They have also enabled me to explore another component of my identity, my womanhood.

When I initiated my research on the radical right in the 1970s, I thought I was studying a movement made up exclusively of men. My education had not trained me to expect otherwise. None of my history courses contained much information on women, nor were any of my history professors women. Significant works on fascist and extreme right-wing women in Europe and the United States, let alone Latin America, had not yet appeared. Thus I was surprised to find mention of female Liga members in newspaper articles and Liga Patriótica Argentina publications. Lacking models of analysis of women's participation in other rightist movements, I did not know what to do with the cases I was finding. I inserted them in a file and stowed it away.

Two years later, when I was writing my dissertation, the pioneer of Latin American women's history, Asunción Lavrin,[9] asked me to give a paper at a multidisciplinary conference on Latin American women. When I told her that I did not have anything to contribute, she insisted that I go through my notes. Surely the organizations I was researching had said something about women or recruited them. I found the forgotten file and the wealth of data it contained.

I realized that the Liga Patriótica Argentina had a dual strategy for strengthening the status quo. Men were in charge of attacking laborers and leftists; women were largely responsible for implementing a peaceful message of class conciliation. They taught women factory workers to read, write, and respect authority and carried out charitable projects among the poor. The expectation was that Liga-style education and philanthropy would reconcile workers with the existing order.

As I pondered the impact of gender on radical rightist movements, I became more aware of how gender affected my professional life. Not long after the conference, I applied for a tenure-track teaching position at a small midwestern college, and the departmental chair interviewed me in person. Some weeks later my dissertation adviser told me that the chair had called him and asked if I could speak loudly enough to be heard in the back of a classroom. Despite this concern, he hired me and asked me to teach the history of women in the United States, among other courses. When I informed him that I had never studied this material, he replied that since I was a woman, I could teach it.

Although my chairperson treated me cordially, his sexism and presumption irritated me. The sexually provocative and hostile behavior of some male students in my new setting fueled my anger and alienation. Was this what I had worked toward all these years? Did it all come down to my gender? Because I had rarely encountered such brazen discrimination during my schooling, I had not thought much about women's issues. These new experiences increased my awareness of the need for feminist change.

However reluctantly undertaken, the readings in preparation for the women's history course proved valuable. They gave me the framework I needed to study right-wing women. Furthermore, they helped me understand that women are always part of the story, even if they lurk in the background. When women are missing, one must ask where they are and how their insertion will alter our perception of these events. Recovering women's acts and voices is not only important for its own sake; doing so adds nuance and complexity to historical accounts.[10]

Women were part of the story of radical right-wing movements in the Southern Cone. Some organizations, such as the Liga Patriótica Argentina and Ação Integralista Brasileira, made efforts to recruit them and assigned importance to their activism. Women Integralistas as well as Liguistas set up free schools, clinics, and other social welfare projects designed to convince workers that they could advance in the capitalist system. These pacific attempts to co-opt them complemented and helped disguise the men's violent encounters with leftists and workers. In addition, by the mid-1930s Brazilian women had won the right to vote at all levels, Chilean women at the municipal level. Integralistas and Nacistas tried to attract female adherents in order to gain their votes, indicating their desire to attain power through electoral means. Some movements had few female members, but even that information is useful because it indicates that these groups had little interest in mobilizing popular support through elections. The presence and absence of women tell us much about extreme right-wing organizations, and one must not take either for granted.[11]

Perhaps ironically, given my interest in assuring women their rightful place in historical accounts, my initial writings on right-wing women in the 1980s aroused some feminist disapproval. An anonymous reviewer reacted ambivalently to an article I submitted to a journal by noting it did not focus on the "real women," the feminists. I detected a similar unease or lack of enthusiasm from other reviewers, which reflected the fact that women's participation in extreme right-wing movements is deeply disturbing to a feminist sensibility. It calls into question the belief held by many feminists — that maternal traits of love, acceptance, and nurturance characterize women and set them apart from men. Or it suggests that women have channeled and used different definitions of maternalism to serve a variety of causes, including racist and murderous ones.[12] Women in the groups I have studied asserted that the blatantly anti-Semitic forgery, the *Protocols of the Elders of Zion,* was accurate and that Jewish imperialism was a grave threat to their nations.[13] Nothing distinguished these beliefs from those of men in these movements.

By the mid-1990s my book on radical rightist women and men in Argentina, Brazil, and Chile was nearing completion, and I was contemplating the direction I was going to take after I finished it. I wanted to present a paper at a forthcoming Latin American Jewish Studies Association conference, and I thought it might serve as the springboard for a new topic. At previous meetings of this organization, I had spoken on rightist anti-Semitism, but it was time to move on. I hungered for a more positive approach to the study of Latin American Jews; unconsciously I was also looking for a means of exploring aspects of my Jewish identity that went beyond opposition to fascism and persecution.

An idea came to me one day as I sat in the library, sifting through scores of publications on Argentine Jewish history. I suddenly realized that women were absent from these works. If women are always part of the story, as I believe, then they should be part of the story of Argentine Jews.

Actually, one group of Argentine Jewish women appeared in the historical literature, as well as in films and fiction—prostitutes.[14] This focus may reveal more about Argentine views of Jewish women than about the women themselves. The possibility that Argentines have regarded Jewish women as the sensual other is a hypothesis that should be tested. Still, Jewish women were active in arenas other than prostitution.

My work in progress traces the experiences of Jewish women of Ashkenazi, Sephardi, and Arabic-speaking origins, and of different social classes, and situates them in their communities and Argentina. It begins in 1880, on the eve of their arrivals, and terminates in 1955, the end of the Peronist administration. Immigrant and first-generation women responded in diverse ways to the challenges and opportunities of being Jewish, Argentine, and female in a modernizing and cosmopolitan society. They melded influences from their varied backgrounds with those of the local milieu as they entered the schools, professions, factories, political parties, and Jewish institutions. Women faced discrimination in both the Jewish and Catholic communities, yet the wider society also accorded them a large measure of acceptance, particularly in the educational and professional realms. Jewish women carved out places in the collectivity and the nation through their participation in communal causes and larger struggles for social and political justice. Although they arose after my period of research, the Mothers of the Plaza de Mayo are but one of the groups in which Jewish women have played a role disproportionate to their percentage in the population.

Given their prominence, it was difficult for me to understand the dearth of studies on Argentine Jewish women. The reactions my work elicited in Argentina, however, helped explain the gap. Some Argentines, particularly Jewish and non-Jewish women, expressed enthusiasm for the project. Yet not all Jewish women approved of it. One teased me—only half-jokingly—for being uninterested in men, implying that my focus was too narrow and that I was a lesbian. Several older Jewish women, and many Jewish men of differing professions and political persuasions, could not understand why I would restrict myself to studying women; for some, this indicated a radical feminist, perhaps even man-hating agenda. Some leftists hinted that by researching Jewish women I was promoting divisions among Argentines; they would have preferred to see me explore workers as a whole or (if I insisted on studying women) female workers. Contacts who gave me names of persons to interview generally supplied those of men who knew little or nothing about the women in their movements or communities. In their view, only men could serve as historical witnesses. Several longtime colleagues did not know I was Jewish. My topic revealed my identity—for in their view, only a Jew would study other Jews—and this discovery stunned them. I wished I could contradict their ethnocentric notion, but I could not. It irked me that my identity and choice of subject matter marginalized me in their eyes. These responses indicate some of the issues that may have dissuaded scholars from pursuing the topic.

The many writings on Argentine Jewish history focus on male actions and perceptions. We know little about what women did or how they perceived the events they participated in or witnessed. Nor do we know much about what they considered important in their own lives or how they formed their identities. For these reasons, I conducted free-flowing interviews with women of diverse ethnic and class origins and pursuits.

Despite their ancestry, some interviewees, generally Socialists, claimed that they were not Jewish because they did not practice the religion or belong to communal institutions. To a greater extent than the local Communists or anarchists, the Socialist party for many years insisted that its members give up religious practices and ethnic loyalties. I learned to be careful to say that I was studying women of Jewish *origin*. I even had to explain that just as first-generation Argentines whose parents were born in Italy were of Italian descent, children born to Jewish mothers were Jewish. These informants and other Argentines see class and political allegiances as overriding conditions of birth in determining one's identity.

These deeply held opinions made me reflect on an age-old question: what makes me Jewish, beyond my roots? A preoccupation with anti-Semitism no longer suffices. I do not practice the Jewish religion or belong to Jewish organizations, nor do I speak Yiddish or Hebrew. While I enjoyed visiting Israel, its culture seemed completely foreign. I felt a common bond with some of the Argentine Jewish women I interviewed but not with all. Most of my daily contacts in the United States are with non-Jews. In the southwestern city in which I live, U.S.-style Ashkenazi foods are difficult to find, and I have lost the taste for many of these cholesterol-laden dishes anyway. Like many other Jews, I would like to see a more egalitarian world, but I share these beliefs with numerous non-Jews.

Perhaps what makes me Jewish is an appreciation of our long and complex history. As in Argentina, it includes persecution and resistance but also toleration, acceptance, and intermingling. Men and women have served as protagonists in this ever-changing historical process, which has sparked the creation of multiple and shifting identities.

My journeys through history also have taken many turns, and at each juncture a different side of my identity has emerged, ready to be explored. Since the time I read Ibarguren's memoir, I have chosen research topics designed to help me understand the past and my place in it. I have not found answers to my deepest question—what makes humans so inhuman?—but my work has enabled me to heal familial and personal wounds.

NOTES

I thank Marjorie Agosín, Judith Laikin Elkin, Yolanda Chávez Leyva, Nicol Partida, and K. Lynn Stoner for the encouragement, materials, and comments they offered.

1. Carlos Ibarguren, *La historia que he vivido,* 2d ed. (Buenos Aires: Editorial Universitaria de Buenos Aires, 1969).

2. Sandra McGee Deutsch, *Counterrevolution in Argentina, 1900–1932: The Argentine Patriotic League* (Lincoln: University of Nebraska Press, 1986).

3. Sandra McGee Deutsch, "The Right under Radicalism, 1916–1930," in Sandra McGee Deutsch and Ronald H. Dolkart, eds., *The Argentine Right: Its History and Intellectual Origins, 1910 to the Present* (Wilmington: Scholarly Resources, 1993), 47–58.

4. Sandra McGee Deutsch, *Las derechas: The Extreme Right in Argentina, Brazil, and Chile, 1890–1939* (Palo Alto: Stanford University Press, 1999), 83.

5. Edy Kaufman, "Jewish Victims of Repression in Argentina under Military Rule (1976–1983)," *Holocaust and Genocide Studies* 4 (1989): 479–499.

6. Judith Laikin Elkin, "We Knew but We Didn't Want to Know," *Jewish Frontier* (February 1985): 7–11.

7. Although the rightist dictatorship of Augusto Pinochet (1973–1990) of Chile outlasted the Argentine military regime of 1976–1983, radical rightists exerted a more pervasive influence over government, culture, the Catholic church, and the military in Argentina from the 1920s to the 1980s than in the other two countries. For lengthy discussions of these points, as well as those raised in the following paragraphs, see Deutsch, *Las derechas.*

8. Sandra McGee Deutsch, "Anti-Semitism and the Chilean Movimiento Nacional Socialista, 1932–1941," in David Sheinin and Lois Baer Barr, eds., *The Jewish Diaspora in Latin America* (New York: Garland, 1996), 161–181.

9. Among her many works, see *Women, Feminism, and Social Change in Argentina, Chile, and Uruguay, 1890–1940* (Lincoln: University of Nebraska Press, 1995).

10. At the time, Gerda Lerner, *The Majority Finds Its Past: Placing Women in*

History (New York, 1979), influenced these thoughts. More recently, Aurora Levins Morales, *Medicine Stories: History, Culture and the Politics of Integrity* (Cambridge, Mass., 1998), has inspired me.

11. See, for example, Sandra McGee Deutsch, "The Visible and Invisible Liga Patriótica Argentina, 1919–1928: Gender Roles and the Right Wing," *Hispanic American Historical Review* 64:2 (May 1984): 233–258; "What Difference Does Gender Make? The Extreme Right in the ABC Countries in the Era of Fascism," *Estudios Interdisciplinarios de América Latina y el Caribe* 8:2 (July–December 1997): 5–21.

12. For discussions of these points, see Claudia Koonz, *Mothers in the Fatherland: Women the Family and Nazi Politics* (New York: St. Martin's, 1987); Victoria González and Karen Kampwirth, eds., *Radical Women in Latin America: Right and Left* (University Park: Pennsylvania State University Press, 2001); Kathleen M. Blee, *Women of the Klan: Racism and Gender in the 1920s* (Berkeley: University of California Press, 1991).

13. Deutsch, *Las derechas*, 234, 279.

14. Donna J. Guy, *Sex and Danger in Buenos Aires: Prostitution, Family, and Nation in Argentina* (Lincoln: University of Nebraska Press, 1990); Nora Glickman, *The Jewish White Slave Trade and the Untold Story of Raquel Liberman* (New York: Garland, 2000); Victor A. Mirelman, *Jewish Buenos Aires, 1890–1930: In Search of an Identity* (Detroit: Wayne State University Press, 1990). One of the few books that discusses aspects of the history of Argentine Jewish women beyond prostitution is Myriam Escliar's *Mujeres en la literatura y la vida judeoargentina* (Buenos Aires: Milá, 1996).

The Paradox of Communities

GRAEME S. MOUNT

Chile and the Nazis

Chile did not become a World War II belligerent until February 1945. Until January 1943 it was a neutral country, like Switzerland, Sweden, or the Irish Free State, maintaining diplomatic relations with both Axis and Allied countries. Except for Argentina, all the other Latin American republics had severed their ties with the Axis early in 1942 after an Inter-American conference at Rio de Janeiro, Brazil.

Chile had had extensive ties with Germany since the mid-nineteenth century. The Chilean army managed to defeat the Araucanian Indians and in the process opened land south of the Bío-Bío River (near Concepción) to European settlement. Germans had a reputation as honest, hardworking Europeans who lacked a powerful government that might intervene on their behalf. At the same time, German settlers became available. Germany's liberal revolutions of 1848 failed, and in their aftermath some of the would-be reformers decided to migrate elsewhere—to the United States and Australia, as well as to South America. Karl Anwandter, a pharmacist and deputy in the Prussian Diet (parliament), led dozens of well-educated professionals and their families to what they hoped would be a land of freedom. Like Puritans who left Stuart England for Massachusetts in the seventeenth century, many of the immigrants were self-serving. Convinced that events of 1848 doomed Germany to a terrible future, they wanted to escape the forthcoming turmoil and raise their families in a more peaceful environment. Economically ambitious Germans, who could never hope to own extensive tracts of land in Europe, followed the political dissidents. Most of the German settlers were Protestants, but some were Roman Catholics and a few were Jewish. Aboard the *Susanna* when she left Hamburg for Valdivia in 1850 were A. C. Goldberg and C. B. Israel.

Despite the liberal origins of Chile's German community, many German Chileans lacked strong convictions about the horrors of Hitler. Allied propaganda about the Kaiser's Germany during World War I had exaggerated, or even invented, cases of German wrongdoing. What evidence was there that the stories of the Third Reich were not also exaggerations or falsehoods? Many could admire Germany and German achievements as a whole, even if they disliked its incumbent government (which they regarded as but another temporary phenomenon). Supported by the German embassy in Santiago, Nazis gradually infiltrated existing newspapers, both German-language and Spanish-language. News and commentaries from established, prestigious newspapers appeared credible. Like Christians in the United States, Canada, and Switzerland, who did not want to admit large numbers of Jewish refugees from the Third Reich, some German Chileans blamed Jews for crucifying Christ and other misdeeds. The Reverend Martin Kannegiesser, pastor of Valparaíso's Lutheran church, is quoted as having said: "[The Old Testament] proves that a people chosen by God erred and is now damned."[1]

There were several other reasons for Chile's ongoing neutrality and then, from January 1943 to February 1945, its nonbelligerence. Like citizens of the United States, Chileans were proud of their country's identity as an independent nation. Despite the fact that the United Kingdom and France had gone to war against Nazi Germany in September 1939, the United States maintained diplomatic relations with the Axis powers until Japan attacked Pearl Harbor and Hitler declared war on the United States in December 1941. Ernesto Barros, Chile's foreign minister for six months in 1942, argued that Chile had as much right to maintain diplomatic relations with adversaries of the United States as the United States had had to maintain diplomatic relations with adversaries of Great Britain and France. Nor did Chileans feel that they owed the United States any favors. When Chile fought and defeated Bolivia and Peru in the 1879–1884 War of the Pacific, then annexed some of their lands, U.S. authorities—particularly Secretary of State James G. Blaine[2]—disapproved. The Hawley-Smoot Tariff Act of 1930 had effectively excluded Chilean exports from the U.S. market. Chile had a presidential election in February 1942, and the governing Radical party did not want to alienate voters of German extraction. Nor did Chilean authorities care to jeopardize their shipping or their coastline by antagonizing the Axis powers, especially after the destruction of the U.S. fleet at Pearl Harbor. Successive Allied victories in 1942, along with the U.S. willingness to arm Peru and Bolivia and thereby tilt the military balance of power against Chile, convinced the government of President Juan Antonio Ríos (1942–1946) to close the German, Italian, and Japanese diplomatic posts after all.[3]

Argentina too remained neutral for most of World War II. Like Chile, Argentina had been at the periphery of Spain's empire. Before the mainland Spanish American colonies gained their independence in the first quarter of the nineteenth century, Spain focused on the places with precious minerals, especially Mexico and Peru. After independence, large numbers of Germans and Italians chose to relocate there. Argentina's Germans also included Jews. Some are buried at the cemetery at Bariloche, which after 1945 gained notoriety as a haven for fugitive Nazis. During World War II, many Argentines felt little reason for loyalty to the British and the Americans. Traditionally, Argentina and the United States had been competitors, not partners. For generations, Argentines had regarded the United Kingdom as an outlet for their beef and wheat, but in 1932 that situation changed. Faced with high unemployment at home and with the Hawley-Smoot Tariff in the United States, Commonwealth prime ministers met in Ottawa and granted tariff preferences to each other. In the aftermath of the Ottawa conference, the United Kingdom bought greater volumes of beef and wheat from Canada, Australia, New Zealand, and South Africa, less from Argentina.

Not all aspects of Argentine and Chilean neutrality were negative from an Allied standpoint. Chilean diplomats could assist Poles in Axis-occupied Europe. Argentine diplomats helped with the evacuation of Canadians from Japan after Pearl Harbor. The Canadian government selected Argentina as Protector of Canadian interests in Japan, in part because Buenos Aires was the only capital with both Canadian and Japanese diplomats at the time. Moreover, the Swiss were serving as Protector for so many Allied countries that they could not give the time and attention available to the Argentines. The U.S. State Department disapproved of this arrangement, because it allowed the Argentines to justify their neutrality. Pressured by Washington, Canada reluctantly thanked the Argentines for their services and, like almost everyone else, asked the Swiss to take responsibility for Canadian interests in Japan.

Three key players who strongly favored maintaining normal diplomatic relations between Chile and the Axis powers were Carlos Ibáñez, Tobias Barros, and Conrado Ríos. Ibáñez, an officer in the Chilean army, had seized power in a coup d'état and governed by nonconstitutional means from 1927 to 1931. In 1938 he went to jail for complicity in an attempted putsch by Chilean Nazis, fifty-five of whom died in the effort.[4] An unsuccessful presidential candidate in 1942, he had financial support from the German embassy, and, it would appear, from the Japanese legation in Santiago as well.[5] Tobias Barros was another army officer who, like many of his peers, had gone to Germany for training, albeit in the Weimar period. He returned to Germany as his country's ambassador in Hitler's Berlin. In his memoirs Barros later described General Alfred Jodl, one of the Nuremberg defendants, as one of his closest friends.[6] He regarded World War II as a clash of conflicting imperialisms, without moral overtones. After all, the Soviet Union was one of the Allies. Ambassador Barros deplored the cruelty of Allied air attacks in Germany but accepted without protest German actions on the Eastern Front. He ridiculed such Allied achievements as the liberation of North Africa, and he regarded an Axis victory as both inevitable and desirable; an Allied victory would mean Soviet domination of much of Europe. For his efforts, Hitler's government awarded Barros the Order of the German Eagle.[7] Conrado Ríos was Chile's ambassador in Buenos Aires. He believed firmly in the harmonization of Argentine and Chilean policies toward the rest of the world. As long as Argentina maintained normal diplomatic relations with the Axis powers, he believed that Chile should do so too.[8]

Yet another pressure group that favored maintaining normal diplomatic relations with the Axis belligerents was the Asociación de Amigos de Alemania (AAA; Association of the Friends of Germany). One Chilean army general, Arturo Ahumada, was president of the AAA, and two others — Francisco Javier Díaz and Carlos Vergara — were directors. These men shared the traditional Chilean distrust of the United States and the conviction that Hitler offered stability in the world. According to Marcial Martínez of Chile's internal security organization, the Dirección General de Investigaciones, the AAA wanted to promote Nazi values in Chile by working with "respectable" Chileans. Members of the governing Radical party attended AAA meetings and joined the generals in toasts to Hitler.[9] The German army had been training Chilean army officers since 1885, and in so doing had created a legacy of goodwill. Given what they had come to admire in Wilhelmine and Weimar Germany, some officers simply could not convince themselves that Germany had had an evil government since 1933.

Even after Hitler's defeat and suicide, his legacy survived in Chile. Carlos Ibáñez won Chile's presidential election of 1952 — taking fewer than half the votes in a field of four candidates. In January 1954 he appointed as his foreign minister none other than Tobias Barros. In June of that same year, Barros became minister of defense. Under his leadership, one could not anticipate a purge of Nazi sympathizers in the armed forces. Because relations with Argentina had been tense, within days of taking office, President Ibáñez sent Conrado Ríos back to Argentina as Chile's ambassador. Argentine President Juan Perón had welcomed Nazis and Nazi sympathizers to Argentina as possible modernizers. When Perón fell in 1955 and went into exile, some of these people thought that they should migrate again. Given his World War II track record, it would have been out of character for Conrado Ríos to be concerned about such matters.

Of Nazis who moved from Argentina to Chile when Perón fell, the most notorious is Walter Rauff. Rauff had been an SS captain who found more efficient ways to exterminate Jews with gas. Transferred to Italy to take charge of intelligence operations, he was there when the war ended. With the assistance of Bishop Alois Hudal, an Austrian who headed a Roman Catholic college in Rome, he helped fugitive Nazis to escape. In 1949, his mission accomplished, he too went to South America, first to Buenos Aires, then to Punta Arenas in Chile. There he operated a fish-packing plant. After the military takeover of 1973, the régime led by General Augusto Pinochet appointed Rauff director of DINA, its secret police. When the Israeli government requested Rauff's extradition, Pinochet's foreign minister replied that it was "inappropriate to expel a [Chilean] citizen who has lived twenty years in the country."[10]

Another fugitive from the Third Reich who won political asylum in Pinochet's Chile was Vlado (previously Vladimir) Svescen, a Croatian from the collaborationist Ustashe government of 1941–1945. There he had served as chief bodyguard to Ante Pavelic, head of the Ustashe régime.[11] According to historian John Cornwell, Pavelic "had plotted the assassination of [Yugoslav] King Alexander" as he arrived in Marseilles in 1934.[12] The French foreign minister, Louis Barthou, died at the hands of those same assassins; Barthou had invited Alexander to discuss common strategy for the containment of Hitler.

Communist Josip Broz Tito defeated the Ustashe and reunited Yugoslavia. Cornwell accuses the Ustashe of responsibility for the murder of two million Serbs (who were Orthodox in religion), in addition to large numbers of Jews, Gypsies, and Communists. The Ustashe's goal was to create a totally Roman Catholic Croatia by means of "enforced conversions, deportations, and mass exterminations." Cornwell says that "even hardened German troops registered their horror," and that Pope Pius XII was well aware of the Ustashe régime's intentions when he welcomed Pavelic to the Vatican in 1941.[13] In Tito's view, Ustashe officials were war criminals who deserved punishment; in Pius XII's, they were Christian martyrs persecuted by a Communist tyrant.

In 1947 Perón and his wife, Evita, went to Europe as guests of Generalissimo Francisco Franco of Spain. On June 26 they visited Pope Pius XII in his private library at the Vatican, where they talked for half an hour. Ten days later, on July 5, the Argentine embassy in Rome began to issue visas to Croatians. Among them was Vlado Svescen.[14]

When Perón went into exile in 1955, Svescen found a safer haven in the Dominican Republic, then controlled by the notorious dictator Generalissimo Rafael Leonidas Trujillo, a practitioner of torture. Gerald Clark, a reporter for the highly respected *Montreal Star,* described Trujillo's jail on Fortieth Street for political prisoners, La Cuarenta:

> Trujillo's men slowly exterminated political foes by subjecting them to the *pulpo* (octopus), an electrical device with several arms that were attached to the skull by screws. The shocks came in gradual doses. An electrified rod was also used to shock the genitals; and then later came castration, nail extractions and other methods of inducing confession and slow death. The agony was known to be slow, because survivors could hear the victims' screams over an amplifying system deliberately hooked up to the cell blocks.[15]

That was the regime which Svescen served between 1955 and 1961, when assassins shot Trujillo dead as he returned from an extramarital adventure in Haina, west of the capital city, Ciudad Trujillo (Trujillo City), which he had renamed for himself.

The following decade, Svescen resurfaced in Chile, where the Pinochet regime offered him a position as a security adviser. While in that capacity, he purchased weapons in Chile and transferred them as "humanitarian aid for Croatia" to Budapest in Hungary and to Dubrovnik on the Dalmatian coast.[16] Almost certainly, those weapons played a role in the disintegration of Yugoslavia and Croatia's successful battle for independence.

The values of the AAA survived in the Chilean armed forces long after World War II. In 1986 — fewer than eleven years after the death of Hitler's collaborator, Franco — I visited the Alcazar, a fortress in Toledo, and read the signs. From July 21 to 28, 1936, forces loyal to Spain's democratically elected republican government besieged the Alcazar. Forces loyal to Franco, then engaged in what would be a successful attempt to destroy the republican government, withstood the siege. In January 1973, nine months before Pinochet's coup, the Chilean army congratulated Franco and his Falangist followers for withstanding the siege. The Chilean air force followed suit in 1975, as did the Carabineros (Chilean police) in 1976.

Others who congratulated the Falangists for defeating the "Communists" included branches of the Argentine military and Spanish veterans of the Blue Division, who had fought beside German forces on the Soviet front between 1941 and 1944.

Nazism has other manifestations in modern Chile. Chilean Nazis still commemorate their failed putsch of September 5, 1938. Men dressed in brown shirts and black boots march each year to the place in the Santiago General Cemetery where swastikas surround a small-scale replica of the Washington Monument. Engraved on the monument are the names of fifty-five Nazis who died in 1938. Canadian writer and reporter Lake Sagaris, a resident of Chile, identified Sergio Onofre Jarpa, appointed Pinochet's minister of the interior on August 10, 1983, as a former member of Chile's Nazi party.[17]

Colonia Dignidad, near Parral, a few hours south of Santiago in the southernmost part of the Seventh Region, was the creation of Paul Schäfer, a veteran of the German army of occupation in northern Italy from 1943 to 1945. After the war Schäfer became an evangelist and persuaded German philanthropists to donate so that he might open a utopia for German orphans in Chile. The first settlers arrived in 1961, when Jorge Alessandri was president of Chile.

Inside Colonia Dignidad discipline was fierce, and children dressed as they had in Germany during the 1930s — the boys in lederhosen, the girls in blouses and with their hair in long braids. Escape was difficult. Sagaris reported that the colony's doctor, Gisela Seewald, used electric shock treatment and that both adults and children suffered such terrible beatings that "they lost control of their mental and physical functions."[18] Colonia Dignidad outlasted three constitutional governments, those of Jorge Alessandri (1948–1964), Eduardo Frei Montalva (1964–1970), and Salvador Allende (1970–1973).

When the armed forces overthrew President Allende's government in 1973 and General Pinochet became head of state, Colonia Dignidad entered its golden age. The Pinochet family and members of the Pinochet regime admired the efficiency, cleanliness, and apparent modernity of the place. According to Sagaris, Mrs. Pinochet vacationed there, as did Manuel Contreras, founder of DINA. Monica Madariaga, Pinochet's minister of justice between 1977 and 1981, was another frequent visitor. Amnesty International cited Colonia Dignidad as a "prison camp and center for training and experimentation with torture techniques."[19]

Perhaps it would be more accurate to label Colonia Dignidad neo-Nazi rather than Nazi. Wolfgang Müller, a resident who escaped, said:

I don't think this is really a Nazi camp, but the methods used, the discipline and the cult to a superior being [Schäfer] is what they did for Adolf Hitler in Germany. . . . I know that there are two ex-members of the SS in Dignidad, but I don't think there's anything political or Nazi. In the discussions that we had in the dining room on the basis of some movies, the consensus was anti-Nazi and the persecution of the Jews was criticized.[20]

Colonia Dignidad survived the Pinochet era, plus that of the first post-Pinochet president, Patricio Aylwin, and closed only in November 1996, during the presidency of Eduardo Frei Ruiz-Tagle. By then the evidence that Schäfer was a sexual predator who had attacked the children in his care was so obvious that the police could no longer turn a blind eye.[21]

This does not appear to be the end of neo-Nazis in Chile. Sagaris identifies Miguel Serrano as "the official leader of Chilean Nazis."[22] In 1997 he had a high profile. That year marked the fiftieth anniversary of the establishment of Chile's naval and army bases in the Antarctic, Base Prat and Base O'Higgins, respectively. Serrano wrote an article for a Sunday edition of *El Mercurio* in which he claimed to have participated in the creation of Base O'Higgins. One of his companions — later Pinochet's Minister of the Interior — was Sergio Onofre Jarpa, with whom, he said, he shared a common ideology. These bases, said Serrano, were a Chilean response to British ambitions in a region claimed by Chile. During the Ibáñez presidency, Serrano served as Chile's ambassador to India, where he lobbied for Indian support for his country's Antarctic claims at the U.N.[23]

Also in 1997 Chile and Argentina had a territorial dispute in the ice fields southeast of Puerto Montt. Given the ubiquity of the ice, there were problems determining the actual border, a problem that concerned governments in Santiago and Buenos Aires. A group calling itself the Movimiento Nacionalista Chileno (MNCh) opposed compromise. MNCh graffiti in Osorno read, "CAMPOS DE HIELOS SUR CHILENOS" (The Southern Ice Fields are Chilean), and "SOLO LOS TRAIDORES ENTREGAN TERRITORIO!" (Only traitors surrender territory!).[24]

On February 23 the Puerto Montt newspaper, *El Llanquihue*, featured a story from Vodudahue near the ice fields, some 118 kilometers southeast of Puerto Montt. About twenty-two families had settled there, and the settlers had seen young men with short hair on patrol, making maps and sketches. The military types had no contact with the settlers, who suggested that they might be Argentines. *El Llanquihue* quoted one settler, Carlos Sánchez:

It is strange to find so many people, all between 25 and 30 years of age and with short military haircuts, who have no connection with anyone in the settlement and who call themselves tourists. These people have been spotted making maps and studying the landscape, near the rivers Vodudahue and Baceló.[25]

Two days later *El Llanquihue* determined that the paramilitary types were Chileans, not Argentines. Fernando Ramírez, a history professor from the University of Chile who had been studying the Vodudahue area since 1993, identified them as such and noted that a developer from the United States, Douglas Tompkins, wanted to create a utopia in the region. The young people, said Tompkins, were members of the MNCh "who fit the profile outlined in *El Llanquihue*: short hair, military-style clothes, who give orders to each other."[26]

The following day, *El Llanquihue* carried an interview with General José Sepúlveda, chief of the Carabineros in the Tenth Region. Sepúlveda emphatically denied that the young short-haired men were Argentines, and he doubted whether they were nationalistic paramilitaries. He thought that they were probably outdoor types who enjoyed mountain climbing, and he saw no harm in their activities as long as they carried no weapons. However, directly beneath the interview with General Sepúlveda appeared confirmation that the MNCh definitely was in the area. *El Llanquihue* reported:

> Led by young Marcelo Saavedra Fuentes, teacher at the University of Concepción, National head of the MNCh and creator of the general plan of southern sovereignty, . . . the group has taken an initiative against the presence of U.S. citizen Douglas Tompkins, who has developed a project called "Pumalin Park."[27]

El Llanquihue cited the Concepción newspaper *El Sur* as its source.

The issue remained contentious, at least in the pages of *El Llanquihue*. On February 27 an editorial said that whether the young men were Argentines or Chilean paramilitaries, the government of Chile had neglected the Vodudahue area. On March 1 it said that following a helicopter tour of the region, General Sepúlveda agreed that they were superpatriots, followers of Marcelo Saavedra. On March 4 it carried a lengthy letter from Douglas Tompkins.

Tompkins expressed concern about the MNCh. As a pilot, he found it unimaginable that Argentines would attempt to invade Chile through such rugged terrain as that around Vodudahue. If they had any such intentions, he said, they would invade by air or through a route with mountain passes. Nor could he share General Sepúlveda's lack of concern about the MNCh vigilantes. They were not simply tourists or backpackers, he said, or "firemen with spare time." They had threatened Tompkins with death. "They are extremists, supposedly followers of Miguel Serrano, whom I have seen in pictures published in newspapers dressed in a Nazi-style black coat saluting the Nazi flag on Hitler's birthday." Members of the MNCh, said Tompkins, "are racists who hate Jews and Amerindians." He could not understand why the MNCh would disapprove of his environment-friendly projects.[28]

Two days later Serrano responded. He expressed resentment that a foreigner like Tompkins would have ambitious plans for a strategically important area on Chile's periphery, a place rich in resources and potential. Foreigners were taking control of Chile, lamented Serrano. General Pinochet had tried to limit the amount of land a foreigner could buy to one thousand hectares, but Tompkins had purchased three thousand.[29] These were legitimate concerns, not exclusively those of nationalistic fanatics. Three days later *El Llanquihue* reported that Tompkins wanted to build eight landing strips, and a deputy in Chile's House of Representatives, Sergio Elgueta, wondered about the implications for Chilean sovereignty in a peripheral area. Under the circumstances, Elgueta thought that the thousand-hectare limit had merit.[30] On March 13 one Juan Eduardo Correa expressed negative thoughts about Tompkins in a letter to *El Llanquihue*. Until 1995 Tompkins had worked in conjunction with a Chilean organization, EDUCEC. This would guarantee Chilean control of his lands. By 1997 he represented a U.S. organization, Bosque Pumalin Foundation, whose goals were unclear.[31] Any Canadian with memories of American challenges to Arctic sovereignty between 1969 and 1988 should be able to understand the attitudes of Elgueta and Correa. It is also understandable that patriotic young men might feel an obligation to strengthen their country's claims in a peripheral region neglected by their national government.

Nevertheless, it is clear that undesirables from the Third Reich and its ally, Ustashe Croatia — Walter Rauff, Vlado Svescen, and Paul Schäfer — did move to Chile, where they served the Pinochet regime. Chilean nationalists who had no direct contact with the Third Reich, most notably Miguel Serrano and the members of the MNCh, appear to have shared some common values with Nazis. Whatever the validity of Tompkins's charges against Serrano, by his own admission Serrano collaborated with

Ibáñez and shared the values of Onofre Jarpa. Members of the MNCh appear to be more than patriotic gentlemen who considered their country's territorial claims in jeopardy.

In July 1989, four months before the Berlin Wall opened, General Pinochet told Chilean journalists Raquel Correa and Elizabeth Subercaseaux that Communists worried him considerably more than did Nazis. "Hitlerism has disappeared," he said. "Stalinism has not."[32] That Hitler's heritage survived through Rauff, Onofre Jarpa, and those who celebrated the events of September 5, 1938, appeared of little concern.

Nor was ongoing Nazism of concern to a great number of people, some of them in surprising places. One was Henry Kissinger, himself a refugee from Hitler's Germany. In his memoirs Kissinger defends Pinochet's coup d'état and makes no apology for friendly relations with Pinochet's regime.[33] Also apparently unconcerned, despite the attempt to extradite Rauff, was the government of Israel. In 1992, when making arrangements for a research trip to the archives of the Chilean Foreign Office, I went to the Chilean embassy in Ottawa. Two years earlier Pinochet had left the presidency but remained commander-in-chief of Chile's armed forces, a role he held until 1998. The official who helpfully made arrangements for my visit to the archives mentioned that his previous postings had been in South Africa and Israel. For much of the Pinochet presidency, he said, the only countries that would sell weapons to Chile were South Africa (which still practiced apartheid) and Israel. "My task," he explained, "was to keep the weapons coming." Even on May 31, 1994, when I was conducting research for this essay in the Foreign Office on Santiago's Calle Bandera, military helicopters hovered over the building because Israeli Foreign Minister Shimon Peres was inside concluding an arms sale. Under the deal that Pinochet had concluded before stepping down as president, the civilian authority would have minimal control over the armed forces until his retirement in 1998. Whatever Peres managed to sell would benefit Pinochet and his colleagues.

Carlos Cerda, a Chilean novelist who spent the Pinochet years in East Germany, returned home in 1990, when East Germany collapsed and Pinochet vacated Chile's presidency. In 1993 he released what became a best-seller, *Morir en Berlín* (To Die in Berlin). In one scene a Chilean refugee named Mario visits the East German community of Weimar. Weimar, his East German guide notes, was home to such distinguished and civilized Germans as Johann Goethe and Friedrich Schiller. It was close to Buchenwald, one of Hitler's death camps. Many residents of Weimar were totally unaware of what was happening at Buchenwald. So it must also be in Chile, suggests the East German guide. Many saw what they wanted to see, equally unaware of or indifferent to the horrors of the Pinochet regime, despite the fact that thousands were tortured, executed, or forced into exile. How right the fictional guide was!

NOTES

1. Christel Krause Converse, "The Rise and Fall of Nazi Influence among the German-Chileans" (Ph.D. dissertation, Georgetown University, 1990), 247.

2. See David Healy, *James G. Blaine and Latin America* (Columbia: University of Missouri Press, 2001), 54–99.

3. This is a brief summary of my book, *Chile and the Nazis* (Montreal: Black Rose, 2001).

4. Mount, *Chile and the Nazis,* 16–17.

5. Ibid., 19–20.

6. Tobias Barros Ortiz, *Recogiendo los pasos: Testigo militar y político del siglo XX*, vol. 2 (Santiago: Planeta Chileno, 1988), 159, 297–298.

7. Mount, *Chile and the Nazis,* 74–75, 80, 82, 83, 86–88, 107–108, 124.

8. Ibid., 2, 82.

9. Martínez's 1942 report appears in the Archivos Diplomáticos de Relaciones Exteriores, vol. 1970, Santiago.

10. Jorge Camarasa, *Odessa al Sur: La Argentina como refugio de Nazis y criminales de guerra* (Buenos Aires: Planeta, 1995), 34.

11. Ibid., 114.

12. John Cornwell, *Hitler's Pope: The Secret History of Pius XII* (London: Viking, 1999), 249.

13. Ibid., 249.

14. Camarasa, *Odessa al Sur,* 93, 105.

15. Gerald Clark, *The Coming Explosion in Latin America* (Toronto: Musson, 1962), 278.

16. Camarasa, *Odessa al Sur,* 113.

17. Lake Sagaris, *After the First Death: A Journey through Chile, Time, Mind* (Toronto: Somerville House, 1996), 205.

18. Ibid., 43.

19. Ibid., 47.

20. Cited in Sagaris, *After the First Death,* 56.

21. "24 Horas," TVN, January 27, 1997; *El Llanquihue* (Puerto Montt), January 28, 1997; see also the newsmagazine *Ercilla,* no. 2054, March 10–23, 1997; *El Mercurio* (Santiago), March 20, 1997; "24 Horas," TVN, March 21, 1997; *El Mercurio* (Santiago), March 23, 1997.

22. Sagaris, *After the First Death,* 58.

23. *El Mercurio* (Santiago), February 16, 1997.

24. Witnessed by the author on visits to Osorno in January and February 1997.

25. *El Llanquihue,* February 23, 1997.

26. Ibid., February 26, 1997.

27. Ibid., February 26, 1997.

28. Ibid., March 4, 1997.

29. Ibid., March 6, 1997.

30. Ibid., March 9, 1997.

31. Ibid., March 13, 1997.

32. Raquel Correa and Elizabeth Subercaseaux, *Ego Sum* (Santiago: Planeta, 1996), 57.

33. Henry Kissinger, *White House Years* (Boston: Little, Brown, 1979), 653–683; Henry Kissinger, *Years of Renewal* (New York: Simon and Schuster, 1999), 749–760.

DIANA ANHALT

"Are You Sure They're Really Jewish?"
A SELECTIVE HISTORY OF MEXICO CITY'S
BETH ISRAEL COMMUNITY CENTER

Whenever I revisit my childhood, I focus on that place in my mind where I store my memories. If memories were lined up in rows, like asparagus stalks, I could find what I need immediately. But memories don't behave that way. They're more like beads that pop their string and roll away into the far corners of the mind. My only comfort is in knowing the memories are there—somewhere—even if I don't always find them.

What I have managed to salvage are those things no one else in my family bothered to keep track of. I have a particularly strong recollection of the religious side of my childhood—odd, considering my parents were about as close as you could get to being atheists and Jews simultaneously. Perhaps I have held on to those memories because there wasn't much religion in my home, and what little we had stands out.

What little we had was transmitted to me by Beth Israel, founded—approximately—in 1953, some three years after our arrival in Mexico City. Despite all predictions to the contrary, it has managed to endure, although more than fifty years after its founding it is beginning to dodder and grow shaky in the knees. It also continues to generate controversy. (Before my marriage in 1965, an acquaintance suggested I be married elsewhere. When I asked why, she replied, "Well, I'm not sure they're really Jewish.") I could tell you lots of stories like that, but I'm getting ahead of myself.

To start at the beginning: In November 1950 my parents, Belle and Mike Zykofsky, precipitously left New York. They pulled my sister and me—I was eight, my sister was five—out of school and moved to Mexico. We arrived shortly before the school year was to end. (Mexico had long winter vacations in those days.) That left my sister, Judy, and me with no organized activities until the school year started again in February. So we often spent mornings in Sanborncito, a soda fountain in the neighborhood, where the owner allowed us to read the comics and where I accosted anyone I overheard speaking English. Occasionally, I took them home with me. That's how my parents met the Scodells, a Jewish couple from Miami with three children. (They were in Mexico evading the IRS.) Through the Scodells, my parents met a number of American Jews, and these would go on to establish what later became known as the Beth Israel Community Center (BICC), the only English-speaking congregation in Mexico and among the first in Latin America.

It's no accident that the need for such a congregation would evolve during the 1950s. Under the leadership of President Miguel Alemán (1946–1952), Mexico was just beginning to recognize its potential in an increasingly industrialized world. Alemán encouraged the establishment of American businesses, fostered a political climate hospitable to North American interests, and facilitated the expansion of new industry. As U.S. firms moved south, the need for increased services and additional U.S.-oriented institutions to attend the growing influx of Americans increased.

Furthermore, following World War II, some young Americans, victims of postwar unemployment and in search of adventure and opportunity, were attracted by Mexico's accessible cost of living, its proximity to the United States, and the feasibility of actually settling there either to work or to pursue an education under the G.I. Bill. They were joined by a handful of fortune seekers, draft dodgers, tax evaders, and political dissidents, of the sort who have traditionally fled across the border in search of sanctuary. In addition, an insignificant number of Jewish Americans — usually those affiliated with left-wing organizations — believed the kind of fascism that had swept Germany some twenty years earlier was on the rise in the United States, and they certainly didn't want to be around should that occur.

I think my parents might be included in that last group, but that wasn't their principal incentive for fleeing the Bronx. They fled the Bronx because they were Reds. During the late 1940s and throughout the 1950s — the so-called McCarthy years — former membership in suspect organizations or a controversial petition signed years earlier could, like ghosts from the past, return to haunt former progressives and result in the loss of a job, a subpoena, or both.

Thus, for a wide variety of reasons, there was an influx of American English-speaking Jews to Mexico during this period — Jews who felt, and generally were, excluded from Mexico City's tight-knit Ashkenazi and Sephardic Orthodox synagogues and unofficial prayer houses. While the Americans might have shared an ancient religious heritage with those already residing in Mexico, the resemblance stopped there. Most had been born in the United States and educated in American schools. They had, for the most part, cast off their European or Sephardic traditions and generally spoke no Spanish. (A handful could get by in Yiddish.)

As a result of their upbringing, experiences, and frames of reference, the Americans differed substantially from their European or Sephardic counterparts who, following centuries of persecution and migration, had now converged in Mexico City. As compared with the United States, the Jewish migration to Mexico was a relatively small and recent one. (At present, it has yet to reach fifty thousand.) Only after World War I, following the drafting of the Immigration Laws of 1921 and 1924, which curtailed the flow of immigrants to the United States, would Jewish migration to Mexico increase significantly. Once there, these families had every intention of laying down permanent roots; most of the Americans didn't.

At the beginning, a small group of American Jews, including my parents, met occasionally. "Sometimes we'd go to Passy's Restaurant to socialize and eat strudel," Helen Zoller, a founding member, told me. "We called ourselves the American Jewish Club, but we were mainly a social organization."[1] Another old-timer told me, "Well, we played cards. Gin rummy, pinochle, craps . . ."[2]

At one of the social gatherings in 1953, Helen, attending for the first time—"I still remember, I wore a green suit"—expressed her anguish at not having a place of worship. "You've got to realize," Helen told me, "we were very young. We had small children but no families—no mothers, no fathers, no aunts—just each other. We were pretty much alone."[3] She suggested the group form an English-speaking temple in Mexico City. By then, others were also beginning to recognize their need for a place where, in addition to socializing, they could worship and educate their children in the Jewish tradition.

The "temple," such as it was, was to be named the Beth Israel Community Center, and the founders specified it would be both Conservative and English-speaking. However, I sometimes wonder whether the original members—some twenty families in all—had any notion of the enormity of the task they had undertaken and the challenges they would face. I don't think so. Certainly if they had, they may have better defined their goals and purposes and included a clause in their bylaws, first drafted in 1955, to the effect that English was to be the official language of worship. But they didn't. It probably didn't occur to them that years later their identity would be threatened.

They did identify themselves, however, as "a conservative synagogue"[4] and in so doing would become among the first established in Latin America. Some of the founding members, including my parents, who were only marginally involved, would have preferred a Reform temple, because they felt more comfortable with its liberal humanism. But by then, they realized the already established Orthodox community might take offense. Despite their compromise, the Orthodox congregations did take offense, and even today, some fifty years later, Beth Israel is an outcast of sorts, the *goyishe* temple. (Some of our members have joked, although it might be true, that when an Orthodox Jew passes our front door, he spits three times and crosses the street.)

At the beginning, most of the members, shuddering at the responsibility building a synagogue might imply, had opted instead to rent their own clubhouse, to be used only for social affairs, on Calle Citlaltépetl in a section of Mexico City known as the Colonia Hipódromo. "We decorated it — Chinese-style — and we survived through schnorring. When we needed a tank of gas we'd all chip in, and if we needed food someone would provide it. We didn't know from nothing," Helen told me.[5]

As news of their existence spread, others soon joined them. In 1955 they held their first Shabbat service in someone's living room. A member officiated, and the congregation shared mimeographed copies of Sabbath services taken from the "Union Prayer Book." According to a witness: "On a Friday night . . . two men stood before a small table. . . . One held a prayer book in which the portions he was to read were carefully underlined in pencil. . . . The man's voice was not quite steady. . . . When he came to a paragraph printed in Hebrew he handed the book to the man standing beside him."[6]

Within a few weeks, the borrowed living room proved inadequate. Attendance had increased. So they proceeded to elect a board of directors and set out in search of a home. At the beginning, they approached already existing Jewish temples and organizations, only to be rejected. Not one would rent them space "principally because its husbands and wives wanted to sit and pray together."[7] Or as one early associate put it: "They just didn't like us because we were different."

The Hungarians, however, weren't so fussy. They had established a social club, the Emuna, in a building rented to them by the B'nai Brith on Calle Puebla 212 and within months of that first living room service, agreed to permit Beth Israel to use their premises, rent free. To cover what expenses they had, a board member approached the ten people who could best afford it and asked each to contribute one hundred dollars. "We used that money to cover costs. We also sold yarmulkes for twenty cents each," one of founding members told me.[8] At about this same time, the board started proceedings to legalize their status as a center of worship.

If the early 1950s were marked by an influx of American English-speaking Jews, there were a number of others who, while not American, also spoke English and welcomed Beth Israel's more liberal stance. Richard Pick, the temple's president on two separate occasions, told me he and several others who had belonged to the German congregation, Haktivkah Menora, a small unofficial synagogue with some fifty members, would choose to join Beth Israel: "We felt welcome in the English-speaking, American atmosphere."[9] In addition, a handful of French Jews, some Hungarians, and a few Czechoslovakians chose to join Beth Israel as well, and English would become the lingua franca.

The congregation had temporarily solved the space problem, but they still had to find a religious leader. With that serendipitous good fortune which marked its early years, they found two adventurous young men willing to take risks. Joel (Jack) Schecter, then a student at the Jewish Theological Seminary at Columbia University, presided at High Holiday services celebrated at the Emuna in 1955 or 1956. He remained until after Succot, celebrated in the Zollers' backyard. Everet Gendler, also a rabbinical student, traveled to Mexico the following year, fell in love with the country, and in 1958 signed a contract with Beth Israel. (He would remain for two years.)

By the time Rabbi Gendler arrived to assume his new post, Beth Israel had moved into a house at Virreyes 1140, formerly the Japanese embassy. During those first years of expansion and growth, the founders continued their search for more ample premises, but by 1964 they realized their membership had peaked and was unlikely to increase. As a result, they purchased and subsequently remodeled and enlarged the Virreyes building. Several years later, once construction was completed, the property was deeded to the government in accordance with Mexican law.

During these years, 1955–1960, Beth Israel forged ahead. Fueled by the energy of its young members and impervious to Mexico's Orthodox sector, more inclined to maintain a low profile, they began to be noticed. They would join the World Council of Synagogues, become a founding member of the United Synagogues of Conservative Judaism, and sit on a handful of local bodies as well. (At present, BICC belongs to the International Organization of Conservative Synagogues and continues to have close ties with the community's Comité Central, the Organización de Servicios a Enfermos, the Bitajon, and the Keren Hayesod, among others.)

At the same time, the synagogue established Hebrew classes, a Bible study group, a youth group, a men's club, a choir, a sisterhood, and a Sunday school program, perhaps the first of its kind in Mexico. (Most of the members' children attended the American School and received no religious instruction, while non-American Jewish children generally attended Jewish schools.) In addition, they published a directory, a monthly bulletin, and a yearbook and sponsored fashion shows, teas, card games, bazaars, plays, and annual dances. Such functions attracted hundreds of people, many from outside the community.

Although temples have traditionally contributed time and money to a wide variety of causes, Beth Israel, in particular, its sisterhood, was at the forefront in promoting activities that did not necessarily benefit the Jewish population. They raised funds for the victims of natural disasters, donated heart surgery equipment to the cardiac unit at the American British Cowdray Hospital, supported the Red Cross, and collected money for the United Community Fund. When they decided to support the Colegio Francisco Goitia in San Isidro, a school for the physically handicapped, their work generated so much publicity that the government responded by establishing the Central Pedagógica Infantil (Children's Teaching Center). Helen Zoller remembered how they had even worked alongside a group of nuns whose convent was located near the Villa de Guadalupe: "We felt a responsibility. Many of the Mexicans were so poor and they needed so much, so our programs reached out to the community."[10]

While other temples were predominantly centers of worship — as plain as hard-boiled eggs — Beth Israel was evolving into a community center. (We were, no doubt, regarded as frivolous and not to be taken seriously.) But, of course, there were religious observances as well, and for the children, a wide variety of celebrations — Hanukkah, Succot, Purim.

My favorite was Passover. Since none of the early members had extended families in Mexico, it became common practice to hold one large community seder. I still remember the first one, held in 1955 at the Jewish-owned Chapultepec Restaurant. My mother bought me a blue plaid dress for the occasion, I found the *afikomen,* and I was allowed to drink real wine instead of grape juice. (One of my friends got drunk.)

If those early years are suffused with a kind of glow, that's to be expected. Memories, like ghosts, are highly selective: They only put up an appearance when they feel like it and are never exactly what they seem. In reality, as its founders discovered early on, running a temple was a complicated business. How do you attract new members, define the temple's objectives, find qualified religious leaders?

To begin with, rabbis were in short supply. The Conservative seminaries produced—and continue to produce—few rabbis each year. In addition, a newly organized synagogue could hardly afford to compete with stateside salaries, and Mexico, after all, is off the beaten path. Thus it was not unusual for Beth Israel to find itself "between rabbis." (With the exception of Samuel Lerer, who presided over the congregation between 1968 and 1999, rabbis tended to remain no more than two or three years before moving on.)

Attracting new members has been equally difficult. Throughout the 1960s, American companies would begin to replace their foreign hires with local employees. As a result, Beth Israel, along with some of the American churches and community organizations, would face the challenge of trying to preserve its identity as a foreign institution.

Consequently, as older members died, left Mexico, or changed congregations, Beth Israel's identity as an English-speaking Conservative synagogue was challenged. New members—and on occasion some of the old-timers—were less likely to understand or sympathize with the temple's original goals. Some would attempt to impose more Orthodox practices, replace the English sermon with Spanish, and introduce an authoritarian leadership at odds with the more open style that marked Beth Israel's early years.

With age, the building housing Beth Israel has acquired a certain respectable solidity. It manages to look imposing but not pretentious. Its angular white structure is fronted by a short stairway and was once distinguished from the surrounding homes by its higher visibility from the street. But this too is being lost as insecurity and the threat posed to Jews worldwide increase. At present, a highly patrolled security entrance along one side of the building has replaced the main entryway. The walls grow higher, and the ivy covering them thickens.

The interior is equally sober. Most dividing walls were torn down, leaving one very large wood-paneled meeting room, capable of being partitioned, when necessary, with provisional seating for four hundred. The room's sparse decoration consists of ten narrow, floor-to-ceiling stained-glass panels containing abstract versions of the burning bush and other biblical themes and executed predominantly in peacock blue and turquoise with hints of magenta, yellow, orange, red, and green. The building also houses offices, classrooms, meeting rooms, and a *mikva,* or ritual bath.

The *mikva* is a recent addition. At one time Ashkenazi congregations used the community baths located in the Colonia Hipódromo. Beth Israel employed it for conversion purposes only, but as the Jewish population drifted away from the old neighborhoods, each of the newer temples constructed their own *mikvas* and refused to allow Beth Israel to use them for conversions. For a short time, Rabbi Lerer bypassed this restriction by conducting ritual baths at Lake Tequesquitengo, a two-hour drive from Mexico City. (Needless to say, this practice, when it became known, scandalized the entire community.) Today, as synagogues in Mexico, including our own, grow increasingly more conservative, no Jewish woman can be married without the *mikva*.

Yet despite its increasing conservatism, Beth Israel is still scorned, in other words, not quite kosher, in the eyes of the pundits. Although we have managed to survive for almost fifty years, we continue to be regarded as outsiders.

Some of the differences separating us from other communities are obvious: Most of our services are still conducted in English, although our membership is predominantly Spanish-speaking, and we are one of only two Conservative temples in Mexico. The other, Bethel, was established with our assistance and encouragement in 1961 to serve the Spanish-speaking community, and some of our members have since left to join them. In addition, Beth Israel often found itself at the center of considerable controversy as a result of a series of conversions.

As reported in the *Atlantic Monthly,* in the 1960s a group of Mexicans from the town of Venta Prieta, who claimed to be descendants of the lost tribes of Israel, "met a rabbi from the capital who agreed to perform conversions. With the help of visiting teenagers from a temple in Pennsylvania, the Venta Prietans rehabilitated their primitive synagogue and started studying Hebrew."[11] The "rabbi from Mexico City" was Beth Israel's rabbi, Samuel Lerer. At the same time, he conducted numerous conversions in Mexico City, a practice in part responsible for altering the makeup of our congregation. Needless to say, this practice has been much criticized.

And these aren't the only practices that have been criticized. To my knowledge, the first Bat Mitzvah in Mexico was held in Beth Israel in 1964, and our temple was the first where men and women sat together and where women were allowed onto the bema, although not for the purposes of reading scripture.

In my eyes, however, what distinguished us from other synagogues in Mexico was not primarily the language we spoke or the doctrines we followed but rather our tolerance: We were, to my knowledge, the first congregation to participate in ecumenical services sponsored by the

English-speaking Christian community; the purchase of seats or special distinctions is unheard of; on the High Holidays every member in good standing is given an honor; and assessments are generally determined according to one's ability to pay.

Our tolerance is visible as well in the makeup of our membership. Board member Peter Katz expresses it this way: "We are the most heterogeneous temple in Mexico. You can find all backgrounds and ethnic groups here — Aleppo, Damascus, Greece, France, Germany, the United States, Mexico, etcetera. They're all represented."[12]

Yet from its inception, our greatest asset has been a healthy respect for the democratic process. Board members are popularly elected. Women continue to sit on the board, although they have never presided, and some attempt has been made to follow parliamentary procedure. Most important, particularly in a country with an authoritarian tradition, the board has been able to limit the authority of our spiritual leaders to religious affairs. Unfortunately, over the years, respect for such practices has been on the decline.

At a stormy general meeting some four years ago, the membership, by a slim margin, voted to institute one sermon a month in Spanish. The old-timers and native English speakers protested: "You are challenging our identity. We could hire a Spanish-speaking rabbi for half the price."

While we remain an English-speaking congregation and a Conservative one, I worry that we may be losing our democratic tradition and our reputation for fairness and tolerance. At times I believe that as the nature of our membership has altered we have strayed far afield from the ideals of the temple's founders.

Internal rebellions have split the congregation and resulted in the resignation of valuable members. Expenses are up, and profits are down. We are digging into our resources. In the past few years the complexion of the board has changed dramatically. Newcomers are now in the majority. (Yet what can you expect of a congregation where many of the old-timers have died, left Mexico, or are no longer willing or able to serve?) And who is to say that the more recent arrivals are not equally well intentioned and intent on fulfilling their vision of creating the "perfect temple"? In our world — the only one we know — continents shift, an entire species is eliminated, and cities are swept into the sea. Change is a constant, and to insist otherwise is to live the life of a snail.

When I chose a title for this essay, I purposely included the phrase, "A Selective History." I did so in full knowledge that much of what I write is based on my personal memories, perceptions, and, no doubt, prejudices. The Beth Israel I remember and write about may be no closer to reality than shadow is to substance.

Each of us chooses our memories — to the extent we are able to choose — much as we do our shoes. Are we comfortable with the shoes on our feet or the memories in our head? Do they fit? Can we live with them? No matter how objective one tries to be, we are powerless against the conspiracy of memories, all too eager to mold the past to suit our liking. As for the future, we have nothing to go by, only speculation. And hope.

NOTES

1. Helen Zoller, interview with author, May 21, 2002.

2. Armin Vann, interview with author, September 17, 2002.

3. Helen Zoller, interview with author, May 21, 2002.

4. Constitution of Beth Israel Community Center.

5. Helen Zoller, interview with author, May 21, 2002.

6. "Dreams Made Realities," Beth Israel Community Center Year Book, 1958.

7. Helen Zoller, interview with author, May 21, 2002.

8. Armin Vann, interview with author, September 17, 2002.

9. Richard Pick, interview with author, September 19, 2002.

10. Helen Zoller, interview with author, May 21, 2002.

11. Barbara Ferry and Debbie Nathan, "Mistaken Identity: The Case of New Mexico's 'Hidden Jews,'" *Atlantic Monthly,* December 2000, 85–96.

12. Peter Katz, interview with author, September 12, 2002.

A D I N A   C I M E T

Dancing around the Political Divide

BETWEEN THE "LEGAL" AND THE "REGAL"
IN THE MEXICAN JEWISH COMMUNITY

Four years ago, I was invited to collaborate with a major American Jewish publication that covers developments in Jewish communities around the world on an annual basis. The publication focuses on significant communities of Jews in the contemporary world, but each issue also includes reports on smaller communities; although less significant numerically and politically, these serve as barometers of the intergroup relationships between local populations and Jews.

The Mexican Jewish community had been the subject of much of my published scholarly writing. It had been my home, where my family lives, and had nurtured the roots of my Jewish identity. My participation in this work would not have been the subject of any further writing if a certain incident had not propelled me into the midst of a conflict in which issues of legality, morality, power, and political cronyism were played out. I therefore became an inadvertent protagonist, a role that activated my interest in issues that I had described only historically in the community.

In general, the governing body of the community, the Kehillah, has in Mexico exercised its political power through communal authoritarian bureaucracies. Community leaders who had time, energy, and sufficient financial resources to take on the job joined the head of the Kehillah, who worked tirelessly for the organization but with little transparency in the decision-making process. These individuals received respect and honor, because all recognized that they got the voluntary nonpaying job "done."[1]

Shimshon Feldman, the head of the Ashkenazi Kehillah, had worked this way for more than forty years, since the Kehillah's inception in 1958. His style did not invite much participation; few invitations were extended to outsiders to join the volunteers. The message was clear: there was no need to think or question the leadership; in any event, it did not pay to do it. Feldman groomed one of his sons for the main leadership position. As the father retired, the younger Feldman took over the institution. Although the latter aimed at its "modernization," he perpetuated his father's methods and was equally dictatorial in style and practice.

During one of the years I reported on events in the community for an American publication, a major, unexpected change took place in the Jewish community in Mexico: the well-established communal structure of the Ashkenazi community, the Kehillah covering half of the forty thousand Jews in Mexico, was dismantled and replaced by a new group: the Ashkenazi Community Council. Although the Kehillah was created in 1957–1958 as an umbrella institution for all Ashkenazi organizations, it saw itself as an extension of the early congregation Nidkhei Israel. This congregation was started in 1922 with the building of a synagogue in what is today the historic center of Mexico City, and it expanded slowly to include diverse activities for its members, including education, economic support, health care, and geriatric care.

In 1997 internal changes (a rabbi was dismissed by one of the member congregations that belonged to the Kehillah) opened up possibilities for change. New self-appointed leaders announced their objectives publicly after the reorganization: they moved to new premises, chose a new name for their organization, and promised to become an umbrella for all other Ashkenazi organizations that existed, shedding the Orthodox association of the Kehillah so as to attract the Conservative Congregation Beth El that had dared to be independent. They also pledged themselves to sustain internal freedoms, making communal life in Mexico the "coherent, well-organized and efficient system" that they saw as necessary. Whatever had malfunctioned in the past, this group was going to correct.

It was then that communal politics were revealed as anachronistic and lethal. While the Mexican political system is currently at pains to modify its political culture, democratize its political structures, and expand participation to attain consensus from the broader membership, what went on in this small community was at the very least surprising, if not shameful: surprising, because the national message has not rubbed off on the community itself; shameful, because, as a community and a structure for voluntary association, the Ashkenazim are well aware of the attacks leveled at the anachronisms and failures of the national political system to agree to submit themselves to an arbitrary and authoritarian scheme.

When I reported the change as constituting a coup d'état within the Jewish community in Mexico, key leaders were offended and sought to redress their grievance. That it was important to record the change is hardly an issue. Yet the reporting of the event somehow became a "problem." What, exactly, was the problem? Was my description inaccurate? It became a problem only when, more than a year after its publication, my description made some leaders in the community uncomfortable. Their reaction was not to refute my statement with another view of the events in print. Rather, rallying colleagues from the other organizations and communities (including Sephardic and Oriental) in Mexico, they called into question not the "organizational change" but the description of the "outsider." They demanded that the American organization in charge of the publication, with which they have contractual arrangements for mutual support, dismiss the writer. In addition, they requested sole authority and recognition as observers of the community's activities.[2]

The community leaders did not see the change in governance as a coup d'état in which a cadre of new politicians decided to take control with the acquiescence of a selected few of the old guard. That was not flattering. Instead, they saw themselves as selfless volunteers who had the "interest of the community" at heart. They felt strongly that taking over the reins of the Ashkenazi community in the manner in which it was done was not an act of self-promotion but an attempt to improve the communal arrangement: they felt the old structure of the Kehillah had outlived its usefulness and was surviving by sheer inertia. They wanted to modernize the structure, coordinate all subgroups, and further integrate all communal cultural efforts under their tutelage, without clearly explaining why this was necessary and without obtaining public support. They claimed that they were representing and responding to a "democratic and unified" request of the community. They did not acknowledge that the planning and execution of the change was organized in absolute secrecy and that votes and information about their intention were never taken or made public until the takeover was a fait accompli. Ironically, the inertia they criticized contributed to their success. Few wanted to challenge them; most did not care or had learned the lesson that it does not pay to care. For these new leaders, any other way of seeing their accomplishments was a misinterpretation on the part of the observer. Indeed, the "united" community in Mexico, through the Central Committee, was going to make sure that that did not happen again. Their "intentions" had always been clear to everyone in the community, they claimed, and now they had to make sure all outsiders understood it as well. The record shows that although they achieved some changes, their overall style and practice have remained the same.

This story is important because it reveals the ways in which the leadership of the central governing organization goes to battle to control the image of the community in the media. The battle is waged without skimping on moral costs. Wanting to be the official and exclusive painters of their self-portrait, they are willing to silence and censor other viewpoints. While their attempt begins as an effort to have absolute control of how external others view the community, they are actually seeking to attain unqualified control of the internal activities of the community: promoting an embellished self-image to the outside world legitimizes their control and authoritarian style at home. An examination of the inside operations of the leaders will confirm their unqualified control.

Jewish communities in the Diaspora have always been confronted with the problem of control. The case in Mexico is no exception; after all, a cultural group that is outside the borders of a state, without any enforcement powers, is left vulnerable to disintegration, and its members will behave in unpredictable ways. With few or none of the mechanisms a state has to enforce laws and a moral order, the Jewish communities of the Diaspora have relied on the authority of their leadership to impose norms of behavior. Rabbis have headed these communities since time immemorial. Their training in law and their examination of issues concerning the code of behavior for Jews based in the Torah as well as in other texts such as the Gemara, the Talmud, and the Halacha have made them undisputed authorities for the Jewish masses. Yet despite these elaborate legal codes, a flexible exchange was maintained to allow Jews from different locations to communicate and navigate relationships based on a shared acknowledgment of authority but also on respect for its morality.

This task has always been a challenge.[3] Regardless of relative Jewish success in transmitting identity, the political issue faced by each community cannot be dismissed: how should control be enacted? Each generation must revisit this question. The problem is thus very old and is not specific to the Mexican Jewish community. But each community must devise its own solutions.

Organized Jewish communities have always served multiple purposes: they have been a cushion to help and to orient newcomers by advising them about acceptable ways to integrate into the new societies; and they promoted their interpretation of the identities that can and should be maintained as well as what can or should be shed. The leadership, lay and religious, has always played a crucial guiding role in these activities. They have helped to mitigate the experience of alienation, loss, and disorientation that some may have. Authority figures have therefore always played an important cohesive and integrative role as well as a psychological one. At the center of all this has been the issue of morality and law as regards interpersonal behavior. Part of the ethos of the Jewish identity, linked to tradition and religion, is the message that there is a higher order of interpersonal behavior at stake: the need to live with consistent principles and integrity and to arrive at righteousness and not just mere fairness. Justice, as a guideline in the treatment between and among people, is considered a virtue.

Issues of governance and dispensing justice have multiple layers for a Jewish community. The Law of the land, "Dina d'malkhuta dina," has been understood as a code and ethic to be reckoned with. At the same time, regardless of the concerns and implications of dealing with the Law of the land, Jews try to maintain a world unto themselves, in which their concept of ethics can be put into practice. The aim is not only to protect this worldview but also to ensure practical protection for the members and minimize the potential for assaults from the outside.

Given that law, legality, and a moral view of the world are linked, Jews have maintained their own court system to keep this perspective alive. In the Diaspora, where a single structure of thought has not prevailed, the Jewish court is the only internal institution that can establish a practical legality of sorts. It is a forum where Jews can deal with disputes between Jews and ensure the survival, at least among themselves, of their moral standards and code of ethical treatment. The system of courts, arbitration, and self-imposed acceptance of their law highlights the extraordinary effort put into maintaining a distinct identity based on righteousness. It is not gratuitous that the notions of Solomonic morality have taken on mythical status and have even entered popular folklore.

Justice has also been a seminal concept in Western thought, from Plato's Thrasymachus's discussion and potential criticisms of justice when defined as the advantages of the stronger to the Aristotelian arguments highlighting the treatment of equals as equals. In time, different facets of the term "justice" were elucidated, and justice was also linked to impartiality. The element of moral reciprocity in attaining a state of justice also came to the fore: justice was a quality of life offered to others deserving of respect. But modern thinking (from Hobbes to Marx) has underlined the fragility of the idea and the ease with which it can be abused. For justice to exist, we are repeatedly made aware, there must be a coercive power to enforce particular obligations so that control against injustices can be realized. Yet often those with power can avail themselves of the idea of justice and incorporate it into activities that in fact negate its essence. Jewish communities understood long ago that in the absence of enforcement agencies to oversee the protection of justice there must be mutual agreement among members of the group to avoid "large" mutual harm, a way to take advantage of the reality of "ubiquitous cooperation." This commitment requires maturity and respect; a sense of justice is necessary for any society to ensure that people can trust each other. Jewish communities developed a set of internal rules that function as surrogate protection. The content of these combine custom, convention, and public utility, binding members to a common definition of the "public good." Communal justice presumes, then, a social contract by which all members of the community abide.

But disputes, disagreements, and conflicts are essential and unavoidable. Disagreements can be intellectual as well as practical. People who in principle share many values and objectives and even accept the fact that they will not do harm to each other because they see themselves as a group often end up doing exactly that, harming others, both indirectly and directly. They may or may not be aware of their actions. "Dinei Mamonot," the laws on monetary rules; "Dinei Nephashot," laws that apply to people regarding death sentences (unused since the Sanhedrin court was dismantled and the state was dissolved); and "Dinei mideoraizah and dinei midrerabanan," laws based directly on the Torah as well as added rabbinical laws, were developed because they were necessary as norms to contain and monitor exchanges among Jews. Yet the abstract ideas have not been perfect shields.

Special types of judges are required, and these must train to become experts on the legal codes. There are different types of hearings, from a single judge to a type of arbitration that aims at *pshara* (equalizing) to a full "Din torah," a court made up of at least three judges that hears the contending parties. The fact that a *din torah* (Law of the Torah) exists as a forum does not imply that it is immediately used; it is a measure of last resort. Communities may use lay arbitrators who are members of the community in good standing who alone or in combination with rabbis attempt to arrive at justice.[4]

The only way to overrule a statement made by a rabbi is to find a more studious and larger group of rabbis that would agree to differ ("Ein beit din yachol levatel beit din chevro ela im chen gadol mimeno bechochma u'bemino"). In other words, the opinion of a judge or group of judges is meant to be upheld until, and only until, a higher court rules otherwise, its interpretation based on the higher knowledge of its members. Thus one court is not pitted against another. There is always a protocol, and specialists are required to handle it with respect and impartiality. Because no real enforcement agencies exist in the Diaspora communities, mutual respect and agreement to enforce the result are essential. Traditionally, the community has relied on the authority that stems from knowledge and impartiality. Gossip and ostracism assist the authorities to secure cooperation. When the unruly behavior of a member was noticed, the threat of a ban to excommunicate a Jew from his community loomed large. The possibility of being shunned was terrifying. Even today excommunication is a strong deterrent against further transgression and a source of great shame and social discomfort.

Today not all Jews follow the old prescription to keep all disputes "in-house." Although it is possible to use the Mexican legal system, some Jews opt for the internal resolution of conflicts, which range from business disputes to divorce.

This raises the question of how the system and the law are applied and if indeed the principles defining Jewish ethics are sustained by the newly organized Ashkenazi Community Council. In a relatively small community such as the one in Mexico, whose boundaries are quite defined, it is less easy to dismiss the old tradition of searching for solutions within the communal walls. As a result, it is not clear if it is indeed the moral standard promised or the success of coercive measures that maintains the system. As we follow a real case and examine the actions and reactions of the community leaders and rabbis, we are able to get a sense of the moral justice that is meted out.

Two acquaintances are in similar fields and have complementary specialties. One of them, an affluent entrepreneur, hires the younger to join in a business venture. The original arrangement revolves exclusively around specific work, yet in time a partnership is proposed as an incentive for the younger associate. The preparatory work, including a search for investors, proceeds, but a downturn in the economy makes it difficult to continue and there is a constant and unexpected need for additional funds. The project first slows down and then is completely halted. During this period, it becomes evident (by chance) that the entrepreneur had attracted funds to the project on the basis of an inflated valuation and had been misappropriating the surplus. With the project halted, the limited partner asks for the officially unused money back. Further, he has uncovered enough information to mistrust the entrepreneur.

This unleashes a battle in the interpretation of the original agreement and the rights and obligations of the parties. The fraudulent behavior is denied. The parties are unable to come to an agreement. Monies are never released or returned. The protesting limited partner turns to the community board to seek protection and a resolution. Thus begins a review process by the community board, with arbiters who listen as both sides present their interpretations of the contract. The problem has already been presented when the defendant arbitrarily decides to make a series of marginal, unsubstantiated charges over and above the original arguments. This not only distracts from the original quarrel but also sets the tone for an increasingly broad and aggressive adversarial exchange.

While bad-faith strategizing may occur in all court systems, once incorporated into the Jewish system, it erodes a process in which moral principles and a desire for an expeditious solution are expected. Instead of being rejected, such maneuvers were allowed to proceed, which ensure an escalation of the dispute.

After protracted efforts, the communal judges rule that the founding business partner needs to return a sum of money, though not the original sum invested by the plaintiff. Both parties are dissatisfied: the junior partner for having had to answer fabricated charges and not recouping his investment; the defendant for being forced to return money and thereby acknowledge his misappropriation of funds. To appease the defendant, who was a member of one of the community boards, the court ruled that the plaintiff had to apologize to the defendant for the disturbance caused by the suit at the same time that the court ruled that the defendant had to return some funds to the plaintiff. The plaintiff refused to apologize, which the defendant used as an excuse not to make good on the judgment. The appeal to the courts was in effect neutralized.

Because the community has no enforcement mechanisms, the only way to achieve an equitable resolution is for both parties to accept the verdict and abide by it. Yet the system had allowed irrelevant countersuits to be brought to the table, reducing the offense to a pardonable ritual. The defendant then continued to bring up extraneous issues and refused to pay what he owed. Protests and requests by the plaintiff and deadlines were repeatedly ignored. Arbiters have come and gone, requiring new judges to familiarize themselves with the expanding conflict. Each of the parties requested new judges, and the dispute continued to fester.

Letters, documents, and meetings multiplied as both parties continued to try to make their cases. Over the years, members of the community have followed the case as if it were an ongoing soap opera; each party has attempted to convince the outsiders of the merits of his position, gaining support but also making life in the community very uncomfortable for themselves and for members of their respective extended families. But the board allows official recognition and public praise to be offered to one of the parties and then the other. As one is honored for an activity or remains active in his public role, humiliation is inflicted on the other. This further exacerbates the efforts of both parties in their search for support from the official board. Despite several court assessments and decisions against the senior partner, he manages to flout his obligations. The tacit compliance of the leadership only serves to add another layer of grievance for the plaintiff.

Community arbiters issued four rulings. Each was slightly different, but all followed along the same line. What started as a decision by a panel of arbitrators ended as a statement from a multicommunal court that included lay leaders and rabbis of all Jewish subcommunities in Mexico. However, as the dispute remained unresolved, a new method was used. Coercion was exercised through social pressure: any wedding or Bar Mitzvah of either side was seized on by the board as an occasion to try to bring the parties to an agreement. Thus, for instance, before a wedding in the defendant's family, he was told in private that no rabbi would perform the ceremony if the social obligation he had incurred were not attended to. Promises were then made to avert any public discomfort, but these were not kept. As the battle continued unresolved, the leadership started to lose face and applied coercion indiscriminately. The upcoming Bar Mitzvah of a member of the plaintiff's family was used to try to limit his options: either he agreed to some lesser judgment or no rabbi was going to perform the ceremony. In using these tactics, new "assistants" took on the sanctioning roles in the synagogue. The most notorious consequence of this was that the privacy of the negotiations was violated, and the distinction of right and wrong was lost. In its desperate search for a solution, the leadership continued to exert pressure, and the plaintiff was almost forced to accept the conditions of the defendant to bring the dispute to a close. Publicly, in the synagogue, they pressed him to resign himself and accept less than was his due. Ruling or no ruling, they saw it as a way to restore "harmony."

This incident illustrates the tone and tenor of the methods employed: not only was the plaintiff who had "won" the case publicly humiliated, but the display of abuse and power was now overt and desperate and extended to other members of the family. This last episode took place in a synagogue, on the Sabbath, in front of minors and extended family members, making a further mockery of the system. It was therefore a blatant attempt to get the weaker, injured party to forgo his long quest for justice. Whether intended or not, that moment signaled that a powerful member of the community, with allies who were prepared to desecrate the Sabbath, could prevail.

Eventually, after years of disagreements and attacks, a financial settlement was forced on the parties.

The practices of domination and control that the Ashkenazi Community Council displayed are not uncommon. Abuses and irrationality are often resorted to in a desperate search to establish order. In the case discussed here, it was only after constant pressure and threats by the plaintiff to take his suit to the Mexican court system that a "resolution" was reached. There is no doubt that the members of the community board worked to maintain some type of cohesion within the community. The question is, is this the way the "system" was expected to function in a Jewish community?

A close-knit group has many obvious challenges to address if it wants to maintain itself. Historical group identities and cultural meanings are elements that the community in Mexico, like any Diaspora community, will try to maintain. Communal norms and their explicit content help to solidify a particular common experience for the group: members should feel that they maximize their welfare by living together. Thus the community reinforces two types of rules: those that espouse cooperation between and among members and those that impose punishment for failure to cooperate. But if control and power must exist, as they do, the question is still, in what form?

The original historical communal arrangements were not based on displays of erratic control for the sake of control. The intent was to ensure harmony and justice. Members of the community can usually regain order and harmony and affirm cooperation through arbitration that blunts the sharpest confrontations.

But confrontations can get out of hand, in part as a result of the leadership's mishandling of the cases before them. It is then that the misuse of power becomes apparent. The inertia of the majority keeps it from challenging the leadership, which reverts to the well-oiled pattern of abuse of its power. Leadership is equally feared and devalued in this community. The subtle, covert calculus of each member is simple; the community seems to survive with the minimum of quality and the minimum of effort. The emperor has no clothes: everybody knows this, and everybody behaves accordingly.

The deterioration of the system into arbitrariness, although not a new phenomenon, is disgraceful. The more the style becomes embedded, the more it should be rejected. People are punished eventually for misbehaving, but no distinction is offered, to anyone seeking redress. The public display of arbitrariness, for example, the scenes in the synagogue, only confirms the message. Gossip, the informal network of information, ensures the transmission and appraisal of the events. If the leadership cannot distinguish between deviancy and correctness in its members, the members quickly learn that the greatest payoff results from the least action.

The Kehillot have always supervised and organized the internal life of its members. In social terms, the benefits have historically been greater than the costs to the majority. Overseeing activities from birth to death for members, the community boards hire rabbis and Mohels (circumcision specialists) and organize minyans (the minimum of ten men necessary to perform daily joint prayers), food supervision, and education. In Mexico, as is the case elsewhere, priority has been given to the poor, the orphaned, and the old.

The Mexican Jewish community, a community that developed only in the twentieth century despite the much earlier arrival of Jews and Marranos, has built an impressive network of organizations to cater to all these needs, more so than many larger and more economically powerful communities have accomplished in other locations. Jews from different places mingle here: Syria, Turkey, the Balkans, and eastern Europe. Each had its own language, traditions, and ideals; yet slowly, together and separately, they managed to create an extraordinary network of service organizations. But what they have built does not excuse how they run it. Among the many reasons for a community, living together as a group ranks high. Therefore, how justice is dispensed and injured parties are treated remains the real test of communal excellence. Whether principles are upheld and moral reciprocity is observed remain key criteria in the evaluation of a community.

Although this essay focuses on the Ashkenazi sector and its leadership, there is evidence that all Jewish subcommunities here adopt a similar style to assert their control. They all promote themselves as "champions of the public." Most of the leaders reveal themselves to be shortsighted, with little ability to distinguish right from wrong. If most of these organizations do not follow democratic practices and guard only operational objectives, it is necessary to conclude that the leaders of today, no matter how selfless a task they see themselves performing, fall short of what ought to be. If elected leaders have legitimacy to control and enforce certain behaviors, we expect them to be selected according to standards of knowledge and expertise. Since that is not yet the case in these communities, the least we can expect, and I would like to hope we would demand, is certain qualifications. The communal leadership cannot justify its position. There are minimal demands that should be met, for example, knowledge of Jewish sources and languages. Ignorance of this is not just shameful but also dangerous. After all, how can such a person read and comprehend historical legal documents? Where is the sensitivity to distinguish a Sabbath from a regular day? It is a fact that almost none of the leaders today speak either Hebrew or Yiddish. Leaders of an ethnic community must be versed in history and traditions. Not only do they need to know to whom to consult, but they also need to understand and be sensitive to precedent and what is of value to the community and its members. There is a refinement of Jewish cultural empathy that leaders need to attain if they are to remain committed to decency, help, and the upholding of Jewish moral principles. If the public life of the community is devoid of moral content and its leadership adopts haphazard measures to secure its own power, communal procedural forms become empty shells without meaning.

NOTES

1. Adina Cimet, *Ashkenazi Jews in Mexico: Ideologies in the Structuring of a Community* (Albany: SUNY Press, 1997), chap. 2.

2. Adina Cimet, "Mexico," in *American Jewish Year Book: A Record of Events and Trends in American and World Jewish Life* (New York: American Jewish Committee, 1998), vol. 98, 211–220, 199; vol. 99, 254–263.

3. Robert C. Ellickson, *Order without Law: How Neighbors Settle Disputes* (Cambridge, Mass.: Harvard University Press, 1994).

4. Louis Ginzberg, *On Jewish Law and Lore* (Philadelphia: Jewish Publication Society of America, 1955).

A Literature of Transformation

NAOMI LINDSTROM

The Heterogeneous Jewish
Wit of Margo Glantz

Margo Glantz (b. 1930) is a celebrated Mexican critic and writer
known for her biting wit, awareness of gender issues, and encyclopedic
knowledge of both literary and mass culture. She has always been known
for her comic gifts, but it is only in recent decades that she has also been
singled out as a Jewish Mexican writer. Before examining the characteristic forms in which Glantz's comic spirit manifests itself, some but not all
of which may be called "Jewish wit," let me summarize some relevant biographical facts. These are culled principally from Glantz's heterogeneous
text *Las genealogías* (1981).[1] This work is, among other things, a composite
portrait of her parents, the circles in which they moved, and the environment in which Margo Glantz and her sisters were raised and includes tran-
scripts of tape-recorded conversations, photographs, and reproductions
of documents.

Glantz is the daughter of the Yiddish poet Jacobo Glantz and his wife,
Lucía. Originally from Ukraine, having lived in Russia during the avant-
garde period of the first years of Soviet rule, the Glantzes immigrated to
Mexico in 1925. The couple's home in Mexico City was in some respects a
center of émigré eastern European Jewish culture. Yet the Glantzes never
sought to create for themselves and their daughters an exclusively Jewish
environment. Rather, they benefited fully from the cultural advantages of
living "among the nations." Jacobo Glantz's statements reveal his attach-
ment to the Russian language and its literature and intellectual culture as
well as to writing in Yiddish. The parents, neither of whom was especially
religious, moved in diverse artistic, avant-garde, and socially progressive
circles. Jacobo, in particular, made a point of contacting innovative poets
and artists wherever he was located. While a young poet in Russia, he knew
the work of the avant-garde Symbolist writers and had various degrees

of personal acquaintance with some of these legendary innovators. For a while Jacobo ran an art gallery, and at times the Glantzes hosted literary gatherings. Familiar with the radical tendencies that were common in eastern Europe, in Mexico Jacobo Glantz associated with anarchists and socialists. Jewish thought and culture were certainly high among the concerns of the Glantz household. At the same time, the Glantzes kept up to date on progressive social thought and innovative artistic tendencies.

Early in her career, Margo Glantz attracted notice with research and writing projects that did not draw directly on the Jewish components in her upbringing. At the same time, many of her best-known essays continue her parents' fascination with the avant-garde in art. The first of her critical works to claim international attention was "Onda y escritura: Jóvenes de 20 a 33" (1971). (The main title refers to the two major innovative tendencies in Mexican narrative of the late 1960s and early 1970s, designated *onda* and *escritura;* the subtitle refers to young writers between twenty and thirty-three years of age.) This work, which brilliantly captures the ebullience of the late 1960s–early 1970s youth movement, presents a critical introduction and a sampling of the writing of the then-young writers of Mexico. In addition to showcasing new writers, "Onda y escritura" demonstrates Glantz's extensive knowledge of the counterculture of the 1960s and early 1970s, especially as is it is expressed in rock music.

Since the 1981 publication of *Genealogies,* winner of the Magda Donato Prize, the author's identity, especially her Jewish identity, has become a topic of critical analysis. Elizabeth Otero-Krauthammer sums up the general perception of the text: "[T]o speak of *Genealogies* by Margo Glantz is to speak of the author herself and of a process of searching for identity."[2] In a similar vein, Magdalena Maiz-Peña asserts that "Margo Glantz . . . throws herself into the search for herself, for her origin, for her identity, of her way of being between two cultures: the Jewish one and the Mexican one."[3]

These observations, though certainly not incorrect, apply better to some portions of *Genealogies* than to others. I believe that there has been a tendency to overlook those elements of the work that are less germane to its author's identity and that touch on cultures other than the Jewish and Mexican ones that spring most readily to readers' minds. The broadranging *Genealogies* ventures well beyond what is required to locate or define the author's identity, and not all of it is concerned with being either Jewish or Mexican. For example, it would be quite a stretch to find Glantz's quest for identity in her father's critical appraisals of the work of other writers or his recollections of Russian intellectual life in the early Soviet years. *Genealogies* is composed of so many "multiple voices and narrative levels" and contains so many varieties of discourse that it presents "the phenomenon of 'heteroglossia,' according to the concept developed by Bakhtin."[4] Not all these voices and discourses are focused on the identity of Margo Glantz. As is typical of Glantz's writing, *Genealogies* has multiple themes, including the workings of memory and the ways in which creative artists live their lives.

This essay is not concerned with who or what Margo Glantz is. Glantz provides a vivid picture of herself in *Genealogies:* she is a Jewish cultural critic who is accustomed to associating with progressive intellectuals and artists rather than living in a self-enclosed religious community and who is bohemian and eclectic in her cultural practices. Throughout *Genealogies,* Glantz draws attention to the deficiencies of her Jewish education, recalling painful moments in which her parents' contemporaries expressed shock at her ignorance. To give an instance that is memorable for its oddity, Glantz insists that she can barely comprehend Yiddish, though she recalls extensive exposure to the language when she was a child. She also refers repeatedly to moments in which she wandered away from Judaism, such as her first communion and her out-marriage.

Rather than attempt to add to Glantz's self-characterization, I look at the ways in which her writing continues but also renovates and diversifies a Jewish vein of humor and critical observation. Attempts to define a distinctively Jewish wit have never been very successful, since they inevitably posit as Jewish features that may also occur in humorous expressions from other cultural traditions. Looking through published works on Jewish humor, one realizes that most of the authors soon abandon the struggle to characterize the phenomenon and instead give an abundance of examples. However, it is possible to point out certain tendencies that are often identified as hallmarks of Jewish humor and that are very evidently typical of the wit of Margo Glantz. The first is the use of humor to express doubts about the value of prevailing social practices and assumptions, consistent with the tendency to critical questioning that is inherent in the tradition of Jewish thought generally.

The second is a habit of self-mockery and self-deprecation. In certain witticisms, the target of satire is the Jewish people as a whole. According to the psychoanalyst Theodor Reik, whose work *Jewish Wit* is one of the most sustained attempts to study the phenomenon, "Jewish wit is characterized by a merciless mockery at the weaknesses, faults and failings of the Jews."[5] Glantz seldom takes up this variant of the tradition of self-mockery. She instead presents herself as a comically flawed individual. In

particular, Glantz turns the spotlight on the inadequacies of her education and the lacunae in her cultural knowledge, a habit that stands out
because it runs counter to what readers of Glantz know about her. As Beth
E. Jörgensen summarizes the general perception: "Margo Glantz's writing presents a bewildering proliferation of topics, sources, and forms. . . .
Glantz performs a dazzling display of cultural prowess" [and demonstrates
a] high level of erudition."[6] But, according to Glantz's own account, her
apparent erudition has shameful pockets of ignorance, and she has repeatedly failed to master languages other than Spanish. At the same time,
her mind is cluttered with the ephemera of celebrity culture. If her weaknesses represent those of a larger group, it is less likely to be Jews than
media-bombarded culture consumers in the age of globalization, unable
to climb out of a morass of information and images that are not merely
aesthetically unworthy but also manipulative.

The third characteristic — taking a comic or at least ironic view of disturbing subject matter — is a strategy that I will discuss in more detail. This
last feature is so widely associated with Jewish humor that studies of Jewish wit often overlap with research into the comic treatment of wretched
situations, as witness such titles as David A. Harris and Izrail Rabinovich's
The Jokes of Oppression: The Humor of Soviet Jews (1998) and Steve Lipman's *Laughter in Hell: The Use of Humor during the Holocaust* (1991).

An examination of Glantz's work, especially her *Genealogies,* in search
of manifestations of Jewish wit turns up few examples of outright jokes
of the type that fill popular anthologies of Jewish humor. This scarcity
stands in contrast to the abundance of information that *Genealogies* contains about other eastern European Jewish folkways. Traditional baked
foods and their preparation occupy an especially prominent and respected
place in the text, reasonably enough since one of the Glantzes' numerous
business ventures was a bakery.

Humor with a special Jewish spin is one of Glantz's themes in *Genealogies.* She characterizes "true Jews" as "a minor people with a major sense
of humor" (14). But readers should not expect jokes of the type epito-
mized by stories in which stereotypically Jewish characters are stranded
on a desert island and quickly re-create the idiosyncrasies of Jewish life
in eastern Europe. Nor does one find any of the more didactic anecdotes
in which characters identified as Jewish acquire some fundamental insight
into life that is then recapitulated in the form of a judicious piece of advice
to listeners.

On one occasion, Glantz quotes her father telling what she announces
in advance as "that Jewish joke." The joke turns out to be an insipid anec-

dote. A husband complains that his wife's deafness is ruining their marriage, is advised that the problem can be resolved with a hearing aid, and
then complains that she takes hers out when he addresses her (48). Not
only is the joke not very clever, since its punch line is easy to guess in
advance, it is not even distinctively Jewish. In context, it seems Jewish because we know that Jacobo Glantz is the narrator and because one character is identified as a rabbi. But, like many of the jokes one finds in treasuries
of Jewish humor, this anecdote could easily be modified to function in a
different cultural context. In fact, the humor is identical to that of the well-
known Spanish proverb, "The worst deaf person is the one who doesn't
want to hear."

It is significant that Glantz quotes this pallid example of Jewish joking
style in a passage in which she expresses frustration about trying to find
worthy material with which to reconstruct her family's past. In addition,
Glantz calls the hearing-aid joke "that Jewish joke, one of so many," suggesting that she does not consider preformulated jokes the most valuable
manifestation of the Jewish comic tradition (48).

There are at least two explanations for the near-absence of the standard repertory of Jewish humorous anecdotes. First, Glantz has a well-
established record of both promoting and practicing innovation in narrative construction; she admires writers who tell a story in an unexpected
way. As Jörgensen puts it, Glantz's texts "defy reading habits based on
skimming page after page of text in linear sequence."[7] The same criterion
of novelty can be applied to humor; in Reik's words, "wit belongs to literature—witticisms are also works of art."[8] As an adept of narrative experimentation, Glantz cannot admire the stories constructed along the lines
of retold jokes, which rely heavily on such stock elements as the lead-in
and the punch line.

Some pages after Glantz becomes discouraged by the feeble joke about
the hearing aid, she reproduces a different, more complex Jewish anecdote
that her father tells her. This story is not announced in advance as a "Jewish joke," and it is not really a joke. Yet it is an excellent example of the
much-noted Jewish penchant for utterances that are simultaneously comic
and sorrowful. As Reik writes, a "peculiarity of Jewish wit" is that "you
laugh at it, but it is not merry."[9] In this narrative fragment from *Genealogies,* Russian anarchists kill a Jewish Red Guard and leave his naked body
outdoors; and "girls came to get a look at the blond frizz in that place"
(82). In this case, the anecdote is not from the supply of Jewish jokes but
from a literary work that Jacobo Glantz once heard Isaac Babel read aloud.
The originality of literary creation stands out favorably in contrast to the

circulation of time-worn jokes. So does the complexity of a narrative that remains undecided between a comic spirit and a melancholy expression of horror.

Second, Glantz favors heterogeneous new patterns generated when cultures come into contact. Focusing Jewish humor directly on Jewish subject matter, as in jokes that begin "A poor Jewish tailor went to his rabbi for advice . . . ," is too monocultural for Glantz. Her wit often seems Jewish in style but with subject matter that is ethnically unmarked. Conversely, as a critic, Glantz shows admiration for writers whose comic manner is irreverent and critical, regardless of whether they are known to have a Jewish connection.

Glantz's approach bears out Reik's argument that given the experience of the Diaspora, one cannot realistically expect to isolate features of humorous expression exclusive to Jews. In Reik's assessment, Jewish humor overlaps considerably with the comic expression of the societies in which Jewish communities were established. For this reason, it is impossible to single out any comic element that occurs exclusively in the Jewish tradition.[10] Yet one can identify certain features that occur with greater frequency or occupy a more prominent place in the comic utterances of Jewish speakers and writers. What Reik says of Jewish wit generally should prove especially true of the humor of Margo Glantz, who makes a point of the multiplicity of her cultural sources. One would reasonably expect her humorous style to reflect not only her Jewish and Mexican background but also her empathy for avant-garde art and her desire to be up to date regarding new developments in culture at all levels.

In attempting to characterize Glantz's wit, the first question we must ask is, What strikes her as funny? Looking through Glantz's cultural criticism and creative writing and thinking of her oral performances of her work, one is tempted to conclude that she can inject a comic element into to any phenomenon, no matter how upsetting. One of her specialties is the insertion of diverse elements, including side comments and incongruous or bizarre notes, in the narration of wretched events.

A classic example of this practice, often identified as a coping mechanism of a beleaguered Jewish population, appears in chapter 25 of *Genealogies,* which recounts an episode in which a gang of Mexican fascists attacked Jacobo Glantz in the street. After a paragraph of somewhat rambling warm-up, Glantz begins telling in her own voice how her father narrowly escaped lynching. One of her lexical choices stands out oddly in the midst of this hair-raising episode: "They tried to place my father on the train tracks so he would be run over, while others threw stones and shouted *traditional* insults" (93; my emphasis). Glantz's use of *traditional* is a sardonic comment on the stereotypical nature of hate speech, which relies on a small stock of set insults. The reader is struck by the contrast between the serious crime of attempted murder and the relatively minor offense of lack of originality in denigrating language.

As the narrative of the attack continues, the voices of both elder Glantzes enter the text and embellish the main story with an abundance of highly heterogeneous details. These additions range from the mundane to the peculiar. In one, the captain of the squadron of firefighters sent to help Jacobo Glantz runs up and throws his cloak over the moaning victim, saying, "Don't cry, Jew, here I come to save you" (96). His utterance, which resembles the stiff dialogue of the hero of a serialized adventure novel, evidently stuck in the minds of the Glantzes. Both parents recall the captain's quaint greeting (94, 96), which manages to be melodramatic even in the context of a real crisis.

The unexpected twist does not attenuate the horror of the near-lynching. Reik distinguishes Jewish humor concerning dreadful situations from "gallows humor" in which there is "a sudden freeing breakthrough from a tragic situation." But "[i]n Jewish jokes, there is nothing comparable: no escape, no deliverance from a momentary emergency, but rather a moment of truth in a permanent emergency."[11] The elder Glantzes' recollection of a curious detail has the effect of complicating the narrative. The ironic, incongruous, and partially comic touches commingle with the central anecdote, making the chapter more complex than the retelling of a near-lynching.

One could find many examples of Glantz's ability to wrest humor from lamentable situations. For purposes of this discussion, though, I would like to focus on just one sorry state of affairs that Glantz has especially mined for its comic potential. This subject matter is the immersion in mass media and marketing that typifies current existence in all but the most isolated of societies. Even more comical is the situation of a self-aware consumer who can perceive but not escape his or her own inculcation with media-generated emotions and desires. An example is the narrator-protagonist Nora García, a semiautobiographical creation of Glantz's whose musings fill the short stories of *Zona de derrumbe* (2001; Landslide Zone; the Spanish word used in the title to mean "landslide" can also refer to a general state of collapse). Gripped by a craving for Ferragamo footwear, Nora composes an account of her obsession and considers titling it "The Story of a Woman Who Sought to Make Her Path in Life in Designer Shoes" ("Zapatos" 81). In one of the self-referential notes that appear in Glantz's criticism and fiction, Nora shares a trait with her creator: Glantz is known for showing up at her speaking engagements in shoes that call attention to themselves through their unusual elegance or eccentricity.

Using the characteristic strategy of self-deprecation, Glantz often illustrates through her own case the culture consumer who is taken in by the unworthy allure of the mass product. Throughout her career, Glantz has had a conflict-filled relationship to popular culture. She seems driven to collect information about commercial mass entertainment, alternative counterculture, and eastern European Jewish folklore. Sometimes commercial mass culture itself is the direct target of Glantz's satirical scorn, although she by no means condemns every work that reaches out to a broad public. At other moments Glantz turns her mockery on the consumers, especially herself.

Glantz possesses a sharp critical awareness that some artifacts of commercial mass culture are banal and sexist, yet she becomes as involved with them as with worthier texts. Her intimate knowledge of these works is not purely the scholarly thoroughness of a student of popular culture. Rather, she portrays herself as vulnerable to sentimentalism and sensationalism. In chapter 59 of *Genealogies*, Glantz describes her childhood patterns of cultural consumption. The chapter begins with Glantz claiming, "[F]rom childhood I knew Catullus intimately" (146). She goes on to tell of her exploration of her father's highly eclectic library. As the chapter continues, the initial image of Glantz as a child genius absorbed in high culture grows more problematic. With her fondness for the heterogeneous, the young Margo commingles lines of poetry from an anthology with the Lord's Prayer and recites the resulting mixture as a form of stress reduction. She combines the reading of her father's books with listening to "The Tango Hour" on the radio and consuming chocolates with cherry centers. While the tango has come in for scholarly scrutiny, Glantz's attraction to it is hardly analytical: "Gardel remembers that 'twenty years are nothing,' repeating 'remember, brother, what times those were, twenty-five Aprils' . . . and I break out in disconsolate tears, even though back then I wasn't yet twenty-five Aprils old" (147). One comic element here is Glantz's startling willingness to reveal embarrassing private pleasures. Another is the irony of a young person with a sharp mind who lives in a home rich in intellectual resources yet succumbs to the mass culture that, in the mid-twentieth century, is already inescapable.

When Glantz delivers lectures and conference papers, she often leaves her audiences almost helpless with laughter. Of course, she is a very witty speaker and possesses excellent comic timing. But I believe also that her listeners laugh partly from the shock of hearing a distinguished scholar, who in 1995 was inducted into the Mexican Academy of Language, mix into her learned commentary allusions to the trashiest aspects of popular culture. She is given to referring not only to the sectors of mass culture that are relatively respectable, such as alternative or independent rock music and films by noted directors, but also to areas that are considered embarrassing, such as sentimental romances, bodice rippers, and pornography.

Though in some ways Glantz's extensive knowledge of popular culture is a vulnerable point, it was one of the assets that helped her to stand out among Mexico's many literary and cultural critics. Glantz first gained widespread attention with her research on literature rooted in the youth culture of the period. Her often-cited essays "Narrativa joven de México" (1969; Narrative by Young Mexican Writers) and "Onda y escritura" were composed as forewords to two important anthologies that she compiled. To explain these writers, especially the *literatura de onda* (hip writing), Glantz brings to bear her formidable knowledge of late 1960s hip culture, with special emphasis on rock and folk-rock music, the psychedelic style, and such icons of adolescent rebellion as *Mad* magazine. Glantz's comments on the *onda* are not intended to ridicule the tendency. On the whole, she respects this movement, which she judges fresh and surprising. Besides, *onda* writing hardly needs satirical debunking, since it does not take itself very seriously. Glantz summarizes: "The general tone . . . is that of anti-solemnity achieved by means of colloquial forms of language [and] repeated *mockery at one's own expense*" ("Narrativa joven" 202; my emphasis). Here Glantz is praising the young writers, not known to have a Jewish background, for a strategy that has long been cited as a feature of Jewish wit.

Glantz's essays on the *onda* do not showcase her satirical talents, but they demonstrate that she possesses knowledge of then-hip popular culture far beyond what is needed. For instance, she not only names the rock groups and urban folksingers that have influenced the *onda*, but she understands what the unique contribution of each has been. In addition, her comments on innovative rock reveal Glantz to have some belief in the possibility of cultural radicalism. That is, she sees the potential for loosening up a hierarchical society through cultural forms that call its all-too-fixed bases into question.

Glantz's concern with mass culture extends into her criticism of more established literary works as well. If one looks at her critical essays, leaving aside her extensive commentaries on Sor Juana Inés de la Cruz and scattered writings on the era of the Conquest, a pattern is evident. Glantz has been drawn to works that have a sense of playfulness, do not take their own literary status too seriously, and uninhibitedly offer enjoyment to the reading public. In "Presentación," for example, Glantz discusses some of these well-regarded novels that openly display features of the action-packed potboiler, such as *Los bandidos de Río Frío* (The Bandits of Río Frío) by Manuel Payno. Glantz treats Payno with relative benevolence, since he does not seek to disguise the pulp-serial elements of his narratives. Payno is not sanctimonious and humorless, the two features that most provoke Glantz. She is also fairly kind to José Tomás de Cuéllar, for whose work, *The Magic Lantern,* she provided an introduction. Although she deplores his desire to keep Mexico stratified along class and racial lines, she recognizes the accuracy and insight with which he describes social change ("Introduction"; see also her "De pie sobre la literatura mexicana"). She could savage Cuéllar but refrains from doing so, because he is a satirist and an acute social observer. Both Payno and Cuéllar keep their agendas aboveboard.

For Glantz, it is more fascinating, and amusing, to reveal the trashy and sleazy qualities that certain literary works self-servingly attempt to hide under the guise of respectability. She is especially fond of pointing out that certain of the most-read works of the Spanish American literary canon have been expertly designed to provide titillation. Readers seek in them the same satisfactions that they could find in racy gossip columns or pornography. This observation is the basis for her essays skewering two novels often found on required-reading lists, *María* (1867) by Jorge Isaacs of Colombia and *Santa* (1903) by the Mexican writer Federico Gamboa. (Both novels are named for their ill-fated heroines.) Glantz's work on these novels combines sharp analysis with mockery designed to debunk the pretensions of narratives that, unlike the spoofs and put-ons of the countercultural forms that she respects, take themselves seriously.

Her comments on both novels are acute and clever, but those on *Santa* are not really surprising. Many readers have already noted the salacious quality of *Santa,* which narrates the rise and fall of a celebrated prostitute. There has always been suspicion that its critical examination of social problems is a pretext for sneaking prurient material between the covers of a respectable literary work. Nonetheless, Glantz has some telling comments to make: "What greater pleasure is there than to sin with flesh seasoned with the epithet of *santa* [the name of the heroine, but also the word for *saint* and *saintly*]?" ("Santa y la carne" 47). In her view, *Santa* deserves ridicule, not for its erotic features, but for the insistence with which it denies them. Glantz mocks the author's "moralistic Puritanism" and the pretense that his "discourse is chaste" ("Santa y la carne" 42) In her analysis, Gamboa "was [Santa's] pimp" (42).

Glantz's comments on this novel do not touch on any literary qualities that it may possess. Instead, she is concerned with its appeal to a mass audience. The first sentence of her essay is, "*Santa* is a popular Mexican novel." Since most Spanish-language readers will already know the novel, this line serves not to introduce it but to place it more firmly in the popular terrain. She points out its sales at supermarkets and jeers at it, not for its erotic or titillating features as such, but for the hypocrisy with which it denies them. Forthright, full-strength pornography wins a measure of respect from Glantz, who sees in it the potential to disrupt the social order, but she disdains its tamed and mass-marketed counterparts.

Glantz's analyses of *María* have greater shock value, because on the surface this novel appears to be a model of how to conduct a chaste love. After all, Efraín, the novel's hero and narrator, never goes beyond kissing the heroine's hand, hair, and, on one occasion, forehead. María is a devout Christian, and the two young people pursue their courtship surrounded by family members. *María* is a novel beloved of the general public and is considered suitable, even wholesome, for young readers.

In Glantz's view, *María* is a narrative filled with half-hidden markers of decidedly kinky sex. She casts a suspicious eye on the intimate links among the members of the close-knit household in which María and Efraín carry on their courtship. Many readers of *María* have noticed that its central love borders on incest. Not only are the enamored adolescents cousins, but they were brought up together and call the same people Mamá and Papá. Glantz's analysis takes this observation further. She notes that every family member who crosses Efraín and María's path becomes involved in transmitting encrypted erotic messages between the two. The youngest sibling, who as a child may be caressed by anyone, serves as a useful proxy when the two inflamed young people must keep their hands off one another. In addition, at several points the patriarch of this oddly intimate household appears to be competing with his son over María and openly flirts with the girl, who is nearly his daughter. In Glantz's judgment, "Incest is global, that is to say, it includes the entire family, the living and the dead" ("De la erótica" 34). Moreover, when Efraín recalls María's appearance, his descriptions have a fetishistic quality. Under mid-nineteenth-century rules of bourgeois courtship, he can glimpse little of the body of his beloved and is restricted to imagining what he cannot see. In Glantz's words: "Efraín loves her chastely; he never goes so far as to name her in her totality, to verbalize her body, which remains forever hidden in a ritual garb through which her suitor contemplates her, defining in words that make explicit that contemplation, an erotic peek-a-boo and a system of fashion." ("De la erótica" 31–32) As do a number of current readers, Glantz expresses some wonderment both at the bulky finery that all but enveloped nineteenth-century bourgeois women and at Isaacs's ability to generate a steamy narrative around a virginal, heavily chaperoned heroine: "María barely has feet, hands, a body, but she shows off a wardrobe of silk, tulle, muslin, lace, and pastel colors that stand out against the wild color of a nature that is tropical and, for that very reason, sexualized. María is a pure sign framed by an impure sign" ("De la erótica" 32).

It makes sense that Glantz also mocks works that though superficially allied with sexual liberation, are really blandly commercial artifacts promoting "family values." Her prime example is the film *Looking for Mr. Goodbar,* promoted as part of the sexual revolution but in fact one more warning against the dangers of promiscuity.[12] For Glantz, such a false display of libertinage is not only "the banalization" but also "the persecution of sexual practices" ("Pornografía" 109).

A strategy characteristic of Glantz's critical writing is to move suddenly from the discussion of high-art narrative and film to the analysis of much less exalted forms of culture. An example is her lengthy, funny, and sometimes wandering essay "On the Erotic Inclination to Tangle Oneself Up in Hair." Here the unifying thread is the theme of hair, in many but not all cases eroticized hair. Knit together from various commentaries and reviews that Glantz had composed over the past few years, the essay reels from analysis of cinema classics and canonical literary works to commentary on such low-culture matters as the filmic persona developed by John Travolta through his successive roles. What Glantz sees in Travolta's career, especially his performance in *Saturday Night Fever,* is a well-designed effort to erode the progress made by the 1960s–1970s counterculture; Travolta represents a return to the fixed social conventions of the years "before the Rollingstonian revolution" ("De la erótica" 57). Glantz writes that the image Travolta projects in his disco films is one of submission to norms: "His haircut redeems him and makes him one of the nice, decent boys[;] . . . the absence of sideburns desensitizes faces bare of the infamous fuzz that parents despised" (57); "so let's stick with Travolta so that decent young girls can dance in peace at their fifteenth birthday parties" (58). But Travolta is not the only figure of fun. The element of self-mockery enters in. It is ridiculous that Glantz possesses such a wealth of information about this performer — his earlier roles and various bits of trivia, such as that he made brushed cashmere fashionable. In adding this information to her comments on Travolta, she mocks herself as one more victim of celebrity culture.

There are moments in Glantz's essays when her humor is almost nonsensical. Yet usually she employs humor as social criticism. She is not much concerned with whether a given cultural artifact is situated in high or low culture, but she has very little tolerance for works that advertise themselves as something that they are not.

One finds the same characteristically Jewish approach of cheerless humor that Glantz uses in discussing horrible matters in her commentary on the inescapable reach of the mass media. Finally, Glantz's vast knowledge of popular culture becomes itself the source of self-mocking humor.

NOTES

A preliminary version of portions of this essay was presented as "Margo Glantz's Comic Ambivalence toward Popular Culture" at the Congress of the Latin American Studies Association, Washington, D.C., September 6–8, 2001.

1. The published English translation of *Las genealogías* is *The Family Tree: An Illustrated Novel,* trans. Susan Bassnett (London: Serpent's Tail, 1991). I have chosen to do my own translation of passages from *Las genealogías* that are quoted here. In addition, I refer to this work as *Genealogies* rather than *The Family Tree;* this more literal translation of the original Spanish title leaves open the possibility that Glantz's text is, among many other things, a reflection on the entire concept of genealogy as a method of bringing order to one's origins and sources.

Genealogies and other Glantz works that are listed in the bibliography are cited parenthetically in the text by title and/or page number.

2. Otero-Krauthammer, "Integración de la identidad judía," 868.

3. Maiz-Peña, "Sujeto, género y representación," 78.

4. Otero-Krauthammer, "Integración de la identidad judía," 869.

5. Reik, *Jewish Wit,* 190.

6. Jörgensen, "Margo Glantz, Tongue in Hand," 189.

7. Ibid.

8. Reik, *Jewish Wit,* 211.

9. Ibid., 212.

10. Ibid., 52–56.

11. Ibid., 212.

12. *Looking for Mr. Goodbar* is a 1977 U.S. film directed by Peter Brooks and based on the best-selling 1975 novel by Judith Rossner. Unhinged by a love affair, the heroine begins to seek out sexual partners in bars, which leads quickly to her degradation and death.

BIBLIOGRAPHY

Glantz, Margo. *Con la lengua en la mano* (With Tongue in Hand). Mexico City: Premia, 1983.

————. "De la erótica inclinación a enredarse en cabellos" (On the Erotic Inclination to Tangle Oneself Up in Hair). *De la amorosa inclinación a enredarse en cabellos* (On the Amorous Inclination to Tangle Oneself Up in Hair), 11–89. Mexico City: Ediciones Océano, 1984.

————. "De pie sobre la literatura mexicana" (Standing upon Mexican Literature). *Lengua* 13–36.

————. *Esguince de cintura: Ensayos sobre narrativa mexicana del siglo XX* (Swerve at the Waist: Essays on Twentieth-Century Mexican Narrative). Mexico City: Consejo Nacional para la Cultura y las Artes, 1994.

————. *Las genealogías* (Genealogies). 1981. Mexico City: Secretaría de Educación Pública, 1986.

————. "La húmeda identidad: *María* de Jorge Isaacs" (Humid Identity: *María* by Jorge Isaacs). *Lengua* 84–90.

————. "Introduction." In José Tomás de Cuéllar, *The Magic Lantern*. Trans. Margaret Carson. xi–xxxv. New York: Oxford University Press, 2000.

————. "Narrativa joven de México." *Esguince de cintura* 198–211. Originally meant as the foreword to *Narrativa joven de México*. Mexico City: Siglo XXI, 1969.

————. "Onda y escritura: jóvenes de 20 a 33." (*Onda* and *escritura:* Young Writers between 20 and 33.) *Esguince de cintura*, 212–43. Originally the foreword to her *Onda y escritura: jóvenes de 20 a 33*. Mexico City: Siglo XXI, 1971.

————. "Presentación" (Introduction). Glantz, ed., *Del fistol a la linterna: Homenaje a José Tomás de Cuéllar y Manuel Payno en el centenario de su muerte, 1994* (From the Tiepin to the Lantern: Homage to José Tomás de Cuéllar y Manuel Payno on the Hundredth Anniversary of Their Death). Mexico City: Universidad Nacional Autónoma de México, Coordinación de Humanidades, Dirección General de Publicaciones, 1997, 5–9.

————. "Santa y la carne" (Santa and Meat/Flesh). *Con la lengua en la mano*, 42–49. Mexico City: Premia.

————. "Zapatos: Andante con variaciones" (Shoes: Andante with Variations). *Zona de derrumbe* (Landslide Area), 73–94. Rosario, Argentina: Beatriz Viterbo, 2001.

Harris, David A., and Izrail Raboinovich. *The Jokes of Oppression: The Humor of Soviet Jews*. Northvale, N.J.: Jason Aronson, 1988.

Jörgensen, Beth E. "Margo Glantz, Tongue in Hand." *Reinterpreting the Spanish American Essay: Women Writers of the 19th and 20th Centuries*, ed. Doris Meyer, 188–196. Austin: University of Texas Press, 1995.

Lipman, Steve. *Laughter in Hell: The Use of Humor during the Holocaust*. Northvale, N.J.: Jason Aronson, 1991.

Maiz-Peña, Magdalena. "Sujeto, género y representación autobiográfica: *Las genealogías* de Margo Glantz" (Subject, Gender and Autobiographical Representation: *Genealogies* by Margo Glantz). *Confluencia* 12.3 (spring 1997): 75–87.

Otero-Krauthammer, Elizabeth. "Integración de la identidad judía en *Las genealogías,* de Margo Glantz" (The Integration of Jewish Identity in *Genealogies* by Margo Glantz). *Revista Iberoamericana* 132–133 (July–December 1985): 867–73.

Reik, Theodor. *Jewish Wit.* New York: Gamut Press, 1962.

Preserving the Family Album in *Letargo* by Perla Suez

Long ago, it must be, I have a photograph
Preserve your memories, they're all that's left you.
SIMON AND GARFUNKEL, "BOOKENDS"

In June 2000 the Argentine writer Perla Suez sent me her novel *Letargo*, which had just been released by the Editorial Norma in Buenos Aires. After having read Suez's previously published works, such as *Memorias de Vladimir* and *Dimitri en la tormenta*, both award-winning novels for children, I looked forward to reading *Letargo*, her first novel written for adults.[1] The book came inscribed with the following dedication:

> For Rhonda, with all my affection, as I await her valuable opinion of these, my little gray characters who emerged from the recesses of my memory when I heard their perturbing cries.

Before reading the intriguing dedication, I was captivated by the photograph of a young girl that appears on the book's cover. Her dark eyes seemed to peer directly into mine, penetrating my gaze with a melancholy expression that made me wonder what traumatic story had left an indelible mark on her life. Turning the first few pages, I came across two other photographs, not unlike those one expects to find in an old family album. The first was a formal portrait of an infant girl whose wide eyes stared straight into mine, as if daring me to continue my questioning; on the next page were two stern figures, a young girl, perhaps six years old, dressed in a sailor outfit and standing next to a seated woman, most likely her mother, a somber lady whose black attire creates a stark background for her porcelain face and hands. A smile, even a forced one, is absent from their faces, suggesting that in the pages of this short novel lies a tale of sorrow and suffering. Impatient to see if there were other photographs in this "family album," I flipped through the 109 pages and was surprised to find that a sole image had the last word in the novel: a Star of David engraved on an old, weather-beaten tombstone.

These photographs serve as bookends for the seven chapters that comprise the novel, seven numbered "journals" that relate the journey of Deborah, who travels from Córdoba, where she has lived her entire adult life, to Basavilbaso, the village of her childhood in the province of Entre Ríos. It is fitting for the novel to close with the photograph of a Jewish headstone because the final destination of Deborah's journey is the grave of her mother, Lete Resler, who committed suicide when Deborah was only twelve years old. The trip overland to the cemetery of Basavilbaso transpires in one day; however, the journey reconstructed in the seven journals is a much longer one that transports the narrator back four decades to the two crucial years preceding her mother's death and that of her infant brother in the late 1950s.

As Deborah attempts to reconstruct the memories of those two turbulent years, which marked the end of innocence and premature initiation into the adult world, the narration shifts constantly from the present to the past, from first to third person, from the voice of the fifty-year-old protagonist to that of Deborah, *la niña,* between ten and twelve years of age. At times other voices mingle with her own, piercing the pages of her memoirs: the agonizing shouts of her mother, who suffered from schizophrenia, and the secretive murmurs of her father and maternal grandmother, who spoke to each other in Yiddish in order to conceal the truth from her. Deborah also remembers the stories her Bobe shared, recollections that take the reader far back in time to the distant city of Odessa at the turn of the twentieth century. At that time, her grandmother's family fled the pogroms of Czar Nicholas II, seeking refuge in Lyons, France, before traveling by sea to Argentina, where they settled in one of the agricultural colonies of Entre Ríos, like thousands of other Jewish refugees, including the author's ancestors.[2]

Little did I know that when I read the novel for the first time, I was about to embark on a long journey myself. Exactly a year later, in June 2001, I began to translate the novel, thereby immersing myself in a world that I could only experience from an outsider's perspective, for I am neither Jewish nor Argentine. Although I have spent nearly twenty years of my academic career studying the fascinating history and culture of Argentina and have visited the country on many occasions, the process of translating *Letargo* proved one of my most exhilarating foreign adventures.[3] Umberto Eco writes in his book, *Experiences in Translation,* "every language expresses a different world-view" (12), and "translation is always a shift, not between two languages, but between two cultures" (17). Indeed, as I crossed the borders from source to target language and back again, I found myself faced with the challenge of finding the appropriate words in English to capture Suez's unique worldview. My objectives were to re-create the asphyxiating climate in which a young Jewish girl comes of age and turns to reading, writing, and photography as a means of escaping the madness and rancor that reign within the walls of her house and the intolerance and repression that await her on the other side of the threshold. Above all, I wanted the future readers of *Lethargy* to experience what I felt the first time I read the novel, that after traveling to a distant place and time on a whirlwind trip of a few short hours, their return to the comfort and security of home would be accompanied by a renewed appreciation for the human spirit and a deeper understanding of why some become victims out of desperation, while others rise above trauma and find seeds of hope among the ruins of the past.

When Marjorie Agosín invited me to write an essay for this book, which would "explore in [my] own vision the situation of Argentine Jewish women writers [. . .] from a personal as well as scholarly perspective," I thought about the many Argentine Jewish women authors whose works I have read and studied, and it seemed to me that, in one form or another, their narrative fiction reflects the intimate relationship among memory, history, and writing. Ana María Shua, Alicia Steimberg, Manuela Fingueret, Alicia Kozameh, and Liliana Heker were a few names that came to mind, not to mention Perla Suez, whose novel I proposed to analyze. But then I began to compare the works of these authors with those of other Argentine writers, both male and female, who are not Jewish, and I came to the conclusion that the interplay between memory and history informs their texts as well. Héctor Tizón, a writer from the northwestern province of Jujuy, affirms: "Most definitely, we write with memory, the writer's supreme instrument" (Malusardi, 32). Tununa Mercado, who was born in the province of Córdoba, believes that "writing is nothing more than memory" (32). Mempo Giardinelli, from the northeastern province of El Chaco, observes: "[I]t is in novels where memory appears as the hallmark of the Argentine narrative of the late eighties and the entire decade of the nineties. The powerful urge to write our history, to recover memory, and in some way make each book a triumph over oblivion, is a very notable feature now" (*El país de las maravillas,* 187).

Although the struggle between anamnesis and oblivion is a recurring motif in many Argentine novels published during the past twenty years by those writers whom Giardinelli calls the "Writers of the Recovered Democracy," the problematic relationship between memory and history is present in Latin American literature from its earliest manifestations. In her book *At Face Value: Autobiographical Writing in Spanish America,* the Argentine writer Sylvia Molloy speaks of the important role memory has played in Spanish American letters since the time of the Conquest: "Remembering is not distinctive of the most recent Spanish American literature, nor is it a feature peculiar to the twentieth century. Since *Facundo,* since *María* — one might say since the Inca Garcilaso's *Comentarios reales* — Spanish American literature remembers" (139). "All fiction is, of course, a recollection" (139), Molloy goes on to say, a statement that leads me to ask the questions, if all writers rely on memory as a tool for weaving their tales, what narrative strategies and themes are uniquely Jewish? and more specifically, what tendencies characterize the fiction of Argentine Jewish women writers? Here I examine several interrelated thematic elements that inform the narrative discourse of Perla Suez's novel *Letargo* and appear, in a broader sense, as leitmotivs in the fiction of other contemporary Latin American Jewish women writers, particularly the journey, memory, reverence for the word, and the search for individual and collective identity.

In the introduction to *Jewish Writers of Latin America: A Dictionary,* Darrell B. Lockhart poses the basic question that I would like to address in this study: "What is it that renders a text Jewish?" (xv). In his article, "The Narrative Assertion of Cultural Identity in Three Latin American Jewish Novels," Lockhart writes about the difficult task of characterizing Latin American Jewish fiction and cautiously delineates certain thematic "concerns" that these writers incorporate into their narratives: "Among such concerns may be included immigration, assimilation, religious as well as secular values, Zionism, anti-Semitism, marginalization, intermarriage, Jewish culture, Yiddishkeit or Sephardic tradition, and the Holocaust" (451). Lockhart identifies the following "unifying theme" in the works of contemporary Latin American Jewish writers: "they seek to incorporate and thereby vindicate Jewish reality into Latin American History by means of recuperating the past" (451).

Nearly all of these topics are expressed to a certain degree in Suez's novel *Letargo,* especially the dominant role that memory plays in reconstructing the history of a particular Jewish family while at the same time inserting their intimate *petite histoire* into the collective History of the Jewish immigrant experience in Argentina.

In her introduction to *Passion, Memory, and Identity,* Agosín refers to the journey as a "unifying axis" of the narrative fiction of Latin American Jewish women writers: "Another fundamental theme found in the Jewish literature of Latin America is the voyage, either the one that takes us back to the experiences of the ancestors' expulsions or the one that leads to their arrival in America" (xiii). Both the journey of exile from the old country and the voyage of migration to the new one are incorporated into *Letargo,* in addition to the protagonist's travels across territorial and metaphysical borders. Indeed, the journey, in its myriad forms, appears as a constant element in the narrative fiction of Perla Suez, whose characters travel by boat, train, car, sleigh, and foot, and also by flights of memory that evoke the realities of Jewish persecution under the reign of Czar Nicholas II and during the Nazi regime of Adolf Hitler. Some of Suez's characters retrace the steps that brought her ancestors from Odessa and Besarabia in eastern Europe to San Gregorio, Villa Clara, and Basavilbaso, the Jewish agricultural colonies in Entre Ríos.

Although Suez has lived in Córdoba nearly all her adult life, she spent her first fifteen years in Basavilbaso, where she absorbed the family stories handed down by her grandparents and parents. These legends included tales of adventure, passion, and violence that would eventually find their way into her short stories and novels in fictionalized form. For example, Suez dedicates her short story, "Tan lejos y tan cerca," to "the great-grandfather in me," thus paying tribute to her paternal great-grandfather, who died at the hands of the Cossacks in the pogroms of Odessa, a story Suez heard from her father and wove into this tale years later. In an interview titled "Viaje hacia la memoria," Suez comments on the important role of her family's oral history in the creation of *Letargo:* "I believe that we always speak about the story of our lives and our family; an autobiography is always present. . . . *Letargo* is perhaps the beginning of something that began to take shape within me, something to do with my family and with life in my own little world, which is that of my town (3).[4]

For Suez, writing is a journey in which memory plays a crucial role as she reconstructs her own recollections as well as those passed on to her by others. In "Oral Histories and the Literature of Reminiscence," Naomi Lindstrom observes that third-generation Jewish Argentine writers are concerned with the "recovery and recording" of the past as it has been handed down to them from first- and second-generation immigrants. She stresses that both oral historians and writers are particularly interested in the "meanings to be assigned the material retrieved and reassembled out of reminiscences" (89). Lockhart points out the differences between texts written by Jewish authors of the first and second generations and those of the third and fourth:

> Third- and fourth-generation writers, almost exclusively secular and completely assimilated, often seek a return to and recovery of Jewish identity by salvaging the remnants of their ethnoreligious heritage through literature. Many write texts based on family genealogy and history in an attempt to preserve and/or restore cultural memory. The narrative of nostalgic remembrance is common, often told through the voice of a child narrator. The literary text becomes an exercise of self-identification as authors attempt to blend their Jewish past with their Latin American present in such a way as to fuse the two elements into a single identity. (*Dictionary* xxii)

The migratory experience serves as the focus for many of the verbal histories handed down from generation to generation as a means of preserving Jewish heritage. According to Florinda F. Goldberg, Latin American Jewish writers have a tendency to fictionalize either their own migratory experiences or the journeys of others. Frequently these real or imaginary voyages are presented as an "otherness" that stands as an obstacle between the author's characters and their integration into society (319).

The seven journals that comprise *Letargo* represent, in effect, a travelogue that records the protagonist's quest for identity and belonging. Deborah's trip to her mother's tomb is actually a retrospective voyage to discover her origins and the roots of her ancestors as she struggles to find a place for herself in the present. The adult narrator sums up the purpose of her journey when she writes: "I need to go back to her grave and tell her, as if I were a girl, what I didn't tell her back then" (50). Not only does Deborah wish to unburden herself of all that she left unsaid, she also wishes to revive her loved ones so that they too may divulge everything they kept from her as a child. During this imaginary family reunion, there is no longer a need for secrets: "I want Mama, Papa, and Bobe to ride with me in a taxi, like the one in which I'm riding now, and I . . . want them to talk about everything they need to say, for as long as it takes to say what they couldn't tell me back then" (107). As Deborah travels over the slippery terrain of memory and through the phantasmagoric landscape of her childhood, she recognizes the difficult task of reconstructing the past and inhabiting her home once again: "Nearly forty years have passed, and the more the image of those I loved fades away, the less I'm able to rebuild the space in which I was born, and yet, the desire to reconstruct every moment lived in my house persists, like the echo that those memories left in me" (47).

In his essay, "Ana María Shua: Memory and Myth," the Mexican writer Ilán Stavans comments on the problematic nature of reminiscence: "History might not be a Jewish invention, but memory surely is and so is forgetfulness. To remember is to be selective with the past, to forget what is judged unnecessary. Jews are by nature retellers: their existence is testified by the act of remembrance of events protagonized by God, and that act links Jews to the chain of generations that come before and after" (79). Actually, the question as to whether or not the past can be revisited and faithfully reconstructed is an issue raised not only in Jewish literature but also in postmodern fiction in general. In A Poetics of Postmodernism, Linda Hutcheon outlines the tendencies of those novels that attempt to re-create the past and, in so doing, actually question whether such a reconstruction is possible, thus confronting and subverting the notion of a single, objective authoritative account of the past (92).

In her journals, Deborah attempts to piece together the broken shards of her childhood, creating in the process a fragmented collage of pain and pleasure and a cache of dreams and nightmares, past and present. Painful memories and joyful pleasures, tzures and nakhes, return to her like flashes of lightning: her baby brother lying dead in his crib, her father leaving the Dutchman's boardinghouse with another woman, and her mother, tied to her bed, floating in a cloud of morphine; but also Leon passing a lemon drop from his mouth to hers and Bobe teaching her to embroider. Nevertheless, Deborah recognizes that she is an unreliable narrator: "I don't know if what I saw then is what I see now. As if the past had reopened a wound. I still have the scar" (66). As this passage suggests, the truth Deborah seeks is inscribed in her body. In Remembering the Bone House, Nancy Mairs reminds us, "[I]t is as a body that one inhabits the past and it inhabits one's body" (8). The adult narrator seems to know instinctively that she must activate all five senses in order to discover the girl she once was and thus understand the woman she has become. She writes in the first journal: "The girl is still there deep inside her, although now she doesn't remember everything she wants to recall. But for that to happen, she will have to return to each image, each taste, each sensation of touch, to the smallest memories which remain embedded in her flesh" (21).

The site of this sensorial evocation is the childhood home, a primor-dial space that Gaston Bachelard, in *The Poetics of Space,* calls "our corner of the world" and "our first universe" (4). Bachelard states, "[O]ver and beyond our memories, the house we were born in is physically inscribed in us" (14). Deborah's childhood home is the locus of memory where her Jewish heritage remains in safekeeping. As the matriarch of the family and guardian of the Judaic legacy, Bobe was the one who provided her grand-daughter with a connection to her ancestors. Deborah recalls that it was her grandmother who insisted that her brother be circumcised at home in a traditional *bris* ceremony, rather than in the hospital, as her father wished. It was also her grandmother who kept the Sabbath rituals intact, covering her head with a handkerchief and her eyes with her hands before reciting the prayer over the candles every Friday evening.

If the childhood home is "our corner of the world," as Bachelard says, the kitchen must be the real center of the universe. Indeed, it is a privi-leged space in the narrative fiction of many Latin American Jewish women writers. For Deborah, the memory of her grandmother is inseparable from the dishes she prepared for her as a child: potato kugel, knishes, gefilte fish, and, above all, borscht. In his delightful essay, "Is There a Text in this Gefilte Fish?" Lockhart explains that food serves as a cultural iden-tity marker: "Within the context of culture, food is key to many aspects of Judaic tradition and holds a place of particular significance that is both symbolic and substantive. Moreover, food plays an important role in the construction of identity inasmuch as it is central both to religious rites and celebrations as well as characterizing regional Jewish identities" (105). As Deborah recalls with fondness the aroma and flavor of her Bobe's beet soup, she is transported far beyond her own childhood to that of her grandmother: "The red broth is steaming now, as it steamed before dur-ing the rumble of the husky cries and sables of the Cossacks, when the girl, who was my Bobe, hid outside her house. She asks her grandmother to teach her how to make *borscht,* and Bobe, her eyes dancing with joy, tells her how to prepare it so the *borscht* turns out delicious" (54).

It is Deborah's grandmother, not her parents, who hand down the Jewish traditions in this family. The break in the chain of continuity between first- and second-generation Jewish immigrants appears in the novels of other Jewish Argentine women writers as well. For example, Lindstrom observes that the novels of Alicia Steimberg reflect "the de-cline of Jewish values of family, tradition, and continuity" and, moreover, that the "well-functioning Jewish family and community belong to an im-plicit, envisioned golden age" (95). In *Letargo,* Suez presents the drama of a dysfunctional Jewish family. Given that her mother suffers from schizo-phrenia and her father is an atheist whose Jewish faith has been replaced by Marxism, the family's Judaic heritage would not have been passed on to Deborah had it not been for her grandmother.

Another important marker of cultural identity is language, as David William Foster explains: "Language conflict is an abiding feature of the immigrant experience, and it is often an eloquent marker of the difficulties of accommodation, the nature of assimilation, and the negotiation under-taken between different cultural establishments" (44). Yiddish is the lan-guage spoken by Deborah's father and grandmother whenever they wish to exclude her from their conversations. Suez reveals that in the case of her own childhood, Yiddish was the language the adults used to discuss taboo topics in the presence of children: "I come from a Jewish family and in my house, and in others like mine, you could not talk about sex, nor could you speak of the death of a child. . . . [I]t was hushed up. So they would use the Yiddish language as a code for speaking freely, and I would hear it like a feverish murmur, which is reflected in the novel" ("Una memoria construida por recuerdos propios y ajenos" n.p.).

For Deborah, Yiddish is a language that circumscribes forbidden se-crets, as this passage from her memoirs suggests: "At one point, before my brother is born, I hear Papa and Bobe speaking in Yiddish, and I wonder if what they're saying has to do not only with something I don't know, but also with something I shouldn't know" (23). According to Lockhart, "The protagonist of the Latin American Jewish novel often functions as the me-diator of multiple voices who may or may not aid the reader in sorting out the myriad layers of meaning that constitute the heteroglossic strata of the text" (*Dictionary* xix). In addition to Yiddish and Spanish, French is also incorporated into *Letargo*'s polyphonic narrative, primarily in the form of songs that Deborah's grandmother learned as a child during her family's stay in Lyons and verses that she taught her daughter Lete. In the original novel, the Yiddish and French expressions are not explained, a conscious decision on the part of the author to capture the sense of mystery these two languages represent for the narrator.

Another prominent feature of the narrative is the wide margins that separate certain paragraphs and serve as an indication that in this house, what is not spoken carries as much weight as what is said. As the matri-archal guardian, Deborah's grandmother tries to protect the family from the rumors and gossip of the outside world by imposing absolute silence on her granddaughter, admonishing her, "Don't say anything, Deborah" (73), words that her father repeats to her so as to keep family secrets behind closed doors. Their censorship is in vain, however, and Deborah is not immune to the anti-Semitic comments she hears on the streets, such as "shitty Jew" (65) and "[there goes] the girl with the crazy mother and the Commie father" (75).

A cloud of fear hovers over the house. There is the possibility that Deborah's father will be arrested for subversive activities or will abandon the family for another woman; and a violent drama is played out as Bobe and her father argue and her mother screams in agony. The persistent fog that envelops the house and the constant rain that seeps through the roof contribute to the oppressive ambience. Seeking refuge from the storm, Deborah isolates herself in her room, where she turns to her books and her diary for solace. She also finds a haven in the darkroom, where her father develops photographs taken at the clandestine meetings of the Communist Party. Reading, writing, and photography offer the child Deborah a means of escape from the pain that besieges her, while they serve as tools for the adult narrator's quest for identity.

Reading becomes a ritual of withdrawal for the young protagonist, a private activity in which, comforted by a blanket of words, she surrenders to a world beyond her own small universe. As a child, she memorized entire passages from such favorite books as Lewis Carroll's *Alice's Adventures in Wonderland* and James Joyce's *Dubliners*. Forty years later, these passages return to the memory of the adult narrator who interprets them in a new light. In "The Reader with the Book in His Hand," the first chapter of *At Face Value,* Molloy observes: "The encounter of self and book is crucial: reading is frequently dramatized, evoked in a particular childhood scene that suddenly confers meaning on the whole life" (17). It is no coincidence that as Deborah embarks on her search for her authentic self she remembers the dialogue in which the caterpillar asks, "Who are you?" And Alice replies, "I hardly know, sir" (71). Nor is it a coincidence that as she travels to the cemetery where her mother is buried, she rereads the lines she marked as a young girl in Joyce's story "The Dead."

The protagonist's love of books and her reverence for the word have their origins in the author's past. Suez explains that she inherited her respect for books from her paternal grandfather, a rabbi who defied Jewish tradition and taught her and her brother the wisdom of the Talmud and the Kabala: "Although he made my brother wash his hands before touching a book, I am the one who repeats the ritual in some way through my writing. The image of the book has been with me since I first opened my eyes" (Schilling n.p.).

Like reading, writing is also an intimate act that provides an emotional release for the young Deborah, helping her to ward off her feelings of abandonment. Her diary serves as a confidant whenever she is unable to share her troubles with Sofia, her best friend, or with Leon, her first love. In the only diary entry in the novel that carries a date, May 21, 1959, Deborah writes in the second person, as if she were addressing a dear friend, "What would I do without you?" (83). The adult narrator evokes the memory of her secret diaries, writing about herself in the third person: "The girl goes to her room and writes in a journal. She writes a story that never ends. Then she hides the journal behind a drawer of the wardrobe. She hides it from herself. Many years will pass before she recalls that moment she thought was forgotten" (46).

Forty years will have to pass before Deborah summons the courage to retell the story that she wrote to herself so long ago, a story she now shares with us, the implicit readers of her memoirs. We learn in the seventh and final journal of the novel that Deborah's retrospective journey begins when she suffers an attack of sudden blindness in her home in Córdoba, where she works as a professional photographer and lives with her husband, Leon, her childhood sweetheart. Confined in bed for hours on end, the memory of her mother comes rushing back to her, and she wonders: "How long will I be shut in, closed up in this room, lying in bed like my mother?" (97).

Chapter 7 contrasts sharply with the preceding ones in that the narration is told completely from the perspective of the adult narrator, who speaks in the present moment as she recalls her most recent past. She thinks about the exhibit that she longs to complete, a series of photographs of voyeurs whose lascivious gazes are captured with her Pentax at the most intimate moment of their desire. Unfortunately, her condition renders her helpless, and she no longer views herself as a photographer but as a darkroom itself: "I'm a darkroom, behind a camera, trying to capture in the darkness that which is inaccessible to my eyes" (100).

Suddenly, that which has been forgotten comes back to her in flashes of images like old photographs taken in the sepia tones of melancholy. Visions of her loved ones return like series of snapshots in an imaginary family album: her grandmother sprinkling flour on the kitchen table, her mother nursing her baby brother, her father sitting under the shade of the grape arbor with his raincoat on and a cigarette in his mouth. Deborah becomes the object of her own voyeurism and the witness of her own memory as she spies on herself: playing hopscotch on the sidewalk, contemplating her budding breasts in front of the mirror, looking out the window at the passing train, wishing it could take her far away.

Among the most cherished photographs that Deborah composes in her mind's eye is the family portrait of her father with her baby brother in his arms and her mother holding her by the hand. Susan Sontag writes in *On Photography:* "Through photographs, each family constructs a portrait-chronicle of itself—a portable kit of images that bears witness to its connectedness. It hardly matters what activities are photographed so long as photographs get taken and are cherished" (8). In Deborah's case, however, the treasured family photograph does not exist: "They're still there in the family portrait that was never taken: Papa with my brother in his arms, and Mama holding my hand" (47). According to Sontag, "[a] photograph is both a pseudo-presence and a token of absence" (16). She goes on to say that photographs, especially those taken of people long ago, "are incitements to reverie" and "attempts to contact or lay claim to another reality" (16). Deborah wishes to lay claim to a past that was denied her: a happy childhood with a healthy mother who nurtured her through the difficult years of adolescence, a faithful father whose desires were fulfilled at home, and a baby brother who grew up with her.

After her sight returns, as quickly as it disappeared, she embarks on the journey from Córdoba to Basavilbaso, a symbolic voyage to mourn her loved ones and her own loss of innocence. She needs to make amends with the past and forgive her loved ones so that she can finally find her place in the world. As she travels to the cemetery, she looks at the only photograph of her mother she possesses, that of a young girl in a sailor outfit. One photograph is hardly enough to fill a family album, but Deborah has a new project in mind, one in which her missing family photographs will be compensated by those of other Jewish immigrant families who, like her own, made the long journey of exile to Argentina in search of a new life. Unlike her other photographic enterprises, this one is not a clandestine operation to capture the stolen images of individuals but rather a collective film documentary that will require the cooperation of a vast sector of the Argentine Jewish community:

> . . . *The camcorder is going to linger over each of the tombs, over each inscription, over each headstone, and then, a voice off-camera will speak of those men and those women, of the* pogroms, *of Czar Nicholas II, and after making a sweep, I'm going to open onto the port of Buenos Aires: the arrival of the immigrants, and I'll follow a man to his destination, wherever that is . . . and zoom in on the train station . . . and zoom in over an awning, and then on the villagers, the plague of locusts, and closing*

*the diaphragm, I'll open with the story of Eichelbaum, "The Motionless
Traveler," the voice off-camera. After the flashback, a woman from Bobe's
generation will speak about her life, and then I want to show a series of
photos of Mama as background to the story.* (106–107; original emphasis)

Although each family story is as unique as Deborah's own, their common
threads unite to form the fabric of the nation.

The novel comes to a close as Deborah enters the cemetery and heads
for her mother's grave. On the facing page is a black-and-white photograph of a Jewish tombstone, an imposing image that attracts the gaze
of the reader. The last words of the novel, separated from the preceding
text by a wide margin, capture the attention of the reader as well: "Fallow
fields. Mist. Silence" (108). The words "fallow fields" stand out as a promise of rebirth among the ruins of the past. The seeds of hope lie dormant
beneath the hallowed ground, ready to spring forth as a promise of new
life for Deborah and for those like her who seek their roots in the past and
find a home for themselves and their dreams along the way.

NOTES

1. One year after the publication of *Letargo*, Suez added another distinction
to her curriculum vitae, that of finalist for the Premio Rómulo Gallegos 2001, a
literary prize granted every two years to the best novel published in the Spanish
language during that period. *Letargo* is the first novel of a trilogy. It was followed
by *El arresto* (2001) and *Complot* (2004).

2. Suez's maternal great-grandparents and paternal grandparents were
among those Jews of Ashkenazi heritage who fled the pogroms of Russia at the
turn of the twentieth century and settled in the agricultural colonies of the Argentine province of Entre Ríos. Her paternal great-grandparents did not survive the
pogroms ordered by Czar Nicholas II.

3. All English translations of passages from *Letargo*, as well as other passages
translated from Spanish, are mine. Due to limitations of space, I have included
in this essay only the translations of the original Spanish passages cited from the
novel and other sources. All page numbers refer to the original sources.

4. During the presentation of *Letargo* at the International Book Fair in
Buenos Aires, Suez revealed that the origins of the novel may be found in her
childhood memories of her mother's sister, a strange aunt who lived in the Chaco
and often visited her family in Basavilbaso. She had lost a son and was given a
lobotomy as a treatment for schizophrenia, a condition that Suez, as a girl of ten,
could not understand. After forty years, however, images and voices resurfaced in

Suez's memory of a sad woman lying in bed, surrounded by family members murmuring hushed whispers in Yiddish ("La escritura, un modo de supervivencia" 3–4).

WORKS CITED

Agosín, Marjorie, ed. *Passion, Memory, Identity: Twentieth-Century Latin American Jewish Women Writers*. Albuquerque: University of New Mexico Press, 1999.

Bachelard, Gaston. *The Poetics of Space*. 1958. Trans. Maria Jolas. Boston: Beacon Press, 1994.

Eco, Umberto. *Experiences in Translation*. Toronto: University of Toronto Press, 2001.

Foster, David William. "Recent Argentine Women Writers of Jewish Descent." *Passion, Memory, Identity*, ed. Marjorie Agosín. Albuquerque: University of New Mexico Press, 1999. 35–57.

Giardinelli, Mempo. *El país de las maravillas: Los argentinos en el fin del milenio*. Buenos Aires: Planeta, 1998.

Goldberg, Florinda F. "Literatura judía latinoamericana: Modelos para armar." *Revista Iberoamericana* 66.191 (2000): 309–324.

Hutcheon, Linda. *A Poetics of Postmodernism: History, Theory, Fiction*. New York: Routledge, 1988.

Lindstrom, Naomi. "Oral Histories and the Literature of Reminiscence: Writing Up the Jewish Argentine Past." In *The Jewish Diaspora in Latin America: New Studies on History and Literature*, ed. David Sheinen and Lois Baer Barr. New York: Garland, 1996. 89–100.

Lockhart, Darrell B., ed. "Is There a Text in this Gefilte Fish? Reading and Eating with Ana María Shua." *El río de los sueños: Aproximaciones críticas a la obra de Ana María Shua*, ed. Rhonda Dahl Buchanan, vol. 70. Washington, D.C.: Interamer Collection of the OAS, 2001. 103–116.

———. *Jewish Writers of Latin America: A Dictionary*. New York: Garland, 1997.

———. "The Narrative Assertion of Cultural Identity in Three Latin American Jewish Novels." *Romance Languages Annual* 5 (1993): 451–454.

Mairs, Nancy. *Remembering the Bone House: An Erotics of Place and Space*. New York: Harper & Row, 1990.

Malusardi, María. "Cuentos y novelas de la Argentina: Mapas del alma." *Revista Nueva* (2001): 30–35.

Mercado, Tununa. *La letra de lo mínimo*. Rosario, Argentina: Beatriz Viterbo Editora, 1994.

Molloy, Sylvia. *At Face Value: Autobiographical Writing in Spanish America*. Cambridge: Cambridge University Press, 1991.

Schilling, Carlos. "Perla Suez habla sobre su nueva novela: 'El único consuelo es el libro.'" *La voz del interior* [Córdoba], June 4, 2001, n.p.

Sontag, Susan. *On Photography.* 1973. New York: Farrar, Straus & Giroux, 1977.

Stavans, Ilán. "Ana María Shua: Memory and Myth." *El río de los sueños: Aproximaciones críticas a la obra de Ana María Shua,* ed. Rhonda Dahl Buchanan, vol. 70. Washington, D.C.: Interamer Collection of the OAS, 2001. 79–82.

Suez, Perla. *El arresto.* Buenos Aires: Editorial Norma, 2001.

———. *Complot.* Buenos Aires: Editorial Norma, 2004.

———. *Dimitri en la tormenta.* Buenos Aires: Primera Sudamericana, 1993.

———. "La escritura, un modo de supervivencia." Presentación del libro. Buenos Aires, July 9, 2001.

———. *Letargo.* Buenos Aires: Editorial Norma, 2000.

———. *Memorias de Vladimir.* Buenos Aires: Ediciones Colihue, 1992.

———. Review of *Letargo.* "Una memoria construida por recuerdos propios y ajenos." *Diario Pregón* [Jujuy], July 2, 2000, n.p.

———. "Tan lejos y tan cerca." Córdoba: Foco Cultural, 2000.

———. "Viaje hacia la memoria." *La voz del interior* [Córdoba], June 25, 2001, E3.

Culture, History, and Representation

STEPHEN A. SADOW

Lamentations for the AMIA

LITERARY RESPONSES TO
COMMUNAL TRAUMA

On July 18, 1994, at exactly 9:53 A.M., on Pasteur Street in central Buenos Aires a small truck loaded with explosives slammed into the front portal of the seven-story headquarters of the Asociación Mutual Israelita Argentina (AMIA). The building, with its black marble facade, had long given the impression of invulnerability. However, within seconds it collapsed. The explosion itself and the falling debris killed or maimed most of those inside, many in neighboring buildings, and passersby. Despite intense relief efforts, eighty-five people, twenty-five of them AMIA employees, died, and an estimated two hundred fifty were injured. Many of the casualties were not Jewish.

At first there was massive public outrage. At one rally in the Plaza de Mayo, an estimated 150,000 people from diverse ethnic groups and sectors of Argentine life rallied in support of the victims and for pluralism in general. Nonetheless, with the exception of a few low-level operatives, the perpetrators of the bombing — now known to have had Iranian direction and support — have not been apprehended. Rebuilt in approximately the same spot, the new AMIA headquarters resembles a fortress. It is set back from the street to prevent future attack and is protected by an extensive security system. At street level, the names of the victims written in simple white spray paint on black placards stand in witness.

The AMIA building was familiar to the vast majority of Argentine Jews. Its departments offered job counseling, supplemental retirement programs, after-school activities, and library facilities. Beyond its social service functions, the AMIA was a center of Jewish culture, housing an important Yiddish library, the archives of the community, an active theater, and Editorial Milá, a publishing house that made available Jewish classics in Spanish translation as well as new works of all sorts by promising and established authors.

The magnitude of the attack took the Jewish community by surprise. Though many Argentine Jews remained apprehensive because of a similar unsolved attack on the Israeli embassy two years earlier, the economy seemed robust and the government of Carlos Menem appeared to be pursuing a strongly pro-Israel foreign policy.[1]

To a large extent, Jewish cultural production mirrored this guarded optimism. In Ricardo Feierstein's complex novel *Mestizo*, published in 1994 in a revised version by the prestigious Editorial Planeta, the protagonist, David Schneiderman, is able to identify himself simultaneously as a Jew and an Argentine. Ana María Shua's short novel, *El libro de los recuerdos* (The Book of Memories), tenderly presents the travails and foibles of the Rimetka family. Under the editorship of Feierstein and Perla Sneh, the AMIA itself was about to publish *El libro del Centenario* (The Centenary Book), a celebratory illustrated history of the Jewish community of Buenos Aires.

"El atentado de la AMIA" — the attack on the AMIA — as the AMIA bombing came to be known, then, was *the* turning point in the life of most of Argentina's 220,000 Jews. The sense of physical and psychological security and the broader participation in national life that had been slowly growing since Argentina's return to democracy in 1983 were suddenly threatened. Within weeks of the attack, concrete-filled oil drums stood in front of Jewish institutions as protection against car bombs. Overnight, strict security procedures were in place. Though the police arrested a few suspects, the government's bungling attempts to solve the crime were seen first as inept and later as intentional. Memoria Activa, a protest organization made up of survivors, relatives of the victims, and supporters, was established to pressure the national government and began to rally every Monday morning in front of the Justice Ministry.

In the months after the *atentado,* many Jewish writers and artists, in shock, found it difficult to engage in creative work. Feierstein, who had lost many colleagues in the attack, wrote of the difficulty of thinking and feeling at the same time, of finding words that could portray the intensity of the emotions provoked by the crime ("Las palabras" 10). The Academy Award–winning screenwriter Aída Bortnik argued that speaking out and action were needed more urgently than literature ("Argentinos aquí," 50).

Slowly, however, both fiction and nonfiction works appeared in response to the communal, as well as personal, trauma. Sofía Kaplinsky Guterman, Carlos Levy, Ricardo Feierstein, Isaías Leo Kremer, Marcos

Aguinis, Diana Wang, Alberto José Miyara, and many others have created a body of work that grieves, protests, and attempts to explain the disaster. Directly or implicitly, they bear witness and demand justice for the crime and equal treatment for Argentina's Jews. None of them treats the historical event in the same way. In their highly charged works, anger, grief, confusion, self-assertion, and hope — the complex of feelings related to catastrophic loss — are omnipresent.

Among the first to respond was Kaplinsky Guterman, a poet whose twenty-one-year-old daughter, Andrea, was killed in the AMIA attack while looking for a job. Kaplinsky Guterman's *Del corazón al cielo* (1997; From the Heart to Heaven) is a collection of poems by a mother who has lost her child. She puts no distance between herself and her subject: Andrea's picture is on the book's cover.

The poems are straightforward and unadorned, laden with grief, loss, and rage. There is little imagery, just impassioned speech. The titles — "Mataron a mi hija" (They Killed My Daughter), "Te busco" (I Search for You), "Palabras a un asesino" (Words for a Murderer) — are indicative of Kaplinsky Guterman's direct, forceful style. As a counterpoint, she has inserted after each poem prose commentaries that are calmer for the most part, although no less filled with pain. In both poetry and prose, Kaplinsky Guterman describes Andrea's character, her childhood, her dream of running a kindergarten. In "Vida de mariposa" (Butterfly's Life), the mother remembers, "Al describir las cosas nuevas, brillaba tu mirada, / y tu sonrisa, cristalina, resonaba en ecos donde fuera" (Discovering new things, your face would shine, / and your smile resonated in echoes wherever you went) (28). The mother fantasizes about the moment of the explosion, the nature of the killers, and the many people who were murdered. One poem is an elegy for the victims of the AMIA. She demands justice from the government and thanks her friends and colleagues in Memoria Activa: "Son nuestros amigos, que en los peores momentos, / nos brindaron su apoyo y su aliento" (They are our friends, who in the worst moments / offered us their support and strength) (84).

Carlos Levy, another poet, universalizes the event on Pasteur Street. By the fourth anniversary of *el atentado de la AMIA,* the bombing has become part of world history. One extraordinary poem, "18 de Julio de 1998" (July 18, 1998), describes the invasion of hatred in an ordinary street, one in which children play and rabbis, nuns, and tradespeople might walk: "Sobre esta calle, Antonio, desparramó el odio un es- / truendo esa mañana llenando el aire de pavura" (On to that street, Antonio, hatred let loose a thunder clap that morning, filling the air with fear) (Silber and

Levy 48). Levy sees Jewish names joined in death with those of Hernández, Fernández, and Abdalla. He compares the scenes of destruction written by Homer to others from Treblinka, Dachau, and Auschwitz,[2] then Bosnia, Vietnam, Korea, and Rwanda: "Mientras flota la pregunta inútil del por qué / cada vez que comienza un nuevo día" (While the useless question why floats / every time that a new day begins) (Silber and Levy 49). Levy places the attack in temporal context. It happened three thousand years after Homer told his tales and hundreds of days before. "De nuevo nuevamente" (Once again, just now), a phrase consciously borrowed from the Argentine regional poet Antonio Esteban Agüero, is repeated throughout the poem. Unlike Homer, who is long dead, the Jews are reminded now of what they have seen before. But Jews existed before Homer and will continue to exist now.

Jewish history and identity, albeit the Argentine variety, is the theme of Feierstein's *La logia del umbral* (2001; The Lodge of the Threshold). At the time of the bombing, Feierstein was working for the AMIA, though in another building; his secretary, Mirta Strier, at the AMIA building on an errand that day, died there.

La logia del umbral begins and ends with the explosion on Pasteur Street. Between these boundaries, a panorama of Jewish life in Argentina jumps, bounces, and goes back and forth in time. Argentina is at first seen as a Jewish homeland. Though there is always some concern about being accepted, Argentina *seems* to be a safe haven where Jews can maintain their traditions or opt for assimilation. As this is an emphatically Argentine and Jewish family novel, Israel is relegated to being an escape route rather than a shared Zionist goal.

This is a historical novel, a family saga, but not quite a realistic one. The author of *Historia de los judíos argentinos*, Feierstein uses his vast knowledge of Argentine Jewish history as weaponry in what is here a polemic. As in Woody Allen's film *Zelig*, the characters just happen to turn up at moments that have Jewish historical significance. They believe that a family or a people should transmit its history to the generations that follow. When they try to celebrate their history, they find themselves caught up in it once again.

The novel's group protagonist is the Schvel family (*schvel* means "threshold" in Yiddish). Through four generations, they are at the edge of Argentine society, never quite inside. The Schvels are an extended Jewish *mishpocha* (family or clan) that traces its Argentine heritage to the arrival in 1889 of Moíses Schvel and his wife, Juana, on the steamship *Waser*, the first commercial vessel to bring Jews to the Río de la Plata. The members of the Schvel family are prime movers in the founding and development of Moísesville, the most important of the Jewish agricultural colonies, an enterprise funded by the philanthropist Baron Maurice Hirsh. In a scene rewritten from a historical event, the progenitor, Moishe Schvel, an immigrant from Russia, becomes the first Jew murdered in Moísesville. Because of a misunderstanding, he is killed by a gaucho who, in turn, is torn to pieces by enraged Jewish settlers. Moishe's son, named optimistically Mauricio Argentino Schvel, born soon after Moishe's death, is the first child born in the colonies. After early travails and some experience of the pleasures of rural life, Mauricio Argentino grows up to be the paterfamilias of an enormous clan. Later on, following the historical pattern, most of the family members leave the colonies and move on to Buenos Aires, where they enter business and the professions and become active in political movements. These cousins come in all shapes and sizes. They are physically strong or sickly, devoted to their spouses or womanizers, believers in the occult or realists. More important, the characters are emblematic, finding themselves in professions and social situations typical to Argentine Jews. Bernardo Schvel runs a small business. Miryam is a psychologist. Manuel is the most religiously observant. During El Proceso, the Dirty War, Solomón Schvel's life is threatened by anti-Semitic thugs; fearing for his life, he is secreted out of the country and flown to Tel Aviv.

These people have profound, intense feelings about Argentina. Some remember the satisfaction of rural life; others remember the security and fellow feeling they enjoyed while growing up in an urban neighborhood filled with immigrants from many countries. Manuel Schvel speaks of a culinary blending that signaled entrance into Argentine life:

> Asi crecimos con mate y varenikes, asado y guefilte fish, locro y latkes espolvoreados con azúcar, medialunas de grasa y strudel, café con leche y té en vaso con terrón de azúcar en la boca hasta arribar a la común y económica polenta/momeligue. Una mezcla sabrosa, nutritiva, llena de vida y esperanzas. (Feierstein, *La logia*, 128)

> And so we grew up with mate and varenikes, asado and gefilte fish, beef stew and latkes spinkled with sugar, greasy halfmoons and strudel, coffee with milk and tea in a glass with a sugar cube in your mouth until arriving at the everyday and economical polenta/mameliga. A tasty mix, nutritious, full of life and hopes.

In contrast, Mario Schvel shows his children and grandchild how, during the 1930s and 1940s, national identity cards issued to Jews bore a small perforated Star of David so that the bearers could easily be identified by the authorities. The younger Schvels find this hard to believe.[3]

After a family reunion held in Moísesville during its hundredth anniversary celebration in 1989, the Schvel family decides to create a society to promote Jewish status and history in Argentina. Gradually, they build the membership of the lodge, first with family members, then with Jews, and finally with anyone — particularly anyone who considers himself an outsider — who wants to join. The name of the lodge, La Logia del Umbral, also the title of the novel, describes the situation of the Jewish community in Argentina. Jews, as cousin Marcelo says, are both here and not here; they are on the margin. Argentine Jews are an extended family at the edge of full equality as Argentine citizens.

The first joint task of the lodge members will be to bring a time capsule from Moísesville to Buenos Aires and bury it in the Plaza de Mayo, the most hallowed of Argentine places and the site where Juan Domingo Perón himself buried a capsule in 1950, to be opened in the then magical-sounding year 2000. Among the documents and farming implements, the capsule will contain the actual soil that had been tilled by the Jewish immigrants. The voyage they will undertake between Moísesville and Buenos Aires (a distance of 620 kilometers; a map is included in the text) illustrates the spatial dimension of the Argentine Jewish experience, demonstrating its presence in the Pampas, the suburbs, and the capital. As the old men are no longer strong enough to ride horses, the first leg of the trip will be done in an old-fashioned sulky; from there, they will travel sixty kilometers a day on horseback.

Like many lodges, this one has a large esoteric component. Esoteric interpretations are applied to the family's history. The six-pointed star has deep meaning for them. They decide to wear rings on their left hands bearing the Kabalistic tree, the symbol for the levels of Enlightenment. They accept Kabalistic interpretations of the *mem*, the middle letter in the Hebrew alphabet (and the middle letter in the Hebrew word *emet*, meaning "truth"). Hence the corresponding letter *m* in Spanish takes on great importance in the novel. Coincidently, the Schvel clan bears many names starting with *m*: Moishe (1860–1889), who emigrated from Europe; Mauricio Argentino (1889–1978); Mario (1920–); Marcelo (1948); Mariano Moíses (1972–); and a Manuel and Myriam, for good measure.

The novel is structured to resemble a board game. To reinforce this notion, Feierstein has bound together with the novel, *El juego de la inte-*

gración, or *The Game of Integration,* a complete board game that replicates
the Argentine Jewish experience. By avoiding assimilation, ghettoization,
religious fanaticism, and emigration, a player wins.

Overall, the story moves forward in time, but there is a jerkiness to it,
as side themes are introduced and then abandoned; sections that stop the
action seem arbitrarily placed, and then things straighten out in a rush
toward the end, as the Schvels and some friends make the ten-day "Jewish
gaucho" pilgrimage from Moísesville to Buenos Aires in which representatives of each living generation ride their corresponding part of the way.
Moreover, the pile-up of disparate scenes gives the novel the appearance
of a scrapbook.

The lodge members had wanted to record a historical event at a historical place, and they run right into history. The novel describes a celebration of Judaism in the Argentine context only to have this literally blown
up in their faces. The Lodge of the Threshold is, of course, a metaphor for
Jewish community. The Schvels have been in Argentina longer than many
other immigrant groups. They have farmed and herded cattle on the Pampas. They moved to the city and joined the middle class. They wear their
identities as both Jews and Argentines on their sleeves for all to see. The
main goal of their lodge is to gain public recognition for what to them
is obvious: the Jewish presence in Argentina is worthy of being honored.
The Schvels intended to put their own historical records at a place vital to
Argentine national history, and, on the way, their young scion runs right
into the most painful moment in the history of Jews in Argentina. The
time capsule with its valued relics is destroyed along with the community
records housed in the AMIA building. From that point on, the Schvels' life
and Jewish life in Argentina in general would never be the same. Extreme
insecurity was once again to become part of the Jewish identity in Argentina. What had finally seemed a coherent worldview is smashed almost
beyond repair. Identity found becomes identity lost. The final section of
La logia del umbral is titled "¿Llegada? 18 de Julio de 1994" (Arrival? July 18,
1994). The young member of the clan, Mariano Moíses Schvel, did indeed
arrive—but not where his family had intended. The seriousness of his in-
juries is left unclear. Whether the attackers are homegrown or imported
is unknown. The future of the Argentine Jewish community is shrouded
in dust and smoke and drowned out by emergency sirens. In the novel's
epilogue, Miryam interprets dreams to find predictions of the future, but
her findings are inconclusive.

The short story writer Isaías Leo Kremer mentions the AMIA *ma-
tanza* (slaughter) only once in his fiction; however, it is always there by

implication. Born on a farm and a rabbinical student for a time, Kremer is an agronomist and a frequent traveler through rural Argentina. He has long been associated with the AMIA, and three of his four short story collections are published by Editorial Milá. In person, Kremer is a virtuoso storyteller, a cross between an Argentine *payador* (one who sings an improvised song accompanied by a guitar) and a Jewish *rebbe* (rabbi). His short stories rarely exceed five pages. Many of his stories, written in the characteristic style of the memorialist, are more like vignettes than convoluted tales. In many stories he re-creates the literary style of the times and places he describes, freely mixing Yiddish, Hebrew, and gaucho slang into the dialogue. And Kremer does not shy away from moralizing.

Most of Kremer's multitudinous protagonists are rural Jews; often they are members of the immigrant generation, for example, the blacksmith Kiske Fasolie, the cattle herder Iasha, the simple Buzzie, the circus performer Vanya. Many of the stories are set in the heyday of Jewish colonization.[4] Though Kremer's tales may be poignant, they are often upbeat, giving the impression that those were good times. He is emphatic in his praise of the Jewish colonists as if to say, "We were here first and are part of this place." Drawing from a true story, he describes Noáj, the agronomist of the colonies, who taught the settlers how to grow sunflowers for their oil and by doing so changed Argentina's rural economy. He tells of the two Jewish friends, Boris Kleinkind and Meir Boshomke, huge young fellows, who, while doing compulsory military service, beat up anti-Semites and without permission go home to celebrate the Rosh Hashanah. "Di mame Bruria" (The Mother Bruria) is dedicated to the strength and fortitude of the women of the colonies.

Kremer, however, also believes deeply in a multicultural vision of Argentina: "Soy hijo de ruso, judío y argentino. Algunos de mi compañeros son italianos, cristianos y argentinos. Otros son hijos de libaneses, mohametanos y argentinos también" (I am the son of a Russian, a Jew and Argentine. Some of my comrades are Italian, Christian and Argentine. Others are the children of Lebanese, Muslims and Argentines too) (Kremer, *De cada pueblo*, 9). In *Milonga de la independencia* (2000; Milonga of Freedom), Kremer tells of a pair of elderly friends, don Benito and don Barúj, an Indian and a Jew, both of whose names mean "blessed." In an autobiographical tale, he tells about his longtime friendship with "La Turquita," a girl of Lebanese descent, with whom he constantly argued about Middle East politics.

Kremer's stories are sometimes somber. In his darker stories, he shows his grief and anger over the many tragedies of Jewish history. "El hombre de lc ; tulipanes" (The Tulip Man) relates a Holocaust scene that takes place in Holland. In "No hay simjat Torá en Olimpo" (Simhat Torah Doesn't Happen in Olimpo), he replicates a letter from a Jewish man being held by torturers during the Dirty War in Argentina who knows he will die soon. In "Los dos leones" (The Two Lions), which takes place during the Falklands War, a Jewish British officer, Lionel Samuels, comes upon a shell-shocked Argentine recruit named Ariel Levinas. The shivering, crazed soldier is repeating over and over the Shema Y'Israel, the most sacred prayer in Judaism. Hearing him, Samuels, though ordered to take no prisoners, spares the young man's life.

In contrast, in Marcos Aguinis's novel *Asalto al paraíso* (2002; Assault on Paradise), none of the major characters are Jewish. Jews are present only in the short scene describing the AMIA bombing itself or as they are appear in the minds of others. Instead, the novel is an exploration of why and how the bombing was carried out. Aguinis is a master of the historical novel and, in particular, a specialist in the workings of the Spanish Inquisition. Here he writes what could be called a journalistic novel in that the events described happened very recently. Moreover, the protagonist is a journalist, the non-Jewish Cristina Tibori. In a manner reminiscent of E. L. Doctorow, Aguinis builds fiction on well-known events. Aguinis both invents material and adds information that heretofore had been suppressed. In this "AMIA novel," there are four main characters: one is Catholic, the others Muslim. These figures—Cristina Tibori; Dawud Habbif, the suicide bomber, who believes self-destruction and murder are the methods to recompense the humiliations he suffered in his native Lebanon; Imam Zacarías Najaf, a resident of Argentina who was a founder of Hezbollah but now preaches peaceful tolerance instead of fundamentalism; and Hassem Tabbani, an Iranian diplomat—are "grown" by Aguinis from bits and pieces of the historical record. Of the four, Tabbani is the only one closely modeled after a real individual. *Asalto al paraíso* is an intricately structured suspense novel; its scenes, created with extraordinary attention to detail, shift swiftly to and from the bombed Israeli embassy to refugee camps in southern Lebanon, a television recording studio, terrorist training sessions, Buenos Aires's red-light district, and the offices of Argentina's secret service.

The plot begins on March 17, 1992, with the destruction of the Israeli embassy in Buenos Aires by a car bomb. (This was, in fact, the first terrorist suicide attack in the Americas.) Television reporter Cristina Tibori is sent by her editor to cover the story. At the scene she meets the imam Zacarías Najaf. The cleric understands the logic of terrorism and tries to explain to Cristina that if perpetrators of the first attack are not punished, a second attack will follow. Cristina does not feel a personal connection to the story until, to her horror, she learns that her sister has died in the attack. Cristina then decides that she must find those who are responsible and prevent the probable second attack.

Finding the truth about the embassy's destruction becomes Cristina's obsession, but she makes little headway. (In reality, the perpetrators of the Israeli embassy bombing have never been identified.) Two years later, unbeknown to Cristina, four Islamic terrorists arrive in Argentina from Lebanon and are greeted by functionaries from the Iranian embassy. In secret, officials of the Argentine secret service and the federal and Buenos Aires police forces, for differing reasons, join in a plot to destroy the Sociedad Hebraica, the largest Jewish cultural and sports institution, by means of a car bomb. Through intimidation and even murder, they aid the Iranians in the planning of an enormous catastrophe. At the last moment, Cristina hears of the plot against the cultural center and is able to abort it. However, the Iranians have a backup plan, and four days later the AMIA building is destroyed.

Asalto al paraíso is structured around two interwoven stories. Cristina Tibori is the courageous journalist obsessed with finding the perpetrators of the embassy bombing and her sister's murder. Through her investigations, Aguinis examines the most sordid aspects of the Argentine security forces. Paralleling this story is that of Dawud Habbif, the suicidal terrorist (*shahid,* or martyr) who arrives in Argentina determined to carry out his mission and win the rewards due a martyr in Heaven. Through his thoughts and memories, presented in stream-of-consciousness, Aguinis reveals the mentality of a person willing to die for a religious cause and the historical situation that led him to this intention.

In addition to being a novelist, Marcos Aguinis is a psychiatrist. The novel contains both psychological turmoil and interpretation of it. Obsession and anger are omnipresent. Cristina *must* find her sister's killer. She is willing to put her career and even her life in danger to do so. Dawud Habbif *must* destroy the Jewish center and himself; the horrors of his life prepared for this moment. The imam Zacarías Najaf *must* follow his religious convictions, even when millions oppose him and many threaten him. And Hassem Tabbani, as a representative of the Iranian Islamic government and because of his own hatreds, *must* direct the killing of his enemies.

Asalto al paraíso is, then, a mystery story that mixes fact and fiction, sometimes putting the two in counterpoint. Many Argentine readers would be surprised by the novel's premise that the Sociedad Hebraica had been the intended target. In the novel, the "facts" of the bombing are gradually made clear to the reader. The reader gets a "report" that substitutes for what is lacking in real life. The facts about the *atentado* have never been obvious or available, and no one has been convicted of so much as complicity in the crime.

Remarkably, within weeks of the bombing, Jewish cultural life began to regain its momentum. Headquartered at a temporary location, Editorial Milá continued publishing books of Jewish interests, though for a time it produced mainly sycophantic biographies of "Jewish leaders" such as Vladomir Jabotinsky and Menachem Begin. Other publishing companies such as Acervo Cultural and Dunken picked up the slack with a steady flow of fiction, Holocaust testimonies, and serious studies, such as Diana Wang's *El silencio de los aparecidos* (The Silence of Those Who Appeared), a discussion of the problems faced by children of Holocaust survivors. Acervo Cultural sponsored a novel-writing contest that brought in fourteen manuscripts from all over Argentina and from Israel. The contest winner, *Marcela y Judith* by Enrique Amster, is the story of a woman torn between allegiances in Argentina and Israel. Milá and other publishers eventually brought out three more of the novels. In 2002 the AMIA held a competition for young Jewish writers and awarded Clara Klicksberg Awards for the best writing by Jewish youth. The AMIA sponsored a sculpture project, "Reconstruimos la AMIA" (We Rebuild the AMIA), in which artists had to create works of art from bits of the rubble left by the explosion. Important sculptors such as Claudia Aranovich, Danilo Danziger, and Mariana Schapiro took part. The Israeli artist Agam constructed a highly controversial, multicolored monument to the victims of the *atentado* for the courtyard of the new building.

On August 11–14, 2001, the Cultural Department of the AMIA held an *encuentro*, or get-together, to "stimulate Jewish cultural production and to move on from paralyzing complaining to inspiring debate—to invoke hope" (Feierstein and Sadow 9). The cultural festival was free to all and lasted from morning until late at night. During its three and a half days, approximately one hundred people took part and more than thirteen hundred attended. The focus of the event was what it meant to be Jewish in Argentina in 2001. The presentations ranged from the history of Argentine Jewish cinema to the origins of the ancient Jewish communities of Sepharad, what is now Spain.

Theater and music alternated with the lectures. Three new plays were performed: *Hombre de dos amores* (Man with Two Loves) by Sol Levinton, a short piece about Jewish identity written especially for the Encuentro, scenes from *Liturgías* (Liturgies) by Nora Glickman, and a farce by Ana María Shua. Musical performances included the jazz-influenced klezmer music of Marcelo Moguilevsky and César Lerner, the Mordje Guebirtig Yiddish choir, and Paloma Sneh, a young saxophonist who interpreted Gershwin's "Summertime." Outside the auditorium, there was an exhibition featuring the work of leading artists such as Basia Kuperman, Delia Banchik, and Víctor Chab.

The majority of the critical papers dealt with the lingering questions of ethnic and national identity or with the nature of Argentine Jewish literature. Daniel Silber's talk was titled "Judíos en la Argentina? Judíos de la Argentina" (Jews in Argentina? Jews of Argentina). Laura Kitzis and Enrique Herszcovitz speculated on the identity of Argentina's Jews in the second millennium. Guido Setton pondered whether Jewish Argentine literature really exists. Other topics were more specific: the Yiddish theater in Buenos Aires; the works of individual writers such as Samuel Eichelbaum and Marcelo Birmajer.

During the Encuentro, explicit mention of the *atentado* was remarkably rare but instructive when it did occur. The novelist Silvia Plager declared that the many claims of solidarity with the victims had not alleviated the horrible scars left by the experience. The psychologist Diana Wang told of how her mother, a Holocaust survivor, called to beg forgiveness for bringing her to Argentina. For Wang, the AMIA bombing was a defining moment. She stated dramatically that she had been born as a Jew on July 18, 1994. Before that time, her Judaism had meant little to her; thereafter, it became central to her life. She established a clinical practice specializing in the problems of the children of survivors and established self-help groups around Buenos Aires. In 1998 she wrote *El silencio de los aparecidos*. Wang became active in Memoria Activa, joined a Yiddish choir, and studied Yiddish.

This torrent of artistic activity since the *atentado* is especially impressive, given that since 1999 Argentina's economy had been in free-fall. The government defaulted on its international debt, froze personal savings in banks, and unpegged the peso from the dollar. The middle class, which included most Jewish families, was particularly hard hit. Jewish poverty, almost unknown until then, became common. The number of Jews emigrating to Israel skyrocketed. Many others left for the United States, Canada, Spain, and even Poland and New Zealand.

At the same time, others remained hopeful. In 2002 Editorial Milá published *Recreando la cultura judeoargentina* (Re-creating Judeo-Argentine Culture), the 458-page proceedings of the Encuentro, complete with a CD-ROM containing recordings of all the music. In "Identidad," a poem in this collection, Alberto José Miyara, a Jewish poet from the city of Rosario, sums up the resilience of Argentine Jews after all that has happened to them:

> Soy judío. Tengo agua, tierra, cielo
> y mi voz. Y también tengo esperanza.

> I am a Jew. I have water, earth, sky
> and my voice. I also have hope.
> (Feierstein and Sadow 362)

Though not always as hopeful as Miyara, Argentine Jewish writers and artists have responded forcefully to the destruction of the AMIA building and the death of eighty-five people. Writing from grief, anger, and outrage, they have provided their community with fiction and poetry to help it deal with what happened on July 18, 1994.

NOTES

1. For an in-depth study of the relationship between the Jewish community and the government of President Carlos Saúl Menem, see Melamed, *Los judíos y el menemismo.*

2. Many Holocaust testimonies have been published in Argentina since the AMIA bombing. It is difficult to discern whether this production has occurred as a response to the attack. However, in his Holocaust memoir, *Una vida,* Charles Papiernik recalls that when he first heard of the bombing, his mind was immediately filled with scenes from Auschwitz: "Me encontré otra vez en el Holocausto" (I found myself in the Holocaust once again) (235).

3. The Argentine government has vociferously denied the existence of these identification cards, but the many cards still in existence contradict this denial.

4. In the years since the bombing, a great deal of fiction has been written about the Jewish agricultural colonies in Argentina. Besides Feierstein's *La logia del umbral* and the stories of Kremer discussed here, there are novels such as Armando Bublik's *Poncho y Talmud* and Gregorio Tavonaska's *Ydel, el judío pampa* and story collections such as Dina Dolinsky's *Las doce casas.* During the same period, Feierstein edited the selected works of Alberto Gerchunoff in *Alberto Gerchunoff: Judío y argentino* and the collection *Los mejores cuentos con gauchos judíos.* All of these works emphasize the Jewish contribution to the development of Argentina.

BIBLIOGRAPHY

Aguinis, Marcos. *Asalto al paraíso.* Buenos Aires: Planeta, 2002.

Bortnick, Aída. "Argentinos aquí y ahora." *Raíces* 3.9 (summer 1994–1995): 50.

Bublik, Armando. *Poncho y Talmud.* Buenos Aires: Atlántida, 1997.

Dolinsky, Dina. *Las doce casas.* Buenos Aires: Editorial Milá, 2000.

Feierstein, Ricardo. *Mestizo.* Buenos Aires: Planeta, 1994.

———. "Las palabras y las cosas." *Raíces* 3.9 (summer 1994–1995): 10. Reprinted in Ricardo Feierstein, *Contraexilio y mestizaje: Ser judío en la Argentina,* 15–17. Buenos Aires: Editorial Milá, 1996.

———, ed. *Alberto Gerchunoff: Judío y argentino.* Buenos Aires: Editorial Milá, 2000.

———, ed. *Los mejores cuentos con gauchos judíos.* Buenos Aires: Ameghino, 2000.

———. *La logia del umbral.* Buenos Aires: Galerna, 2001.

Feierstein, Ricardo, and Stephen A. Sadow, eds. *Recreando la cultura judeoargentina 1894–2001: En el umbral del segundo siglo.* Buenos Aires: Editorial Milá, 2001.

Feierstein, Ricardo, and Perla Sneh, eds. *El libro del centenario: Comunidad judía de Buenos Aires 1894–1994.* Buenos Aires: Editorial Milá, 1994.

Kaplinsky Guterman, Sofía. *Del corazón al cielo.* Buenos Aires: Editorial Milá, 1997.

Kremer, Isaías Leo. *De cada pueblo un paisano.* Buenos Aires: Editorial Milá, 2001.

———. *Guachadas y mitzves.* Buenos Aires: Editorial Milá, 2000.

———. *Mateando bajo el parral.* Buenos Aires: Milá, 2002.

———. *Milonga de la independencia.* Buenos Aires: Acervo Cultural, 1999.

Melamed, Diego. *Los judíos y el menemismo.* Buenos Aires: Sudamericana, 2000.

Papiernik, Charles. *Una vida.* Buenos Aires: Editorial Milá, 1997.

Sadow, Stephen A. "La Colonia judía a través de la ficción argentina actual." *Recreando la cultura judeoargentina 1894–2001: En el umbral del segundo siglo,* ed. Ricardo Feierstein and Stephen A. Sadow, 27–39. Buenos Aires: Editorial Milá, 2001.

Silber, Marcos, and Carlos Levy. *Las doloratas.* Buenos Aires: Editorial Milá. 2001.

Shua, Ana María. *El libro de los recuerdos.* Buenos Aires: Sudamericana, 1994.

Tavonaska, Gregorio. *Ydel, el judío pampa.* Buenos Aires: Corrigedor, 1998.

Wang, Diana. "Lo judío en mi obra." *Recreando la cultura judeoargentina 1894–2001: En el umbral del segundo siglo,* ed. Ricardo Feierstein and Stephen A. Sadow, 311–317. Buenos Aires: Editorial Milá, 2001.

———. *El silencio de los aparecidos.* Buenos Aires: Acervo Cultural, 1998.

RAANAN REIN

Nationalism, Education, and Identity

ARGENTINE JEWS AND CATHOLIC RELIGIOUS INSTRUCTION, 1943–1955

In the midst of World War II, as they struggled against the limitations imposed on Jewish immigration while their brothers and sisters were being sent to the death camps in Europe, Argentine Jews were forced to face yet another challenge. In December 1943 the military government that had taken power in Buenos Aires six months earlier published a decree instituting Catholic education in all state schools. In the next decade, the Jewish community of this South American republic had to contend with governments that regarded Catholicism as a basic ingredient of Argentine nationalism. Non-Catholic Argentines, therefore, found themselves in a peculiar situation in which they were not considered "good Argentines." This essay seeks to analyze the reaction of Argentine Jews to the growing influence of the Catholic church in Argentina in general and in the field of education in particular during the 1940s and 1950s. What I mistook at first as a passive attitude on the part of Jews made me appreciate later the moderation, sense of proportion, and pragmatic strategy of Jewish leaders in times of rapidly and radically changing political and social circumstances. At the same time, I became more aware of the gap that existed between anti-Semitic public discourse and its actual influence on the daily lives of most Jews in Argentina.

MILITARY OFFICERS AND CATHOLIC BISHOPS

The religious education decree was sponsored by the then justice and education minister, Gustavo Martínez Zuviría, an extreme, anti-Semitic, Catholic nationalist, known for the novels he had written under the pseudonym Hugo Wast. The decree underscored the alliance between the army officers in power and the church bishops. Signed on December 31, the day the military government dissolved all political parties, it instituted compulsory lessons in the Catholic religion in all state-run schools. The Argentine church had fought to achieve this goal for more than half a century. In 1884 Law 1420 established that education in Argentina would be secular in nature and that only religious personnel outside official school hours could teach religion classes. Schoolteachers were forbidden to teach religion. This law reflected the secularization process that took place in Argentina in the second half of the nineteenth century and the views of the liberal elites, who were strongly influenced by developments in state-church relations in Third Republic France. Since the 1880s the church had striven to restore religious education to the public schools and to take a hand in the spiritual formation of Argentine youth.[1]

After a few decades, the church's efforts began to bear fruit. In the 1930s, in the context of economic difficulties engendered by the worldwide depression, a retreat from political freedom following President Hipólito Yrigoyen's ouster in September 1930, and growing conservatism, the church became notably stronger and more influential. The number of religious communities in the capital increased from 39 in 1929 to 105 a decade later. Acción Católica, an activist organization for lay Catholics, was established in 1928 and boasted eighty thousand members by 1940. At the International Eucharistic Congress in Buenos Aires in 1934, more than a million people attended the masses and took communion.[2] Several provinces decided to reinstate religious education in the schools under their jurisdiction. However, provincial legislation affected a relatively small number of pupils, since most schools were controlled by the national government.

The cancellation of Law 1420 and the institution of religious instruction in all state schools in December 1943 therefore constituted an enormously important achievement for the church. The new decree made religious lessons part of the compulsory curriculum for all pupils and, in its preamble, characterized the previous education law as absurd because it ran counter to the "Catholic nature of the Republic." This pro-church legislation was one form of ammunition in the military regime's battle against the various manifestations of liberalism and Marxism, and it brought the unconstitutionally instituted regime support and legitimation from the religious establishment. In this way, relations of mutual dependency were forged between the military and the clergy, providing the basis for the alliance that would help the charismatic colonel, Juan Perón, to take power in the general elections of February 1946.

Under the terms of the decree, the only pupils exempted from religious instruction were "those pupils whose parents have explicitly expressed their opposition because of their adherence to another religion — and thus freedom of conscience shall be respected." Such pupils had to attend "morality" lessons instead. Other articles in the decree authorized church authorities to control the religious curriculum and textbooks and to participate in a supervisory capacity in the special division set up in the Education Ministry to organize the teaching of Catholic religion and morality.

In Catholic circles, of course, the religious instruction decree was greeted with delight. The central committee of Acción Católica was quick to thank President Pedro Pablo Ramírez and his government for having had the sense to restore to the children of Argentina the "authentic" patrimony of their forefathers, by "returning Jesus to our school and our school to Jesus." The Argentine bishops' conference also praised the decree in February 1944, because it "strengthens the spiritual unity of the nation, by harmoniously linking its present with its past." Protestants and Jews criticized the decree, of course (each of these communities constituted roughly 2 percent of the population at that time); although their children were not compelled to receive Catholic religious instruction, they felt pushed to the sidelines by this identification of Argentina with Catholicism.[3] Complaints were also heard from organizations of secular teachers, Liberals, Socialists, and Communists. Interestingly, although some Protestant communities organized public protests, the organized Jewish public did not do so, and would not cooperate with the Protestants on this issue. The Delegación de Asociaciones Israelitas Argentinas (DAIA; Delegation of Argentine Jewish Associations), the political umbrella organization of Argentine Jews, settled for approving the draft of a manifesto on March 23, 1944: "The executive branch of the nation has thus left intact the constitutional precept that mandated the duty to respect freedom of conscience; consequently all Jewish parents have the ineluctable duty to inform the school administration that they wish their children to be exempted from Catholic religion classes." Failure to do so would be "a serious breach of ethics, since such conduct is intolerably hypocritical or outright deceitful."[4]

Why didn't the Jewish leadership adopt a more combative attitude toward a military regime that considered only Catholics "good Argentines"? It seems that this generation of Jewish leaders, born mostly in eastern and central Europe, were accustomed to quiet lobbying and requests for government protection and not to public protests or the mobilization of public opinion to put direct pressure on the authorities. Furthermore, being at least partially aware of the fate of their brethren in the Old World, they did not lose their sense of proportion. The institution of religious instruction in state schools did not seem to pose too serious a threat to Jewish life in Argentina.

In the following months, the DAIA waged a campaign to persuade Jewish parents to defend their children's right to the exemption. Many parents did not take advantage of this right, because they wanted to avoid conflict with school administrators, because they did not want their children isolated from the other pupils, or simply because they did not care.[5]

The education minister, Martínez Zuviría, and his even more nationalistic successor, Alberto Baldrich, now began to staff the ministry with nationalists and Catholics, and the same process took place in the university and teacher-training institutions. Also, the military regime increased the salaries of church employees and transferred large sums of money to various Catholic institutions.

RELIGIOUS ISSUES DURING THE PRESIDENTIAL CAMPAIGN

In the course of his campaign for president in late 1945 and early 1946, Perón made statements indicating that, if elected, he would pass a law ratifying the temporary decree instituting religious instruction in all the schools—the decree so dear to the church establishment. There were a few liberal priests who had expressed support for the Allies during World War II and who now warned against the colonel "with the fascist and totalitarian tendencies," but church authorities saw Perón as the lesser evil when compared to the bloc of parties running against him within the framework of the Unión Democrática. A third possibility, the National Democratic Party—a conservative party that represented the oligarchy and on which the church had depended in the past—was, for all intents and purposes, defunct.

Accordingly, some time before the elections, the heads of the church published a pastoral letter calling on Catholics not to vote for parties that advocated the separation of church and state, the elimination of religion from the public schools, and divorce. In other words, they were not to vote for the Unión Democrática, which included Radicals, Socialists, and Communists, three groups whose position on religious matters was well known.[6] Years later, church officials would claim that this pastoral letter should not have been interpreted as support for Perón, emphasizing that a similar letter had been published at the beginning of the 1930s, when General Agustín P. Justo was running for president against the leader of the Progressive-Democratic Party, Lisandro de la Torre. In the stormy atmosphere of those last months of 1945, however, the Argentine public perceived the letter as a declaration of support for Perón's candidacy.

Most of the Jews, needless to say, supported the Unión Democrática. In the aftermath of World War II, as the extent of the Jewish Holocaust in Europe became clear, Argentine Jews, most of whom were of European origin, were suspicious of a charismatic leader who reminded them of the Führer and the Duce of the defeated Axis regimes. The support Perón received from nationalist organizations, such as the Alianza Libertadora Nacionalista, and the Catholic church only reinforced their suspicions. At the same time, both the political identity (generally liberal or left-wing) and the class identity (primarily middle class) of many Jews disposed them to remain aloof from a military leader whose candidacy was identified with benefits for the Argentine working class.

A look at the various positions that different people in the church took with respect to this pastoral letter shows that the liberals who counseled against its publication were a minority in the Catholic camp. Most of the clergy preferred to maintain some degree of neutrality, and not a few believed that the interests of the church required it to identify with one of the candidates — Perón. "This is our opportunity, we must not miss the boat," as Archbishop Antonio Caggiano put it.[7] Some priests went much further, and in their Sunday sermons explicitly told their congregations to vote for Perón. Some churches became Peronist propaganda centers, essentially serving as emissaries for candidate Perón even in the remotest parts of the Republic. In view of the small majority that gave him the victory in February 1946, we can assume that the church's contribution to his election was significant.

Perón needed the church for more than simply votes and support, however. The Peronist doctrine had not yet been formulated, and Perón sought to use Catholic values to unify his supporters. In his election propaganda, he portrayed himself as "the Catholic candidate" and associated his social message with the social doctrine of "the true church." That doctrine had been expressed in a number of socially oriented papal bulls, notably those issued by Leo XIII and Pius XI, which sought to define a "third way" between Marxism and liberalism.[8]

PERONIST POPULISM AND THE CHANGING
ATTITUDE TOWARD RELIGIOUS MINORITIES

After Perón's victory, he and his wife made various gestures toward the church, including frequent appearances at official religious ceremonies and a mass performed during the celebration of Loyalty Day (Día de la Lealtad Popular) on October 17, 1947, the second anniversary of the historic mass demonstration of Perón's supporters in the Plaza de Mayo. The Day of the Virgin of Luján, whose cult dated back to the colonial era, was declared a holiday. These gestures probably reflected Perón's recognition of political necessity more than they did any deep personal faith. The church repaid Perón in various ways: it suppressed critics of the regime among its own ranks, and the primate of the Argentine church, Cardinal Santiago Luis Copello, participated in blatantly political and partisan ceremonies and events sponsored by the regime. With good reason, the Argentine historian Lila Caimari in her *Perón y la iglesia católica* has designated the years 1946–1949 as "the Catholic period" of Peronism and "the Peronist period" of the church.

About nine months after moving into the presidential palace, in March 1947, Perón kept his promise: the Congress passed the law instituting religious education in all schools. This was no easy task; Perón had to bring all his influence to bear on the members of the Peronist majority in the Chamber of Deputies, since some of them, coming from solidly unionist and leftist backgrounds, were inclined to oppose it.[9] However, Perón's interest lay in ensuring the Church's support for his regime, and he believed that Catholic education would be an important tool for promoting national unity. On one occasion he declared: "I think that in our country it is impossible to speak of an Argentine home that is not a Christian home. Under the cross we formed our ideas. Under the cross we recited our ABCs. . . . Everything distinctive in our habits is Christian and Catholic." Thus Peronism attempted to make religion a basic component of national identity while presenting Communism — an ideology that was competing for the support of the working class — as atheism foreign to the spirit of Argentina.[10] This definition of the national identity was problematic for the Jewish community, as well as for other non-Catholic groups in Argentina, since it appeared to be shutting them out.

As early as October 1946, in the course of a debate in one of the committees in the Chamber of Deputies concerning Radical opposition to the proposal to ratify the military government's religious education decree, the DAIA passed a memo to the president of the lower house of Congress,

Ricardo Guardo, asking that the decree of December 1943 not be given the force of law. Moisés Goldman and Benjamín Rinsky, the memo's signatories, asserted that a religious education law of this kind violated the legal equality of the Jews of Argentina in both letter and spirit, created discrimination between Catholic and non-Catholic pupils, and limited the freedom of conscience that was guaranteed by the constitution. They stressed that Law 1420, which permitted religious study outside of school, helped to make all pupils feel united and bound to their homeland.[11] Yet in the course of the public and parliamentary debate over the following months, nothing more was heard from the leaders of the Jewish public, in contrast to various Protestant groups. Possibly, the Jewish leaders feared that taking an active stand might identify the community even more strongly with opposition to the regime, making their contacts with the authorities more difficult. As it turned out, this attitude would prove beneficial later on.

The deputies of the majority faction in Congress accepted their leader's will, and the decree became law in March 1947, after turbulent debates that raised basic questions concerning the nature of Argentina's national identity.[12] Speaking out against the law's supporters, a Radical deputy named Luis MacKay, who would later be a minister in the Arturo Frondizi government, called on his fellow deputies not to vote for a law that had the potential to divide Argentines: "Since they are children of so many races, religions, philosophies, and regimes, it is our duty to iron out the difficulties between them with the help of mutual respect and tolerance, to forge the unity and harmony needed in this cosmos that is Argentina."[13] His words were not heeded. It was still the era of the melting pot, not the multicultural project (and not only in Argentina). The bill was passed, and Perón was now able to send a letter to Pope Pius XII emphasizing the importance of the law and the Christian aspect of his social policy.[14]

The DAIA then launched a new campaign to persuade Jewish parents to have their offspring placed in the "morality" classes rather than the Catholic religion classes. The morality lessons, however, were described by at least some of the Jewish children who attended them as strongly Catholic in nature. This is not surprising, since the textbooks and curricula in this field were written by the religious—read Catholic—education division in the Education Ministry.[15] Moreover, the exemption from Catholic religious instruction did not release the Jewish pupils from various school activities of a Christian nature—or from the need to refuse explicitly to participate in them. Often school field trips included visits to churches, and many educational events had religious content. Nonetheless, for the most part, available testimonies make no mention of tension, hostility, or systematic discrimination associated with the introduction of Catholic instruction.

The historian Haim Avni sent in the early 1980s several dozen questionnaires to former pupils in state schools during the years 1944–1954. To the question about problems they or their families had to face when asking for exemption from the religion classes, or whether such a petition was ever rejected, "all the respondents, without exception," answered that they had never heard of such a rejection or of any conflict provoked by such a petition. Most respondents claimed that the exemption from religion classes had no negative effects on their relations with non-Jewish friends or with teachers and school principals.[16]

During the early years of Perón's regime, the church refrained from criticizing the regime publicly, in part because it saw Peronism as an effective barrier against Communism and hoped to use the regime's popularity to rehabilitate its own status among the masses. It was a case of quid pro quo, with each side using the other to promote its own aims. The government gave subsidies to Catholic institutions every year and continued to stress the Christian character of *justicialismo,* the Peronist social doctrine (from *justicia,* "justice"). The new constitution drafted in 1949 preserved the Catholic religion's privileged status.

Nonetheless, the alliance between the Perón regime and the Catholic church was not a solid one. Each side was suspicious of the other, and aware that its own camp included dissenters who opposed overly close cooperation. The church was not happy with increasing state intervention in its traditional fields of activity, such as charity, welfare, and education, or with Perón's self-proclaimed status as sole interpreter of the social significance of "true Christianity." In a speech in 1948, Perón tried to equate being a good Christian with being a Peronist, while in May 1950 he declared, in a speech before Catholic academics, that a two-thousand-year-old doctrine — Christianity — needed to be updated to fit modern life.

It hardly needs to be said that such speeches aroused uneasiness and concern in the church. At this stage, it was becoming increasingly clear that the bishops' wish to maintain Catholicism's privileged status with respect to other religions no longer had a consensus in the Peronist leadership. The government now showed no inclination to restrict the activities of non-Catholics. In fact, it was beginning to present respect for all religions as a feature of Peronism. The regime considered loyalty to Perón and his movement more important than loyalty to any other institution,[17]

and, moreover, sought to apply in the religious sphere the Peronist am-
bition of protecting the rights of minorities and weak, marginal groups
from the encroachments of the privileged. Peronism was presented as a
conglomerate that had a place for every decent Argentine who supported
the Peronist project.

At the beginning of the 1950s, teachers were advised not to urge non-
Catholics to participate in Catholic doctrine lessons but to respect the
principle of freedom of religion. The new Peronist textbooks published
in the years 1953–1955 reflected the desire to defend this principle. In one
second-grade reader, the following dialogue appeared under the heading
"Respect for All Religions":

BEATRIZ: Are you staying for the religion class, Esther?

ESTHER: No. Dad is Jewish, and he has asked that I be taught Morality
instead of religion.

BEATRIZ: Oh, I am staying. This year I am taking my First
Communion.

ESTHER: The teacher won't mind, right? Since she is Catholic.

BEATRIZ: No, Esther. The teacher says that each one of us should follow
the religion of our parents. And we should respect each other's
religions.

ESTHER: Oh! That is good education.

BEATRIZ: Good education and also tolerance.

ESTHER: Jews also respect the Catholic religion, and they are grateful
to President Perón for allowing them to celebrate their holidays
without counting the absences at school.

BEATRIZ: They [the Jews] also make this country great. We are all
brothers and sisters.

ESTHER: Before, Jews used to feel like strangers in Argentina. That's
why they hid their religion.

BEATRIZ: With Social Justice [Peronism] we have even achieved harmony among all of us.[18]

The respect for religious pluralism that characterized the last years of
the Peronist regime is reflected in a statement that Perón made in the book
he published in 1956, while in exile in Panama:

During my government I received, without making any distinction between them, the heads of the Roman Catholic Church, Jewish rabbis,
the representative of the Jerusalem Patriarch and head of the East-

ern Orthodox Church, the Greek Orthodox, Protestants, Mormons, Adventists, etc., because I believed it was my duty not to discriminate between the spiritual leaders of different sectors of the Argentine people.[19]

ON ANTI-SEMITISM AND THE JEWISH RESPONSE

As I was researching Argentine Jewry of the 1930s–1950s, it became clear to me that historiography has so far devoted excessive attention to the question of anti-Semitism in this South American republic. Too often, therefore, the reader of essays on anti-Semitic manifestations in Argentina receives the false impression that all through the twentieth century the lives of Jews there were intolerable. Such was not the case. The anti-Semitic image of the Peronist regime is also unfounded to a large extent. During the Peronist decade, the Argentine government—trying to improve its image at home and abroad—gradually made the struggle against anti-Semitism an integral part of its policy. To some extent, this should not surprise us. Peronist populism showed a greater readiness to promote the social and political integration of groups that had previously remained on the margins of the system. The principal beneficiaries of this attitude were, of course, members of the working class, but immigrant groups, including Jews, also gained something from it. A number of Jewish figures reached positions that had never been open to Jews before, in government ministries and in the judicial system. Argentine populism was a multi-class coalition that included new industrialists—mainly producers of import substitutes for the local market—and provincial business elites. These groups incorporated Jewish businesspeople and entrepreneurs who had been able to advance economically as a result of Peronism and its policy of protecting local manufacture in various fields.[20] Nonetheless, many Jewish (and non-Jewish) businesspeople continued to be strongly mistrustful of Perón. "Strange," wrote Yaacov Tsur, the first Israeli ambassador to Buenos Aires, in his memoirs, "many of these Jews have made a fortune since Perón came to power[,] . . . but despite that it was evident that they did not believe the regime had a future, and feared the signs of extremism in it."[21]

This notwithstanding, when assessing the overall performance of Argentine Jewish leaders during this fateful decade, one cannot fail to appreciate the fact that the leaders of the DAIA managed to walk a thin line during a period that divided Argentine society into two warring camps.

They cultivated good relations with the president—all the time stressing that, as Jews, they were expressing their loyalty to the head of state and the elected bodies of the Republic, not personal allegiance to a certain political party. They refrained from boycotting the small Jewish section of the Peronist party, taking advantage of the channel of communication it provided to the upper echelons of the regime, but they did not allow the Peronist Jewish organization to expand its base of support in the Jewish community. Moreover, they managed to preserve their organization's autonomy at a time when institutions, organizations, and entire social sectors were undergoing rapid Peronization. The Jewish papers praised the regime for its various measures favoring Jews and the state of Israel without joining in the toadyism and the personality cult endemic in the rest of the Argentine media, most of which eventually jumped on the Peronist bandwagon, willingly or otherwise.

At the same time, ironically, the anti-Peronista opposition, especially since the eruption of the open conflict between Perón and the church in November 1954, saw the Jews as strong supporters of the regime. Catholic nationalists circulated anti-Semitic pamphlets, especially in the city of Córdoba, which had always been considered a Catholic stronghold. These pamphlets included accusations against the Jews and Freemasons who surrounded President Perón who were allegedly responsible for the attempt to separate church and state. In this atmosphere of conflict, many Jews feared that, as in other times and places, they would become "victims of a kulturkampf."[22] Therefore, many Jews welcomed Juan Perón's overthrow in September 1955 and the institution of a military government, in part because they hoped for political stability after a particularly turbulent year.

NOTES

This essay is based in part on my recent book, *Argentina, Israel, and the Jews: Perón, the Eichmann Capture and After* (Bethesda: University Press of Maryland, 2003).

1. On the struggle over the place of religion in the schools, see among others José S. Campobassi, *Ataque y defensa del laicismo escolar en la Argentina (1884–1963)* (Buenos Aires: Ediciones Gure, 1964).

2. David Rock, *Authoritarian Argentina: The Nationalist Movement, Its History and Its Impact* (Berkeley: University of California Press, 1993), 101; Alberto Ciria, *Partidos y poder en la Argentina moderna (1930–1946)* (1975; rpt. Buenos Aires: Ediciones de la Flor, 1985), 228–234; Ernesto J. A. Maeder, "La enseñanza religiosa en la década del 30," *Todo es Historia* 227 (1986): 80–92.

3. Lightman to JDC, 17 July 1944, American Jewish Committee Files, Argentine Anti-Semitism (YIVO, New York), Box 2; Loris Zanatta, *Perón y el mito de la nación Católica: Iglesia y ejército en los orígenes del peronismo (1943-1946)* (Buenos Aires: Editorial Sudamericana, 1999), 115-190.

4. Quoted in Haim Avni, *Emancipation and Jewish Education: A Century of Argentinian Jewry's Experience, 1884-1984* [Hebrew] (Jerusalem: Shazar Center, 1985), 95.

5. The same was true after the decree became law in the second half of the 1940s. See *American Jewish Yearbook* 51 (1950): 265.

6. On this pastoral letter and on the church's position during the election campaign, see *Criterio* (Buenos Aires), November 22, 1945; Lila Caimari, *Perón y la iglesia católica* (Buenos Aires: Ariel Historia, 1995), 94-100; Zanatta, *Perón y el mito de la nación Católica*, 400-438.

7. On reactions within the church to the pastoral letter, see Susana Bianchi, "La iglesia católica en los orígenes del peronismo," *Anuario del IEHS* 5 (1990): 71-89.

8. On Peronism and the church's social doctrine, see Cristián Buchrucker, *Nacionalismo y peronismo: La Argentina en la crisis ideológica mundial (1927-1955)* (Buenos Aires: Editorial Sudamericana, 1987), 305-308.

9. Author's interviews with Joaquín Díaz de Vivar, who conducted the congressional debate on behalf of the majority faction (Buenos Aires, June 22, 1989); with Rodolfo Decker, chairman of the Peronist majority faction (Buenos Aires, August 31, 1989); and with Cipriano Reyes, who at that time had already left the Peronist camp and of course opposed the law (Quilmes, September 15, 1989).

10. See Orestes D. Confaloneri, *Perón contra Perón* (Buenos Aires: Editorial Antigua, 1956), 254-255.

11. The full text of the memo appears in Avni, *Emancipation and Jewish Education*, Appendix B, Document 4, 186-187.

12. On the education law and its ratification, see República Argentina, *Diario de Sesiones de la Cámara de Diputados* (1946), 10: 568-879; Virginia Leonard, *Politicians, Pupils, and Priests: Argentine Education since 1943* (New York: Peter Lang, 1989), 82-90; Susana Bianchi, "Iglesia católica y peronismo: La cuestión de la enseñanza religiosa (1946-1955)," *Estudios Interdisciplinarios de América Latina y el Caribe* 3.2 (1992): 89-103.

13. Quoted in Avni, *Emancipation and Jewish Education*, 84.

14. Author's interview with Father Hernán Benítez (Buenos Aires, June 29, 1989) and Perón's letter to Pope Pius XII, dated March 28, 1947, a copy of which was furnished to the author by Father Benítez.

15. See Esti Rein, "The Struggle for Ideological Hegemony between the Cross and the Sword in the Perón Era [Hebrew]," in *Society and Identity in Argentina* [Hebrew], ed. Tzvi Medin and Raanan Rein (Tel Aviv: University Publishing Projects, 1997), esp. 141-143; "Collected Reminiscences of Former Pupils," Appendix A in Avni's *Emancipation and Jewish Education*, 169-174.

16. Avni, *Emancipation and Jewish Education,* 169–172.

17. This is the thesis of Lila Caimari, "Peronist Christianity and Non-Catholic Religions: Politics and Ecumenism (1943–55)," *Canadian Journal of Latin American and Caribbean Studies* 20.39–40 (1995): 105–124.

18. Celia Gómez Reynoso, *El hada buena* (second-grade reading text) [Buenos Aires: Luis Lesserre, 1953], 54. See also Ana Lerdo de Tejeda, *Un año más* (second-grade reading text) (Buenos Aires: Luis Lesserre, 1953), 12. English translation in Caimari, "Peronist Christianity," 11–12.

19. Juan Perón, *La fuerza es el derecho de las bestias* (Buenos Aires: Ediciones Síntesis, 1974), 62.

20. On Peronism as a populist movement, see my *Peronismo, populismo y política: Argentina 1943–1955* (Buenos Aires: Editorial de la Universidad de Belgrano, 1998), chap. 1.

21. Yaacov Tsur, *Credential No. 4: First Diplomatic Mission in South America* [Hebrew] (Tel Aviv: Ma'ariv, 1981).

22. See memo by S. A. Fienberg, 14 June 1955, American Jewish Committee Files, Argentine Anti-Semitism, Box 3.

DARRELL B. LOCKHART

From **Gauchos judíos** *to*
Ídishe mames posmodernas

POPULAR JEWISH CULTURE

IN BUENOS AIRES

You see, every bit the gaucho! Baggy pants, wide belt, knife and
even those lead things to kill partridges; but in the synagogue he's
silent and doesn't know how to pray.
ALBERTO GERCHUNOFF, LOS GAUCHOS JUDÍOS

The Yiddishe Mames of yesteryear didn't get breast implants.
SILVIA PLAGER, AL MAL SEXO BUENA CARA

All research endeavors have a history. For years now I have focused my
research on Latin American Jewish literary and cultural studies. This essay
is born of that interest, although it had a rather long, nagging gestation
period. As a consumer and collector of cultural (by)products, and in an
effort to satisfy my own capricious impulses, I have managed to assemble
a relatively significant and rather curious assortment of materials related
to the Jewish experience in Argentina. Among these items are first edi-
tions of literary texts, films, weighty coffee-table books, postage stamps,
first-day covers that commemorate Jewish colonization, cookbooks, and
a variety of humor books. I have spent a good amount of my time reading, researching, and analyzing literary texts by Jewish Argentine authors.
While I find this challenging and rewarding, it is not always entertaining. I
do, however, find pleasure in watching films, reading humor books, amusing myself with cartoons, or even experimenting with a new recipe. I never
really intended for these leisure activities to turn into an academic exercise. Nonetheless, the more popular artifacts I gathered, the more I began
to contemplate the significance of such items, particularly in relation to
the socioliterary dimensions of Jewish writing in Argentina. Likewise, I
began to reflect on the roots of cultural myths and to what extent Jewish-

ness—as an ethnoreligious identity construct and a semiotic system of cultural coordinates—enters into the broader national consciousness. The title and the epigraphs by Gerchunoff and Plager that I selected should provide a clue to the territory I wish to explore here. Moreover, they are intended to signal the evolution of Jewish popular culture I aim to map out. I begin with Gerchunoff's *Gauchos judíos* and end with the witty musings of Plager and her contemporaries. I do not propose an/other analysis of Gerchunoff's foundational text. Rather I am more interested in the legacy it has bequeathed to subsequent generations, namely, the mythic figure of the *gaucho judío.*

Before entering into a discussion of specific texts, allow me to clarify which definition of popular culture I am ascribing to here. There are several concerns that must be addressed when approaching Jewishness from a Latin American popular culture standpoint. This is complicated by the fact that Latin Americanists have been attempting to determine the boundaries of popular culture scholarship over approximately the past thirty years without much success at achieving a consensus. The principal points of contention revolve around the act of naming. Whose culture, language, geography, and taste "qualify" as popular, and as culture, and why?

We may begin by addressing the conceptual slippage that occurs in translation from Spanish to English. "Popular culture" is not an accurate translation of *cultura popular,* which connotes something more akin to "folk culture" (Hinds and Tatum xiii). If we work strictly from this meaning of *popular,* that is, stemming from *el pueblo* (the people), we are confronted immediately with a set of seemingly irreconcilable dichotomies: rural versus urban, pueblo-folk-indigenous versus foreign, popular culture versus mass or consumer culture, pure-authentic versus contaminated-hybrid, local versus global, and so on. It should be clear on which side of these dichotomies the category of Jewishness would fall.

In their book on popular culture in Latin America, William Rowe and Vivian Schelling address many of these issues and tend to side with the pueblo-rural-indigenous understanding of popular as an oppositional force of resistance against the threat of encroaching urban consumer culture. Jean Franco underscores this when she states, " 'The popular' was formerly an index of Latin American difference, a difference that was measured by *distance* from the metropolis by the class who were closest to the metropolis and as the foundation for nationhood (the independent *gaucho,* the 'authentic' rural population ["Globalization" 209; original emphasis; note the keyword *formerly*]). I return below to the figure of the gaucho as a popular national icon. In 1982 Franco wrote a seminal essay in which she raised several concerns over the terminology used to speak about popular culture ("What's in a Name"). Some fourteen years later she revisited that essay in light of globalization and neoliberal policies in Latin America and came to the conclusion that "older senses of the word *popular* no longer correspond to any stable group, and the idea of 'a culture made by a people themselves' is no longer viable. This has resulted in attempts to describe local, regional, national, or 'Latin' difference in terms of hybridity or nostalgia" ("Globalization" 217). This is precisely the approach that Ilán Stavans takes to popular culture in his book *The Riddle of Cantinflas.* He states that there is essentially nothing left that is original in Latin America and works primarily vis-à-vis the cultural production of kitsch or the kitschification of cultural production.

There has been a gradual move in popular culture studies toward more urban realities and expressions. This is reflected in the journal *Studies in Latin American Popular Culture* (founded in 1981), which focuses mainly on urban cultural practices and production. Similarly, when surveying the essays collected in books such as *Handbook of Latin American Popular Culture* (1985) edited by Harold E. Hinds and Charles M. Tatum or *Imagination beyond Nation* (1998) edited by Eva Bueno and Terry Caesar, one finds topics as diverse as film, sports, music, religion, indigenous art, *telenovelas,* comic strips, tango, photonovels, television, and print media. Critics do seem to agree, at least in recent years, that the dimensions of popular culture are changing in Latin America, and with them so is the manner in which we approach it. Bueno and Caesar state, "[O]ur conviction is that nothing more than the study of popular culture recovers the reality of a country—no matter that part of this reality (depending of course upon the country) is now irremediably open to copying. In the end, popular culture in Latin America occupies a sort of middle stratum between an adopted paradigm of national identity and a lived complexity of social reality" (15). Franco voices the opinion that her "own preferred definition [of popular culture] would be the broadest possible and would include a spectrum of signifying practices and pleasurable activities most of which fall outside the controlling discipline of official schooling" ("What's in a Name" 179). Finally, David William Foster affirms, "By popular culture we mean all those cultural forms that impinge on our daily lives: newspapers, magazines, movies, television, greeting cards, even phatic speech and social rituals" (*From Mafalda to Los Supermachos* 2).

It is within the parameters of these more comprehensive definitions that I locate my discussion of Jewish popular culture as primarily urban in nature, notwithstanding its rural—though primarily mythified—origins. Indeed, there are parallels to be drawn between the rural-to-urban population shift and the development of a Jewishly marked popular culture. A consequence of this shift is the predominance of cultural products originating from the vast metropolis of Buenos Aires, which overshadows to the point of obscurity any cultural manifestations coming out of the interior provinces (Foster's *Buenos Aires: Perspectives on the City and Cultural Production* provides an excellent analysis on this point). This pattern of migration began in the early twentieth century as people flocked to the Greater Buenos Aires area in search of employment, education, and better opportunities in general. The majority of Jews—one of the major immigrant groups to Argentina—first settled in the agricultural colonies of the Litoral region established by Baron Maurice de Hirsch and the Jewish Colonization Association at the end of the nineteenth century. The colonies did not prosper, and Jews soon joined the migration to Buenos Aires (for the history of Jewish immigration to Argentina, see Avni; Feierstein; Mirelman). In sum, the result is that Buenos Aires is home to the largest Jewish community of Latin America, and it would not be difficult to sustain that it is one of the two major Jewish cultural centers (or capitals) of the Americas—New York being the other. Foster makes this comparison as well in his chapter "Jewish Buenos Aires" (*Buenos Aires* 132–149). He surveys the evolution of the urban geographical dis/placement of the Jewish community (the move from the traditional urban ghetto of El Once to outlying neighborhoods) and the participation of Jews in different social and cultural sectors of the city that has afforded them a certain visibility and even power base.

My focus is only partially related to literature as a mechanism of cultural production. I am more interested presently—let me reemphasize—in the kinds of cultural texts that are produced and consumed outside the institution of literature, which often leans, unfortunately, toward a highbrow self-definition. I am aware, of course, that Jewish literature in Argentina exists well on the margins of the canon. Notwithstanding, I will be examining texts that are more commonly referred to as belonging to the nebulous category of "pop" culture. Let me state emphatically that I do not adhere to any negative connotations associated with this term ("pop" music, "pop" psychology, "pop" literature) such that it is seen as vulgar, base, common, in bad taste, and so on. Furthermore, I am not interested in establishing, or paying heed, for that matter, to what I view as artificial hierarchies of cultural production. For instance, in music how can one rank the cultural value of the fabulously kitsch brother-sister duo Pimpinella, the protest-folksinger Mercedes Sosa, the rock group Soda Stereo, the neotango composer Astor Piazzolla, or the ingenious originality and humor of the group Les Luthiers? In the same manner, I hope to show that such diverse cultural components as cartoons, humor books, cookbooks, photohistories, films, and literary texts all participate nonhierarchically in the ongoing creation of Jewish popular culture in Buenos Aires; and furthermore that these products are at once rural and urban, regional and global, autochthonous and hybrid.

Any examination of the Jewish gaucho legacy must necessarily begin with Alberto Gerchunoff (1884–1950) and his foundational fiction, *Los gauchos judíos* (1910; The Jewish Gauchos of the Pampas). It has long been considered the ur-text of Argentine Jewish writing, the master narrative that informs the vast body of literature that followed it. Whether authors write in a parricidal counterdiscourse vein or in a more nostalgic laudatory vein, many return time and again to *Los gauchos judíos* as a point of departure. The text has similarly been the object of a great deal of study and has been translated into English, first in 1955 (this version has been reissued by the University of New Mexico Press [1998] in their series on Jewish Latin American literature in translation). In 2000 Edna Aizenberg published a second, vastly improved translation (*Parricide on the Pampa?*) based on the 1910 original (the first translation was done from a later edition). There are also two recent anthologies of Gerchunoff's work: Eliahu Toker's *Alberto Gerchunoff: Entre gauchos y judíos* (1994; Alberto Gerchunoff: Between Gauchos and Jews) and Ricardo Feierstein's *Alberto Gerchunoff: Judío y argentino* (2000; Alberto Gerchunoff: Jew and Argentine), which consists of an anthology of Gerchunoff's writing accompanied by critical appraisals of his work, photos, and a few sketches. These volumes continue the Jewish gaucho theme and work to solidify Gerchunoff's position as the cornerstone of the *gaucho judío* mythology. The sketch by Moreau included in Feierstein's anthology clearly demonstrates the promotion of a hybrid image of Gerchunoff as the Jewish intellectual writer-gaucho (Fig. 1).

Contemporary readers have often criticized Gerchunoff's overly idyllic portrayal of the immigrant experience, accusing him of being too eager to advance an assimilationist agenda of legitimizing the Jewish presence in the country on exaggerated — if not false — pretenses. Primarily, this has involved an attempt to establish a common denominator between Jewish and Hispanic cultures through the Sephardic history of Spain (Senkman 17–57). Aizenberg keenly remarks on Gerchunoff's carefully orchestrated creation of the gaucho judío figure — what she calls a new ethnic type — and the effort to Hispanicize the Jewish immigrant. "We might ask, how

FIGURE 1. *Alberto Gerchunoff. (From Ricardo Feierstein, ed.,* **Alberto Gerchunoff:** *Judío y argentino [Buenos Aires: Milá, 2000]).*

did Gerchunoff 'create' this new ethnic 'type'? The answer is through leger-demain. Although Gerchunoff does not hide that the Jewish cowboy is in reality an agriculturalist of Yiddish expression, his characters largely speak almost Cervantine Spanish as the author attempts to tie the new-comers to the heritage of Sepharad, where Jews made Spanish their own" ("Jewish Gauchos and Jewish 'Others'" 16–17). Gerchunoff's interest in Cervantes is seen throughout his writing but in particular in his *La jofaina maravillosa* (1938), a series of essays on Cervantes's *Don Quijote*. When *Los gauchos judíos* was commissioned to be included as part of the centenary celebration in 1910, obviously Gerchunoff saw his opportunity to advance the cause of Jewish integration and knew just where to start. Surely he cannot be faulted for his clever appropriation of the most ideologically charged symbol of the nation: the gaucho. Furthermore, he was in a prime position to do so given that his stories from *Los gauchos judíos* first appeared in serialized form in the oligarchic newspaper *La Nación*, where Gerchunoff was employed.

The *gaucho criollo* (the native cowboy of the Pampas) as national hero is also a fabrication. He is not the eighteenth- and nineteenth-century rogue outlaw whose disappearance Sarmiento advocated in his famous *Facundo* (1848). The gaucho as stalwart symbol of the Argentine national character was transformed in the pages of literature through texts like José Hernández's *Martín Fierro* (1872, 1879), the definitive masterwork of the so-called gauchesque genre. The image of gaucho-as-hero is further propagated by Leopoldo Lugones in *El payador* (1916; The Gaucho Minstrel) and Ricardo Güiraldes in *Don Segundo Sombra* (1926), who as the name suggests and the narrator confirms in the end of the novel is truly more of a shadow (read myth) than a man. Aizenberg is quick to draw the parallel between the gaucho and the gaucho judío. "Just as the gaucho is Argentina's 'vast generic figure' and his exploits are the backbone of the nation's most potent national myth, so the *gaucho judío* is Jewish Argentina's larger-than-life archetype, and his deeds are the core of an ethnic saga Argentine Jews consider uniquely their own" (*The Aleph Weaver*, 138).

While Jews may have found it viable and advantageous to embrace the gaucho figure, it is evident that Argentine nativists and nationalists traditionally have not been willing to reciprocate that sentiment. Aizenberg takes the famous Argentine author Jorge Luis Borges to task for his total, vehement rejection of the *gaucho judío* image (*The Aleph Weaver*, 138–148). As far as I am aware, *Los gauchos judíos* is not included in any critical evaluation of gauchesque literature, nor does the figure of the Jewish gaucho appear in any other way, shape, or form in regard to gaucho culture — or better stated, the cultural constructs associated with the gaucho figure. What is more, there is a prejudicial binary opposition embedded in language that makes *gaucho* and *judío* ideologically incompatible. This is made manifest by looking up the terms *gauchada* and *judiada* in any Spanish-language dictionary. While *gauchada* refers to a favor or service done willingly and goodheartedly, *judiada* refers to an underhanded or devious action specific to Jews. This kind of deeply rooted ideologeme is certainly one factor that propagates the idea of *gaucho judío* as being the worst kind of oxymoron.

Regardless of nonacceptance into the national mythology, the figure of the Jewish gaucho has endured in the Argentine Jewish imagination, and this seems to be the case now more than ever. Reaching the one-hundred-year mark since the founding of the original settlements inspired a number of efforts to rescue the written heritage of the colonies from oblivion. Many may have been surprised to discover that *Los gauchos judíos* was not the first work of fiction to provide testament of the rural immigrant experience. The 1987 anthology, *Crónicas judeoargentinas: Los pioneros en ídish 1890–1944* (Judeo-Argentine Chronicles: The Pioneers in Yiddish), contains stories by more than twenty-five authors who originally wrote in Yiddish. The volume is divided into "rural literature" and "urban literature." There are also collections of testimonies such as *Integración y marginalidad: Historias de vidas de inmigrantes judíos en la Argentina* (1985; Integration and Marginality: Life Histories of Jewish Immigrants in Argentina), edited by Sara Itzigshon et al. These are valuable sources for preserving the cultural heritage of the past while at the same time stimulating more activity along the same lines. A much more recent anthology compiled by Ricardo Feierstein makes no qualms about using the well-worn figure of the Jewish gaucho. His *Los mejores relatos con gauchos judíos* (1998; The Best Stories with Jewish Gauchos) contains stories by twenty authors who range from Mordejai Alperson to Marcos Aguinis. The inclusion of Aguinis as a *gaucho judío* author is a bit of a stretch, but it demonstrates that the term is now used more as a trope than as an appellation given to those writers who actually lived the pioneer experience. Aguinis's story "Josecito, el memorioso" does reference the colonial period (at the same time it makes a conscious nod to Borges's story "Funes, el memorioso"). As a high-profile contemporary author—not to mention a very urban one—Aguinis is likely to be one of the few in the anthology the general reading public would recognize (aside from Gerchunoff and Samuel Eichelbaum). His inclusion may be interpreted as a conscious maneuver on the editor's part to trace a kind of literary family tree in an effort to show the link between the rural past and the urban present. Visually, the volume makes a statement with its collage of archival photographs on the front and back covers as well as the inside flaps, which immediately evoke a sense of nostalgia.

In the inventory of literary works that incorporate the *gaucho judío* figure and the Jewish rural past, there is none quite so unique as José Pavlotzky's (1906–1988) *Un gaucho judío/payadas sabáticas: Relato entrerriano en verso* (1980; A Jewish Gaucho/Sabbath Songs: An Entre Ríos Story in Verse). The author models his narrative poem after *Martín Fierro*, even beginning with the same famous verse: "Aquí me pongo a cantar" (Here I sit me down to sing; 13). What follows are 2,699 more octosyllabic verses divided into 109 *cantos* over 87 pages. Pavlotzky is well aware that the octosyllable is the *verso gaucho,* as he declares in the preface to the poem (12). Born in Basavilbaso, Entre Ríos, he was a native son of the original Jewish agricultural settlements. He lived most of his life in the northern province of Chaco where he was a physician and active in the Socialist party. *Un gaucho judío* is a remarkable text for the way it mimics quite authentically the gauchesque genre. Similar to Hernández's poem, Pavlotzky divides his verse composition into major narrative sections: "El padre del gaucho" (The Gaucho's Father), "El gaucho judío" (The Jewish Gaucho), and "Payadas sabáticas" (Sabbath Songs). The first tells of the Jewish colonists who arrived fleeing persecution in czarist Russia, how they embraced their new homeland and freedom. Much of the same integrationist sentiment found in Gerchunoff's text is repeated here. The second part begins the story of the Jewish gaucho Loncho Ostrosky who excels both in his formal schooling and in his informal education as a gaucho. The "Payadas sabáticas" parallels the well-known *payadas* contained in *Martín Fierro.* A *payada* is a singing competition between two *payadores* (gaucho minstrels) in which verses are bantered back and forth in a challenge to keep a story going. In literature, this poetic device is traditionally used as a way for the author to philosophize on various social issues as a means of communicating an ideological message. One gaucho often takes on the role of teacher and the other that of student. In Pavlotzky's *payadas* the two gauchos are Loncho, the Jewish gaucho, and Juan Méndez, the native gaucho. In their banter they discuss a variety of issues. Loncho, the formally educated man, and Méndez, wise in the ways of country life, learn from each other and repeatedly express their mutual admiration and respect. The underlying, though not so discreet, message of the poem is that Argentina is a Land of Promise where men of all ethnic and religious backgrounds can thrive and work together in harmony. What makes *Un gaucho judío/payadas sabáticas* an engaging text in relation to popular culture is precisely the way the author manages to manipulate the two foundational mythologies in such a clever way. Not only does he work with the mythic figures of the gaucho and the *gaucho judío,* but he does so using the traditional discourse attributed to gaucho culture. Pavlotzky's attempt to thus authenticate Jewish identity as being an inherent part of the national popular (pueblo-rural-authentic) culture heritage is an admirable one. Yet the fact that the poem came and went virtually unnoticed and has remained as little more than a bibliographic trivia item is a clear indication that such a project has failed.

While Gerchunoff's version of immigrant life may be too highly glossed over with bucolic images of happy Jews plowing the fields of the new Promised Land and Pavlotzky's homage to Hernández overly romantic, other writers have not been so willing to paint the picture with such a rosy hue. Samuel Eichelbaum, better known for his urban dramas, provides quite a different view of the colonies in his volume of short stories *Tormenta de Dios* (1929; Storm from God) and his one rural drama, *El judío Aarón* (1926; Aaron the Jew). One of the few female writers from the period, Rebeca Mactas (the granddaughter of Mordejai Alperson), also portrays life in the agricultural settlements in a more realistic fashion, describing not only the severe hardships but also the corruption and unforgiving nature of the administrators of the Jewish Colonization Association. Her stories in *Los judíos de Las Acacias* (1936; The Jews of Las Acacias) are decidedly told from a woman's perspective, which offers a fresh outlook in this male-dominated body of literature. They also describe the migration of people to Buenos Aires, many of whom return to the colonies disillusioned when their dreams did not come true in the metropolis (Lockhart, "Rebeca Mactas"). Stephen A. Sadow provides a useful survey with regard to contemporary literature that reconstructs in a variety of ways the era of the colonies ("La colonia judía"). Prominent among such authors is Gerardo Mario Goloboff with his beautiful and evocative Algarrobos trilogy (*Criador de palomas* [1984; The Pigeon Fancier]; *La luna que cae* [1989, Falling Moon]; *El soñador de Smith* [1990; The Dreamer of Smith]). I have come across no text, however, that is quite so original as Marcelo Birmajer's short story "En la noche de bodas" (2000; Wedding Night) in the way it both pays homage to and challenges the gaucho judío master narrative. The explicit inscription of homoeroticism in the text functions as a means of boldly planting new thematics such as queer issues (long considered a taboo subject in Argentine Jewish writing) in familiar territory (Lockhart, "Lo queer").

There is probably no author in Argentina who has so consistently undertaken the programmatic narrative project of writing the Jewish experience as Ricardo Feierstein. From his *Sinfonía inocente* trilogy (Innocent Symphony, 1979–1984) to the novel *Mestizo* (1988, rev. 1994) to his latest achievement *La logia del umbral* (2001; The Lodge of the Threshold) and many texts in the interstices, Feierstein has dedicated himself to telling a sometimes painful, sometimes joyous, but always truthful story. *La logia del umbral,* while consisting of a panoramic telling of the Jewish presence in Argentina, has a particularly contemporary catalyst that sets the novel in motion and links it to the past. Descendants of the Schvel (the surname is Yiddish for "threshold," *umbral* in Spanish; thus the title) family embark on a voyage on horseback from the agricultural colony their ancestors settled in to the Plaza de Mayo in central Buenos Aires. The purpose is to unequivocally assert the rightful place of the Jewish community in Argentine society. Plans for their triumphal cavalcade into the city on July 18, 1994, are violently foiled by the terrorist attack on the Asociación Mutual Israelita Argentina (AMIA), a major Jewish institution in Buenos Aires. This tragic event serves as the genesis for the recounting of the story that led up to it. The message is clear throughout the novel: the history of Jews in Argentina has been a troubled one, with many obstacles, and in the end Jews are still not fully accepted into Argentine society either as gauchos or as intellectuals.

There are at least two feature films (and several documentaries) that incorporate the Jewish gaucho image, one more directly than the other. There also was a musical stage production in 1995 called *Aquellos gauchos judíos* that debuted in the Teatro Nacional Cervantes, perhaps the most important theatrical venue in Buenos Aires. It was written by Roberto Cossa and Ricardo Halac and directed by Jaime Kogan — two leading playwrights and director, respectively — with lyrics by Mauricio Kartun, another major dramatist. *Aquellos gauchos judíos* presents the epic story of the arrival of Jews to Argentina, the agricultural settlements, and the struggle to build a better life in the new Promised Land. The play met with relative success but has never been published.

In 1975 the renowned Argentine film director Juan José Jusid adapted Gerchunoff's text for the big screen. While Jusid's film *Los gauchos judíos* does not adhere entirely to the original stories, it does portray the same idealized vision. It is, in fact, an odd film, a rarity in Argentine film history in that it is a musical. The characters often break into song and dance, which adds to the glossy feel-good nature of the film. Though it is overdetermined by stereotyped depictions of Jews and Jewish life, it is not without merit and even its own charm, and indeed is now considered a classic film (it has been released in DVD format). Its cast of actors is a veritable who's who of Argentine cinema (Víctor Laplace, Pepe Soriano, Luisina Brando, China Zorrilla, among others).

Interestingly, one of the most telling aspects of the film is the initial reception it received, even before it was released to the public. In 1975 José López Rega was minister of social welfare under the floundering second Perón government. Juan Perón died in 1974, and his wife, Isabel, assumed the presidency. López Rega was also the leader of the Triple A (Alianza Anticomunista Argentina), an extreme right-wing paramilitary force formed to fight leftist subversion; it was also tremendously anti-

Semitic. It is general knowledge that López Rega controlled the government under the puppet figure of Isabel Perón. Jusid describes his experience with the censorship officials during this time regarding the making of the film and its release:

> With *The Jewish Gauchos* I had to put up with, let's say grotesque, arguments. . . . One day the censors call me and say, "Okay, Jusid, the government, López Rega and everyone else agrees. You will be allowed to debut the film, but you have to change the title. *The Jewish Gauchos* is an offensive title. A gaucho cannot be a Jew." So I suggested to him that we call it "The Not So Jewish Gauchos . . ." That was a very costly film. They burned the sets in Campo de Mayo in an attack and we had to build them again from scratch. In addition they placed bombs in the cinemas. (Quoted in Goity 87)

Such an incident shows the political and ideological stakes at hand regarding the mere term *gaucho judío* (i.e., who can lay claim to the noble heritage of the gaucho and who cannot). It is at the same time an example of a mild scrape with the anti-Semitism that would get much worse with the neo-Fascist military government that held the country hostage from 1976 to 1983.

In 2001 Argentine cinema again returned to the Jewish colonies with Antonio Ottone's film *Un amor en Moísesville* (shown in English as *Divided Hearts*). Moísesville is the most famous of the Jewish settlements and has become a tourist attraction, especially for foreign tourists interested in Jewish history. Víctor Laplace again plays a principal character, David, in this film next to Cipe Lincovsky (a major female actor of stage and screen). The plot is simple enough; a prodigal son returns to his birthplace, Moísesville, on the occasion of the centenary celebration of its founding. After an absence of many years he is, predictably, haunted by numerous ghosts of bygone years, forced to confront his past, and willing to reconcile differences with his estranged father. The film is somewhat flawed by the sappy, unbelievable love story (David falls for the daughter of the woman he left behind) and weak plot. It was not a box office success and did not receive many positive reviews. Perhaps the saving grace of *Un amor en Moísesville* is the cinematography. What the film does achieve in no uncertain terms is to demonstrate that, like so many other texts, the mythology of the *gaucho judío* origins survives as a salient component of the Jewish Argentine cultural heritage.

While the rural Jewish experience essentially provided one lasting

icon in the popular culture register, the move to the vibrant urban setting of Buenos Aires allowed for a wellspring of different cultural manifestations to flourish. Of course, socioeconomic, political, and educational
advancements as well as notable social changes have created a vast infra-
structure capable of sustaining significant production and consumption
of popular culture. In spite of serious obstacles and setbacks, the Jewish
community in Buenos Aires has been able to thrive because there have
also been many factors that contribute to its success.

Just as the *gaucho judío* myth is associated with rural history, there are
a number of urban stories that have stuck in the popular imagination. The
colectividad judía (Jewish collectivity) in Buenos Aires has always constituted a fairly important aspect of the city's social character. As one of the
major immigrant groups that flooded into the city at the turn of the twentieth century, Jews entered into the social fabric of *porteño* society with
a discernible presence. This presence has been portrayed in literature by
Jewish and non-Jewish authors alike, in both positive and negative ways,
and there are numerous excellent studies that examine these issues. A significant difference between the rural and urban past is that whereas the
Jewish gaucho is largely a romantic fabrication, most of the urban experience is more steadfastly grounded in historical reality. I do not want to
spend too much time on literature here since I want to focus on other types
of textual production. However, I believe that at least one topic medi-
ated through literature is worth mentioning in brief specifically because it
forms part of the Jewish collective memory unique to Argentina, and consequently it forms part of the urban lore. I am referring to the (in)famous
Jewish white slave trade run by the Zwi Migdal, a criminal organization
famous for operating a widespread prostitution ring from approximately
1900 to 1930. The Zwi Migdal essentially deceived and kidnapped young
Jewish women and maintained them in brothels virtually as slaves. They
were known popularly as *polacas* (Polish women), a synecdoche for any
Jewish prostitute of eastern European or Polish extraction. News of this
cruel exploitation of naive young women spread far beyond the borders of
Argentina and has been extensively written about by many historians and
writers. Principal among the historians is Albert Londres, whose *The Road
to Buenos Ayres* (1928; originally published in French, 1923) is largely considered responsible for bringing the situation to the attention of the international community. Mirelman dedicates a good portion of his book to
detailing the rise and eventual ruin of the Zwi Migal (337–378). Likewise,
the Yiddish writers Sholem Aleichem and Isaac Bashevis Singer, among
others, wrote stories and novels centered on the topic. While interest in

the international community was piqued, in Argentina it created a veritable furor. Writers, Jewish and non-Jewish alike, have created a fairly large corpus of works dealing with the Jewish white slave trade. Non-Jewish writers, in part, used it as a weapon against the Jewish community to advance their nationalist agendas and accuse Jews of corrupting Argentine society. This was a ludicrous accusation, given that the majority of prostitutes and those involved in prostitution were in fact not Jewish and that a favorite figure in Naturalist literature is the downtrodden prostitute as victim of circumstance and an unjust society. For the Jewish community, it was a source of embarrassment and an impediment to integration. Jewish writers have tended to be sympathetic in their depiction of the prostitutes, and literature on the subject covers a span of many years from César Tiempo (pseudonym of Israel Zeitlin) to writers as contemporary as Mario Szichman and Nora Glickman. Tiempo is famous for pulling off a literary hoax in which he wrote a series of poems under the assumed identity of a *polaca* named Clara Beter (Bitter). His *Versos de una...* (1926; Verses of a ... [here one is meant to insert "whore"]) earned a great deal of notoriety. It was widely read and the unknown, uneducated prostitute-poet was applauded for her talent and candor. When the truth came out that Tiempo was in fact Clara Beter, it caused a colossal uproar.

Nora Glickman (an Argentine writer and professor who lives in the United States) is undoubtedly the person who has taken up the theme of the Jewish white slave trade with the most fervor. Her seminal study *La trata de blancas* (1984) traces the history of the Jewish white slave trade in Argentina and its presence as a literary motif. Included in the study is a translation into Spanish of the Yiddish author Leib Malach's play *Ibergus* (*Regeneración*, 1926), the first work in Latin America to deal with the topic. Glickman later expanded her study under the title *The Jewish White Slave Trade and the Untold Story of Raquel Liberman* (2000). It is the most comprehensive study to date on the subject and is valuable for the way it combines historical information and a useful survey of the theme in literature and film. The most well-known film and the one that deals most directly with the slave trade is *Camino del sur* (1988; The Road South), a title that recalls Londres's account. The film (an Argentine-Yugoslavian collaborative production) re-creates the "process" by which a young girl in Poland would be transformed into a *polaca* in Buenos Aires. It also offers a reasonably authentic depiction of the period and the squalor of the living conditions while playing into the popular gangster myths associated with turn-of-the-century lower-class immigrant neighborhoods.

In addition to the general history of the white slave trade, Glickman dedicates the second half of the book to telling the personal story of Raquel Liberman. Liberman is probably the single *polaca* whose image and story has attained an almost legendary status in the collective memory of the Jewish community. She is known for bringing about the downfall of the Zwi Migdal through her courageous—often portrayed as heroic—act of testifying against them. She herself has been the subject of several literary works and even a television miniseries (Glickman, *The Jewish White Slave Trade*, 60–61). Her story is re-created through the many materials provided to her by Liberman's descendants. These primarily include facsimiles of documents such as a passport, a work permit, a health certificate, a birth certificate, and a copy of her *ketuba* (marriage contract), in addition to many photos. One especially rare type of document included is facsimiles of correspondence between Liberman and her husband and children written in Yiddish and Spanish, with corresponding translations into English. The death of her husband soon after arriving in Argentina is what occasioned her to seek work in Buenos Aires and leave her children to be cared for by a friend. It was then that she fell into the trap of the Zwi Migdal. The letters lend a sense of intimacy to the story and allow the reader a glimpse into the tragic circumstances of Liberman's life. The book can be considered a popular culture artifact for the way it combines a variety of textual registers into a unified discourse that manages to reevaluate a previously taboo *shanda-far-di-goyim* (shame in front of non-Jews) side of history and turn it into a cause to celebrate triumph over adversity.

Glickman's interest in telling this story does not end with the documentary study. In her play, *Una tal Raquel* (2000; A Certain Raquel), she transforms the historical record into a brilliant artistic representation. The drama is structured through the device of flashbacks, as Liberman's granddaughter begins to question her about her past, from which the story unfolds commencing with her life in Poland prior to immigrating to Argentina. The play follows the course of Liberman's life and includes many of the leaders in the Zwi Migdal as well as the deputy police commissioner Julio Alsogaray, who led the campaign against the organization and convinced Liberman to testify against them. One of the scenes that stands out in the play is the confrontation between the prostitutes and pimps and the general public in a Yiddish theater where they have gone to see a staging of Malach's *Ibergus*. In fact, throughout the play Glickman does a thorough job of representing the conflict between the Zwi Migdal and the Jewish community. She cleverly inserts a number of intertextual references that come from sources as diverse as Aleichem and Humberto Costantini (another Argentine author who wrote on Liberman). The play draws to a close with the granddaughter exuberantly declaring: "Mi abuela era una heroína judía y yo ni siquiera sabía quién era!" (My grandmother was a Jewish heroine and I didn't even know who she was! [59]). Essentially this is the message of the play, which functions as a historical revision of the image of the *polaca*. The most recent literary telling of Liberman's life story is the detailed biographical novel *La polaca* by Myrtha Schalom, complete with photographs.

Food enters the domain of popular culture in a way that perhaps nothing else can, since food is an unavoidable part of daily life. Like language, food is also one of the most significant elements of identity formation and definition. Food and food-related rituals unite ethnic groups around a common practice and set them apart as unique from others. How food relates to culture has been studied in anthropology, sociology, and, more recently, literature, and it is by now clear that our culinary habits and traditions are worthy of examination for what they can reveal and teach us. A popular culture approach to food can provide insight into how we go about attaching value to what we eat. In Jewish culture food is particularly important because of its link to religious ceremony and ethnic identity alike. There are several kinds of texts one can turn to in order to gain a better understanding of the role food plays in our lives. These may include an array of literary texts, restaurant menus, cookbooks, magazines, and television cooking shows. There are two authors, Silvia Plager and Ana María Shua, who I believe demonstrate extraordinarily well how food is negotiated in a popular culture context.

Silvia Plager is a prolific author, not only in the sense that she has written more than ten books, but also because her books are a diverse sampling of her talent as novelist, short story writer, essayist, and humorist. Her cleverly amusing novel, *Como papas para varenikes* (1994; Like Potatoes for Varenikes), is a parody—as the title overtly insinuates—of *Como agua para chocolate* (1989; Like Water for Chocolate) by the Mexican writer Laura Esquivel (for a complete analysis, see Lockhart, "Love and Knishes"). Plager's novel follows a format similar to Esquivel's; a recipe for a typical Jewish dish (latkes, borsht, kreplaj, knishes, varenikes, gefilte fish, etc.) precedes each chapter. There are more differences than similarities, however, between the two novels. Whereas Esquivel's novel focuses on the overly emphasized oppressed life of the protagonist with some elements of humor, Plager concentrates on creating humorous, even ludicrous situations each more outrageous than the preceding one. Moreover, whereas Esquivel places her novel in rural Mexico, steeped in popular (pueblo) tradition, Plager's setting is modern-day Buenos Aires as a postmodern locus of cultural hybridity. Plager also consciously inverts the center-periphery paradigm by making Jewish culture the dominant force, while her Hispanic-Catholic assistant, Eduviges, strives to assimilate through such efforts as adopting Yiddish expressions. Perhaps wary of distancing the novel too far from familiar Hispano-Catholic tradition, the author also astutely has Cathy lay claim to being a cultural heir of Santa Teresa and Sor Juana Inés de la Cruz (14), and this places her within a strong feminist tradition at the same time. There is a good deal of mocking of the magical realist style that comes close to turning Esquivel's novel into a cliché. In *Como papas para varenikes* food is inextricably linked to the insatiable erotic desires of Cathy Goldsmith de Rosenfeld and her suitor-lover Saúl Steinberg. Both are widowed and well beyond middle age, which also breaks another stereotype. Cathy is the owner of a catering business, and she is frequently contracted to cater Bar and Bat Mitzvahs, weddings, graduations, and brises. She is at odds with her nemesis-competitor, Sara Rastropovich, who threatens to steal some of her clients in the Jewish community. Virtually every aspect of the novel has some relation to food, either in a humorous way or in a somber or telling way such as exemplified in the following passage.

> That's how doña Berta was: a Jewish woman with memory. And that's how her daughter Catalina was. Both felt that an unstocked pantry and refrigerator was too close to being like a concentration camp, war, death. Food was life. (19)

The novel ends with a kind of appendix, a text discovered to be a "Kama Sutra para golosos" (Kama Sutra for Sweet-tooths) in which sexual positions are meant to imitate the form of a given Jewish food or symbol (a bagel, a kishke, a Star of David, a menorah). Questions of sexuality are in fact explored quite thoroughly, particularly in relation to Jewish tradition. The novel is a truly original text that combines parody and popular culture with tremendous acuity.

Ana María Shua also blends culture with cooking in an innovative way in her *Risas y emociones de la cocina judía* (1993; The Joys and Emotions of the Jewish Kitchen). I have analyzed this text at length elsewhere (Lockhart, "Is There a Text in This Gefilte Fish?") as an example of the relationship between food and Jewish culture, but it merits mention here as one of the best examples of a Jewish popular culture text in Argentina. The book is highly entertaining and practical, with a simple premise—to provide recipes (over eighty) for traditional eastern European Jewish dishes and to describe in a witty, lighthearted way how such dishes relate to tradition and culture. One of the cleverer accomplishments of the book is how it presents the uniqueness of Jewish-Argentine cuisine as a hybrid product of multiple influences, for example, how the enormous consumption of beef in Argentine society and the Italian influence have made their mark on Jewish food. Shua also amusingly addresses topics such as the problems faced by the modern Jewish working wife and mother who is expected to prepare traditional foods for her family, dietary laws, and the presence of food in Jewish literature (including Gerchunoff's *Los gauchos judíos*). *Risas y emociones* thus enters into a dialogue with readers who share a common background and in doing so creates a sense of community.

In this last division of popular culture production I focus primarily on humor texts. There are many studies on Jewish humor dealing with how jokes, cartoons, popular sayings, and similar expressions of wit reveal a worldview that in large part is unique to the Jewish cultural experience. While there are certainly regional differences—a joke in the United States may not be funny in Argentina, or vice versa—it is also true that Jewish humor seems universal or at least shares many commonalities from one geographic region to the next. A good contemporary example of how humor translates well cross-culturally is plain to see in the fact that the American television situation comedies *The Nanny* and *Seinfeld* are both favorites in Buenos Aires.

The appearance of humor and popular tradition books is a somewhat recent phenomenon on the cultural scene in Buenos Aires. In fact, in the past ten years there has been a minor boom of books that in some manner address these themes. Witness, for example, the success of Shua's series, *Cuentos judíos con fantasmas y demonios* (1994; Jewish Stories with Ghosts and Demons), *El pueblo de los tontos* (1995; The Village of Fools), an anthology of "traditional Jewish humor," and *Sabiduría popular judía* (1997; Popular Jewish Wisdom). These titles, joined with her *Risas y emociones*, form a considerable group of texts that are direct manifestations of the rise in interest in Jewish popular culture in Argentina. Other volumes include the humor anthologies *Del Edén al diván: Humor judío* (1994; From Eden to the Divan: Jewish Humor), *Las ídishe mames son un pueblo aparte* (1994; Yiddishe Mames Are a People of Their Own), Silvia Plager's *Al mal sexo buena cara* (1994; Putting on a Good Face for Bad Sex), and, most recently, Rudy (humorist Marcelo Rudaeff) and Eliahu Toker's *La felicidad no es todo en la vida y otros chistes judíos* (2001; Happiness Isn't Everything in Life and Other Jewish Jokes). The universal appeal of Jewish humor is stressed in their book with material on or by Scholem Aleichem, Woody

Allen, Groucho Marx, and Jerry Seinfeld. Shalom Ediciones in Buenos
Aires was the main publisher of these kinds of texts (it is now defunct).

I would like to proceed with a discussion of three of these books as
prime examples of Argentine Jewish humor writing. *Del Edén al diván*
is typical in its range of humor categories but somewhat atypical for including an extensive selection of sketches, images, cartoons, and carica-
tures. Beginning with a section on humor in the Bible and the Talmud,
the book then separates examples of Jewish humor by geography and ethnicity (eastern Europe, the United States, Latin America, Sephardic humor, western Europe, the Soviet Union, and finally Israel). Like many Jewish texts in Argentina, including literature, the volume contains a glossary
of Yiddish, Hebrew, and Ladino words or expressions to aid the reader
(mainly the non-Jewish reader) in deciphering the linguistic intricacies of
the humorous texts, many of which rely on subtle language code-switching
to deliver mordant drollery, acerbic wit, or irony. Simply put, the joke
doesn't pack the same punch without the proper linguistic codification.
Most of the examples of humor are extracted from literary texts, and this
is the case for the section on Latin American Jewish humor titled "De
la Amazonia a la Patagonia" (From the Amazon to Patagonia). Authors
from Argentina (Mario Szichman, Alicia Steimberg, Samuel Pecar, Ana
María Shua), Brazil (Alberto Dines, Moacyr Scliar, Eliezer Levin), and
Peru (Isaac Goldemberg) are chosen to represent the distinct flavor of Jewish humor in Latin America.

This alone makes for noteworthy and entertaining reading, but what
I find most interesting about *Del Edén al diván* are the cartoons, because
they provide acute observations on Jewish culture almost instantaneously
with a shrewd sense of whimsy. A significant number were drawn by the
well-known artist and illustrator León Poch (see Poch). Not all deal specifically with Jewish popular culture in Buenos Aires, but many do, and
these are the ones I find particularly valuable for assessing how humor—
especially visual humor—functions as a vehicle for representing the negotiation of Jewishness in public urban spaces. The cartoon about the call
for a mohel (Fig. 2) plays with different stereotypes as it underscores the
rural-to-urban historical shift and raises questions of cultural and identity
dissonance. The figure of the *gaucho judío*—once again—with his socio-
historical and cultural attachments provides the basis on which the joke
works. In this case he and his fellow Jewish gauchos represent the norm.
Since he lives a great distance from the city, perhaps clinging to a vanishing
(in reality vanished) lifestyle, he does not have ready access to organized
community services and religious functionaries, such as a mohel. He must

FIGURE 2. *"Hello, this is Samuel. My son was born in this town out here in the middle of nowhere. There's no mohel. I'd like you to send one out to do the circumcision. / Mazel tov, Samuel! I'll send you one from Buenos Aires. / Tell me, haven't you ever seen a **porteño**?"* (From **Del Edén al diván: Humor judío** *[Buenos Aires: Shalom, 1994].*

place a call to Buenos Aires. The first strip sets up the obvious differences between life in the country and life in Buenos Aires, modern versus old-fashioned. When the mohel arrives he appears obviously disoriented as he gets off the train in the middle of nowhere. At first he startles the native Jewish gauchos by his strange appearance, but then he is seen as a curious attraction. Confounded by the attention he has drawn he asks "Haven't you ever seen a *porteño?*" The lines are clearly marked here along identity stereotypes—not between Jews and non-Jews but between city and country Jews. The humor is derived from the surprise last word of his question. The expectation is for him to ask if they've never seen a mohel, since the Orthodox garb is more apt to be associated with him as a religious official and explain their sense of wonderment over the exotic clothing. However, by asking if they've never seen a *porteño,* the humor is derived from the assumption that all *porteños* dress like Orthodox Jews. The cartoon does a superb job of conjugating the *gaucho judío* past with the idea that Buenos Aires is a Jewish city.

The cartoon of the two beggars (Fig. 3) provides a different outlook as it examines Jewish ingenuity and survival techniques in an environment that is predominantly Catholic. Sitting in front of a cathedral, the two beggars are outfitted with semiotic markers that plainly define their outward appearance as Catholic and Jewish. As one would expect, the Catholic beggar is the only recipient of alms from the well-to-do parishioners as they enter and leave. When the priest suggests that the Jewish beggar try his luck in front of a synagogue, it is revealed that both beggars are Jewish as one wryly remarks to his partner that the priest has no business sense. The joke speaks to the fact that Jews may often have to get things done in roundabout ways when dealing with a society that does not accept them as they are.

The final two cartoons work purely on visual cues, since there is no written dialogue. They both show, in satirical fashion, how Jews have come to be a permanent presence in Buenos Aires and how they move about in all social situations, from simply going about their daily business to participating in the national sport. One cartoon shows what may be called a "Jew crossing" (Fig. 4) and indeed could represent any busy day on the streets of Buenos Aires, especially in and around the Once commercial district, which at one time was the predominantly Jewish residential and commercial area. Now most residents have moved to outlying neighborhoods or into the upper-middle-class Barrio Norte, for instance, but many Jewish businesses still remain in and around Once. While the vast majority of Jews in Buenos Aires are secular and dress like any other *porteño*

FIGURE 3. *"I believe, good man, that this is not the place for you. Why don't you situate yourself in front of a synagogue?"*
"Nu, Moishe, How about that? Now he thinks he can teach us how to do business."
(From **Del Edén al diván.***)*

FIGURE 4. *Del Edén al diván.*

(again this is what makes the mohel joke so funny), there are areas like Once where it is not uncommon to see greater numbers of Orthodox Jews in traditional attire. The other cartoon (Fig. 5) shows two teams of Orthodox Jews playing in a soccer match. Of course, what makes it humorous is to see that the players are dressed in their traditional clothing, heavy coats and hats, in opposition to what one expects for a soccer uniform. The combination of stereotypes—Jews wear funny clothes; all Argentines are obsessed with soccer—may be hyperbole, but it also metonymically dem-

FIGURE 5. *Del Edén al diván.*

onstrates that Jewish Argentines glean cultural identity from both sources of their cultural heritage.

The book *Las ídishe mames son un pueblo aparte* is similar to the previous one, but it is dedicated to the single topic of Jewish mothers. It does imitate to a certain degree the same categories: the Jewish mother in Israel, in the Bible and the Talmud, in eastern Europe, and in the United States. The section on Latin America is titled "La ídishe mame posmoderna" (The Postmodern Jewish Mother) and primarily contains literary excerpts from Argentine writers (Diana Raznovich, Ana María Shua, Eliahu Toker, Manuela Fingueret), along with a couple by the Brazilian Moacyr Scliar. The three scenes taken from a longer comedy, *La liberación de la señora Sara* (The Liberation of Ms. Sara), by Raznovich, stand out in the anthology for the humorous situation they present. Raznovich is one of the most astutely talented playwrights of the contemporary theater in Buenos Aires, and she is an accomplished cartoonist. Several of her drawings are included in the volume. The drama plays with all the stereotypical characteristics attributed to the Jewish mother: passive-aggressive, long-suffering, overfeeding, the ability to dole out guilt in large quantities and manipulate her children. After problems arise in their relationship, Bérele and his mother agree to go to couples therapy. The ensuing situation is a hilarious account of the contradictions between seeking freedom from a seemingly oppressive mother and trying desperately to hold on to her at the same time. Bérele's slogan in the play is his repeated statement, "Mame, para que todo cambie vos tenés que quedar igual" (Mame, for everything to change you have to stay the same). In the end the "couple" reconciles, and they go home, where the mother has a big plate of varenikes waiting for her son. Other examples of humor in the book are popular sayings and a comparison of what Ashkenazi and Sephardic mothers tell their sons and daughters. Though the book pokes fun at the stereotype of the Yiddishe Mame, it is in fact an endearing homage to Jewish mothers that crosses cultural boundaries and once again provides a valuable Latin American contribution to Jewish humor — something that all too often goes unnoticed or unrecognized.

Both of these anthology-type humor collections can be considered milestone texts for the valuable contribution they make. They are instrumental in bringing together international sources while simultaneously showcasing the unique tenor of Argentine Jewish humor. Notwithstanding, Silvia Plager's collage of texts in *Al mal sexo buena cara* is easily the best Jewish humor book to come out of Argentina. It is an indispensable tool for gaining a better understanding of Jewish Argentine popular culture. Plager, to date, has not received the kind of critical attention her work as a gifted and perceptive humorist or as a prose fiction author deserves. The book is an obvious product of the author's own upbringing in the Jewish community of Buenos Aires and consists of a systematic examination of the idiosyncrasies associated with that community. Her range of topics includes religion, marriage, social attitudes and protocol, Jewish mothers, sexuality, and even a Jewish horoscope. Likewise, it covers a wide range of sites throughout the city: from the home to the country club, from the *shopping* (mall) to the gynecologist's office. Structurally, the book is divided into different parts that can be read as separate units: a section of popular Jewish sayings, a fictionalized sex manual written by the ersatz Professor Veisaj Bus titled "El matrimonio judío perfecto" (The Perfect Jewish Marriage); the aforementioned horoscope; "Memoirs of a Jewish Princess from Junín and Corrientes" (a major crossroads in a traditionally Jewish neighborhood); "The Thousand and One Faces of a Yiddishe Mame"; and even more absurd, "What a Jewish Mother Carries, Doesn't Carry, Would Like to Carry in Her Purse." The titles themselves provide a good clue to what awaits the reader. Plager's humor is sharp, perceptive, and sometimes scathingly critical or charmingly endearing. On the surface it is an entertaining read, but it is also ripe with interpretive possibilities that are better explored in a full-length analysis (Lockhart, "*Al mal sexo buena cara*"). Space constraints here allow me only to present it as an outstanding illustration of Jewish popular culture imagination in Buenos Aires.

There are in fact many more types of texts that could be included in this study. An example that immediately comes to mind would be photo histories of the Jewish community in Buenos Aires, such as *Judíos & argentinos/Judíos argentinos* (1988; Jews and Argentines/Jewish Argentines), published by Manrique Zago, or the more recent *Comunidad judía de Buenos Aires 1894–1994* (1995; Jewish Community of Buenos Aires), published by the AMIA. They pertain to popular culture for the vast amount of information on every aspect of Jewish life in Argentina, and a visual culture studies analysis could be done on the photographs alone. The AMIA book provides an excellent panorama that ends with the terrorist attack on the institution, which is now entirely rebuilt and functioning better and stronger than ever. A volume that specifically pertains to the AMIA tragedy, *Sus nombres y sus rostros* (1995), was compiled by Eliahu Toker. It contains photos and information about all the victims of the terrorist attack and is meant to be an album of remembrance of those who lost their lives on July 18, 1994.

There is a good selection of films that could be discussed as well that narrate the Jewish experience. *Pobre mariposa* (1986; Poor Butterfly), written by Aída Bortnik, comes to mind as one of the best Jewish films produced in Argentina. Recently the young director Daniel Burman, has made his mark with films like *Un crisantemo estalla en Cincoesquinas* (1997; A Chrysanthemum Bursts in Cincoesquinas), the critically acclaimed *Esperando al mesías* (2000; Waiting for the Messiah), and most recently a documentary, *Siete días en El Once* (2001; Seven Days in Once), and the feature film *El abrazo partido* (2004; Lost Embrace). Films such as *Esperando al mesías* and Eduardo Mignogna's *Sol de otoño* (1996; Autumn Sun) speak eloquently to the post-AMIA reality of Jewish Argentina.

The Jewish community is already moving full steam ahead with regard to defining Jewish culture for the next century. Evidence of this is seen in the conference held at the AMIA in 2001 titled "Re-creating Judeo-Argentine Culture 1894–2001: On the Threshold of the Second Century," organized by Ricardo Feierstein and Stephen A. Sadow. The proceedings of the conference, published under the same title, reflect the kind of issues affecting the Jewish community and the kind of topics people are reflecting on as they examine the past and look to the future. In this essay I have strived to continue along this same line of thinking. This effort is meant to provide some insight into new directions of study and convincingly argue that Jewish popular culture is a significant and important component of Argentine culture; that in fact this hybrid urban phenomenon with rural beginnings, local, global, and multicultural influences, is the remarkable result of one hundred years of cultural cross-pollination.

WORKS CITED

Aizenberg, Edna. *The Aleph Weaver: Biblical, Kabbalistic and Judaic Elements in Borges.* Washington, D.C.: Scripta Humanistica, 1984.
———. "Jewish Gauchos and Jewish 'Others,' or Culture and Bombs in Buenos Aires." *Discourse* 19.1 (1996): 15–27.
———. *Parricide on the Pampa? A New Study and Translation of Alberto Gerchunoff's "Los gauchos judíos."* Madrid: Iberoamericana, 2000.
AMIA. *Comunidad judía de Buenos Aires 1894–1994.* Buenos Aires: Editorial Milá, 1995.
Un amor en Moísesville. Dir. Antonio Ottone. 2000.
Avni, Haim. *Argentina and the Jews: A History of Jewish Immigration.* Trans. Gila Brand. Tuscaloosa: University of Alabama Press, 1991.
Camino del sur. Dir. Juan Bautista Stagnaro. 1988.

Un crisantemo estalla en Cincoesquinas. Dir. Daniel Burman. 1997.

Crónicas judeoargentinas. 1: *Los pioneros en ídish: 1890–1944.* Buenos Aires: Editorial Milá, 1987.

Esperando al mesías. Dir. Daniel Burman. 2000.

Feierstein, Ricardo, ed. *Alberto Gerchunoff: Judío y argentino.* Buenos Aires: Editorial Milá, 2000.

———. *Historia de los judíos argentinos.* Buenos Aires: Planeta, 1993.

———. *La logia del umbral.* Buenos Aires: Galerna, 2001.

———, comp. *Los mejores relatos con gauchos judíos.* Buenos Aires: Ameghino, 1998.

Feierstein, Ricardo, and Stephen A. Sadow, eds. *Recreando la cultura judeoargentina. 1894–2001: En el umbral del segundo siglo.* Buenos Aires: Editorial Milá, 2002.

Foster, David William. *Buenos Aires: Perspectives on the City and Cultural Production.* Gainesville: University Press of Florida, 1998.

———. *From Mafalda to Los Supermachos: Latin American Graphic Humor as Popular Culture.* Boulder: Lynne Rienner, 1989.

Franco, Jean. "Globalization and the Crisis of the Popular." 1996. In *Critical Passions: Selected Essays,* ed. and introd. Mary Louise Pratt and Kathleen Newman, 208–220. Durham: Duke University Press, 1999.

———. "What's In a Name? Popular Culture Theories and Their Limitations." 1982. In *Critical Passions: Selected Essays,* ed. and introd. Mary Louise Pratt and Kathleen Newman, 169–80. Durham: Duke University Press, 1999.

Gerchunoff, Alberto. *Los gauchos judíos.* 1910. Buenos Aires: Sudamericana, 1957.

———. *The Jewish Gauchos of the Pampas.* Trans. Prudencio de Pereda, foreword Ilán Stavans. Albuquerque: University of New Mexico Press, 1998.

———. *La jofaina maravillosa: Agenda cervantina.* Buenos Aires: Losada, 1938.

Glickman, Nora. *The Jewish White Slave Trade and the Untold Story of Raquel Liberman.* New York: Garland, 2000.

———. *La trata de blancas: Regeneración.* Buenos Aires: Pardés, 1984.

———. *Una tal Raquel.* In *Teatro,* 19–60. Buenos Aires: Nueva Generación, 2000.

Goity, Elena. "Juan José Jusid." In *Cine argentino en democracia: 1983–1993,* ed. Claudio España, 86–87. Buenos Aires: Fondo Nacional de las Artes, 1994.

Hinds, Harold E., Jr., and Charles M. Tatum, eds. *Handbook of Latin American Popular Culture.* Westport, Conn.: Greenwood Press, 1985.

Itzigshon, Sara, et al., eds. *Integración y marginalidad: Historias de vidas de inmigrantes judíos en la Argentina.* Buenos Aires: Pardés, 1985.

Lockhart, Darrell B. *"Al mal sexo buena cara: Silvia Plager y la cultura popular judía."* In *Recreando la cultura judeoargentina/2: Literatura y artes plásticas,* 2 vol., ed. Ricardo Feierstein and Stephen A. Sadow, I. 198–208. Buenos Aires: Editorial Milá, 2004.

———. "Is There a Text in This Gefilte Fish? Reading and Eating with Ana María Shua." In *El río de los sueños: Aproximaciones críticas a la obra de Ana María*

Shua, ed. Rhonda Dahl Buchanan, 103–116. Colección Interamer 70. Washington, D.C.: Organización de los Estados Americanos, 2001.

———. "Lo queer en un cuento de Marcelo Birmajer." In *Recreando la cultura judeoargentina. 1894–2001: En el umbral del segundo siglo,* ed. Ricardo Feierstein and Stephen A. Sadow, 150–156. Buenos Aires: Editorial Milá, 2002.

———. "Love and Knishes in Buenos Aires: Silvia Plager's *Como papas para varenikes.*" Forthcoming.

———. "Rebeca Mactas." In *Jewish Writers of Latin America: A Dictionary,* ed. Darrell B. Lockhart, 358–362. New York: Garland, 1997.

Los gauchos judíos. Dir. Juan José Jusid. 1975.

Londres, Alberto. *The Road to Buenos Ayres.* New York: Blue Ribbon Books, 1928.

Mirelman, Víctor A. *En búsqueda de una identidad: Los inmigrantes judíos en Buenos Aires 1890–1930.* Buenos Aires: Editorial Milá, 1988.

Pavlotzky, José. *Un gaucho judío: payadas sabáticas.* Buenos Aires: Berenice, 1980.

Plager, Silvia. *Al mal sexo, buena cara.* Buenos Aires: La Mandíbula Mecánica; Planeta, 1994.

———. *Como papas para varenikes.* Buenos Aires: Beas Ediciones, 1994.

Pobre mariposa. Dir. Raúl de la Torre. 1986.

Poch, Susana. "León Poch: 70 años de arte argentino y judío: La vida de una obra; la obra de una vida." In *Recreando la cultura judeoargentina. 1894–2001: En el umbral del segundo siglo,* ed. Ricardo Feierstein and Stephen A. Sadow, 140–149. Buenos Aires: Editorial Milá, 2002.

Rowe, William, and Vivian Schelling. *Memory and Modernity: Popular Culture in Latin America.* London: Verso, 1991.

Sadow, Stephen A. "La colonia judía a través del prisma de la ficción argentina actual." In *Recreando la cultura judeoargentina 1894–2001: En el umbral del segundo siglo,* ed. Ricardo Feierstein and Stephen A. Sadow, 127–139. Buenos Aires: Editorial Milá, 2002.

Senkman, Leonardo. *La identidad judía en la literatura argentina.* Buenos Aires: Pardés, 1983.

Shua, Ana María. *Cuentos judíos con fantasmas y demonios.* Buenos Aires: Shalom, 1994.

———. *El pueblo de los tontos.* Buenos Aires: Sudamericana, 1995.

———. *Risas y emociones de la cocina judía.* Buenos Aires: Shalom, 1993.

———. *Sabiduría popular judía.* Buenos Aires: Ameghino, 1997.

Sol de otoño. Dir. Eduardo Mignogna. 1996.

Stavans, Ilán. *The Riddle of Cantinflas.* Albuquerque: University of New Mexico Press, 1998.

Tiempo, César. *Versos de una . . . 1926.* In *Poesías completas,* 1–41. Buenos Aires: Stilman Editores, 1979.

Toker, Eliahu, ed. *Sus nombres y sus rostros: Álbum recordatorio de las víctimas del atentado del 18 de julio de 1994.* Buenos Aires: Editorial Milá/AMIA, 1995.

Toker, Eliahu, and Patricia Finzi, eds. *Las ídishe mames son un pueblo aparte.* Buenos Aires: Shalom, 1994.

Toker, Eliahu, Patricia Finzi, and Moacyr Scliar, eds. *Del Edén al diván: Humor judío.* Buenos Aires: Shalom, 1994.

Toker, Eliahu, and Rudy [Marcelo Rudaeff], comps. *La felicidad no es todo en la vida y otros chistes judíos.* Buenos Aires: Grijalbo, 2001.

Zago, Manrique, ed. *Judíos & argentinos, judíos argentinos.* Buenos Aires: Manrique Zago Ediciones, 1988.

DAVID WILLIAM FOSTER

Gabriel Valansi

NEOLIBERAL NIGHTS IN BUENOS AIRES

Gabriel Valansi (b. 1959) is one of a group of eleven Argentine photographers who were featured in a 1999 exhibition, *Myths, Dreams, and Realities in Contemporary Argentine Photography,* at the International Center of Photography (ICP) in New York; he works as both a professor of photography at the University of Buenos Aires and an artistic adviser at the Museo de Arte Moderno de Buenos Aires. He is also a contributor to the photography magazine *Fotomundo* (founded in 1966).

Valansi's work is radically different from that of the other participants in the ICP exhibition, in the sense that it essentially does not directly feature human figures, that it concentrates on a nocturnal cityscape, and that it is determinedly "anti-aesthetic" in its use of not only found objects but also ones that appear to have been abandoned as garbage. Like other photographers in the ICP exhibition, however, Valansi makes almost exclusive use of black-and-white images, albeit ones of enormously high resolution that enable large contact prints. Yet ambiguity of image is essential to much of Valansi's work; although one can draw a certain global sense from the series, there are individual images that do not immediately lend themselves to objective identification, as they appear to fluctuate between impressionistic foregrounded patterns of light and a fragmentation of the outlines of images expected in conventional work. Some viewers might even find the term "surreal" appropriate here, because of the dreamlike landscape. These qualities are enhanced by the nocturnal loss of foreground/background perspective. Although Valansi has dealt with other themes, he is well known for work in Buenos Aires in the dead of night, and it is this cycle of work, a 1988 series titled *Fatherland,* on which I concentrate here (*Fatherland,* in turn, is part of a series of related projects, *Zeitgeist* [2000] and *Epílogo* [2000–2001]).

To speak of the "deep" hours of the *porteño* night is almost to speak of a no-man's land, since one might well ask when during the night the streets of Buenos Aires are empty of human comings and goings, when businesses are closed, and the intense combination of Argentine sociability and the imperative to live it on the street ebbs. To be sure, one of the effects of neoliberalism in Argentina has been to sharpen class divisions and to produce an increasing class of individuals excluded from the sort of prosperity that has made Argentine public life so unique in Latin America—at least a public life in terms of superavid consumption, the display of cultural accomplishments, and, simply, the enjoyment of the virtues of the flâneur. It is a city where in many areas (especially the older commercial ones and the prosperous northern tier of neighborhoods that stretches west along the Río de la Plata) night ends only with the first weak light of morning.

Part of the context of this photography is the fact that neoliberalism cast a pall over the nightlife of the central city (a pall, it must be stressed, that began to be felt in the 1970s, before neoliberalization, which began in the early 1990s), not only by encouraging its move elsewhere, through the construction and promotion of new venues, but also because of the impoverishment of much of middle-class life and the subsequent profound devastation of overwhelming sectors of the Argentine population since the closing months of 2001. In one sense, any perception of a deep night in at least the old central core of the city is an index of that process, to the extent that it is a direct consequence of it.

Moreover, Valansi's work, especially what I examine here, comes on the cusp of the transition from a still more-or-less functioning neoliberalism to what, without putting too fine a point on it, must now be identified as something like the Third Worldization of Argentina: Argentina, especially Buenos Aires, the capital (huge sectors of the country were already becoming increasingly impoverished by neoliberalism well before the last quarter of 2001), is now facing the prospect of having to live like the rest of Latin America. The most immediate manifestation of this is that illegal workers from neighboring countries who poured into Buenos Aires to sustain the underbelly of neoliberalism, as portrayed in Adrián Caetano's Dogma-style film *Bolivia* (2001), have fled back to their respective homelands. If they are going to starve in the streets, they might as well do so back home; besides, the streets may be occupied by starving Argentines.

Valansi's 1998 exhibition, *Fatherland*, was shown at the Fotogalería del Teatro San Martín, the most important official cultural space of the municipality of Buenos Aires. In an interview with Pablo Garber at libroarte.com, Valansi has the following to say about this series of forty photographs:

> *Fatherland* is a continuity of [the] idea of "end of the party," but at the same time it is a register of what I call "the hidden holocausts," which are those holocausts that are not for the media and do not have spectacular results filled with death and desolation. They have a subtle structure and "they are accepted by the free world," but overall, they continue to be holocausts. . . . [The idea behind *Fatherland* is] to try to give clues that have to do with a "neutronic" registry, that is to say, they do not leave behind any dead bodies, or craters, but they do exist. And like Argentina lived its holocausts and lives one now: I tried to tell its story in *Fatherland.*[1]

Valansi makes specific reference to Robert Harris's 1992 novel about the Holocaust, *Fatherland,* and this reference provides enormous resonance to his work, in which he counts on a series of cultural references in the Argentine sociopolitical consciousness. First, Argentina has a special relationship to the Holocaust, not just because Buenos Aires is one of the great Jewish cities of the world (and, therefore, home to many Holocaust survivors), but also because Argentina historically has had a large German immigrant population. Adolf Eichmann's arrest there brought world attention to Nazi influence in Argentina. This influence was strong throughout the 1930s and World War II, and, as is well known, during the first Peronist government (1946–1952), Argentina became a haven for Nazi war criminals such as Eichmann (Camarasa; Goñi).

In addition, that the military regimes of recent decades (1966–1973, 1976–1983) were overtly modeled along neo-Nazi lines has kept alive the sense of a "fascist tradition" in Argentina (Deutsch and Dolkart; Viñas). The slang adjective *facho,* derived from the more academic *fascista,* is commonly used to describe an abiding authoritarian mentality and forms of behavior alleged to embody it. Valansi is Jewish, so it is understandable that he would be particularly sensitive to a *facho* strand in the Argentine national ethos ("Lo que este país necesita es una mano dura" [What this country needs is a strong hand] is a common refrain) and, as his adjective *encubierto* signals, to the ideological processes by which this mentality is ignored, argued away, hidden, or transformed into something else.

The return to constitutional democracy in Argentina and the much-touted trial of the military officers that made up the ruling Juntas, along with many of their most notorious subalterns, were evidence of a shift in the country's institutional climate. Yet the violence of the Ménem years (the 1990s) was manifest—all too apparent, for example, in the virtually officially sanctioned persecution of journalists; the virtually officially sanctioned corruption by agents of the government and segments of the business and banking communities and their cohorts; and the economic upheaval wrought by neoliberalism. All these may be interpreted as the sort of "hidden holocaust" that Valansi has in mind. It was hidden not in the sense that people did not know that violence was taking place but rather because the majority of its victims—the common folk—were never consistently recognized as such. Indeed, the synergetic effects of unchecked neoliberalism and flagrant corruption have brought the country to an unprecedented point of stagnation, exhaustion, and despair. Argentina is not alone in Latin America in terms of major social problems, but it is far easier to point to the photographable consequences of public violence in, say, Colombia than it is to the hidden violence in Argentina.

But Valansi's point would be that that violence is now not quite so hidden. Others may photograph the evidence of that violence in terms of the victims of street crime that has turned the once absolutely safe Buenos Aires into a place as dangerous as any other metropolitan area. For a long time, curiously, Buenos Aires was always safe despite the repressive acts of what the current president, Eduardo Luis Duhalde, once called the "terrorist state," and this was not just because of the facile belief that fascism makes for safe streets. Others may also photograph the creeping way in which a megacity with narrow streets and many buildings now more than a century old can suddenly begin to show clear signs of decay; and at that, even at the height of the prosperity induced by neoliberalism in the early 1990s, public buildings were never very well maintained.

Valansi's photography takes a much subtler approach to the recording of social reality in the context of the ongoing holocaust of economic violence. The absence of human figures from his work, given that the human environment was built by humans to serve specific human needs while also being adapted, expropriated, and reclaimed for complementary and supplementary needs, would seem to negate the need for the buildings. Many people feel that abandoned buildings and sites need to be recycled, rebuilt, or cleared because they constitute eyesores, if not places where crimes and various kinds of delinquency are carried out. It is, therefore, rather difficult to be convincing as regards a poetry of vacancy or the absence of human figures.

In the case of night scenes, certainly vacancy occurs with the conventional rhythm of social life. However, this vacancy is relative; in the case of Buenos Aires, where it has been customary for residents to be out and about at night and where there are many venues to accommodate them, one of the interests in photographing at night becomes as much this greater use of public spaces at night as it is, through counterpoint, the perception of the decline of this use.

Valansi's opening image, the signature piece for the exhibition, is intriguingly mysterious. From a distance, the image appears to be an impressionistic pattern consisting of a dark background with a foregrounded pattern of glowing white spots. A line of smaller white spots snakes up the image vertically and elbows off to the left, only to return to a perpendicular position as it bleeds off the top of the image. Around this central line smaller clusters of dots organize themselves into a combination of rectangles and random groupings. Closer inspection reveals that the spots are the lights that one would typically associate with a nighttime cityscape: high-intensity street lights (or, perhaps, a combination of high- and medium-intensity ones), lighted billboards, car lights (note, however, that it has only been the enormous increase in automobile traffic in the city that has brought the mandatory use of high beams), and some buildings. The pattern that emerges when one realizes this is a nighttime cityscape is that of a part of the city in which a freeway, with its looping access ramps, constitutes the horizontal axis of the image, with an exit to an important arterial that snakes up the image and bleeds off its top margin. Lower-intensity lights that border major and minor streets and mark the parameters of city blocks form the rectangular patterns.

The relative irregularity of these patterns would seem to suggest that this is the central core of the city (as befits a city whose definitive foundation dates from 1580; there was an abandoned attempt to found Buenos Aires in 1536) that, though a long way from being as randomly nongeometric as medieval European cities, is made up of relatively small blocks that are often poorly lighted, whose geometry is often interrupted by diagonals, alleyways, and bisecting and irregularly drawn boulevards. The phenomenon of "streets that don't go through" is frequent in the center city. Since the rectangles in the image are not punctuated by other points of light, one can believe that it is very late at night. That is, there are few white spots that can be attributed to the lights of houses or businesses.

I am describing this perceived layout of the city in such detail because the inaugural image makes a defining statement about the sequence of photographs as a whole. And that is done in terms of the juxtaposition of the freeway and the necessarily older arterial that feeds into it: older, because the arterial was probably there before the freeway, especially given its irregular line.[2] There are not many freeways in Buenos Aires (just as there are, generally, not many in all of Latin America): they are too expensive to build and maintain, and their installation is too disruptive of a residential, commercial, and industrial life that is often precarious enough without the effects of massive relocation. Although there are some design and execution problems with the freeways the military imposed on the city beginning in the 1970s — indeed, it is easy to believe that the freeways could only have been built by a tyrannical regime powerful enough to ignore common needs — there is no question that these roads have been important for the commercial and industrial life of the city, especially in providing rapid access to the Ezeiza international airport, some twenty miles west of downtown and previously extremely difficult to get to because the traveler departing from the administrative and financial center had to cross the entire city before reaching the two-lane highway that completed the journey.

Moreover, confirming the proposition that if you build freeways, the cars will come, the three- or fourfold increase in cars in Buenos Aires that came with neoliberalism would have been virtually impossible without the freeway, and the same is true of the residential development of the suburbs west, northwest, and southwest of the city that have been prized as part of the American lifestyle whose incorporation — or implantation — was crucial to neoliberalism. Thus where this image becomes eloquent is in juxtaposing the traditional arterial, which owes its irregular line to having developed in conformance to geographic irregularities and gradual urban expansion, and the modern freeway, which cuts a brutal swath across the cityscape, creating massive disruptions and dislocations and often constituting an abiding environmental problem for the neighborhoods through which it passes. Although it is possible to control fumes and noise, as many European and American cities claim they are doing, the increase in traffic and traffic-related accidents is not something that can be controlled, since, quite the contrary, an increase in traffic is exactly what the freeway is meant to produce (one of the best examinations of the urban consequences of freeways is Mike Davis's discussion of the issues surrounding the creation of freeways in that paradigm of the freewayed city, Los Angeles).

The large-scale image of the city of the anchor photograph of *Fatherland* is complemented by several other views of the general urban landscape. There is one, for example, that is a map of the midsection of the country, one that is also built on lights indicating population concentrations (I do not know if this is a formal demographic representation or if it is a figurative one created by Valansi). The result is to show the domination of the province of Buenos Aires and, within it, of the city of Buenos Aires: if Argentina is accused of living with its back to the rest of Latin America, the province of Buenos Aires lives with its back to the rest of Argentina and the city of Buenos Aires lives with its back to the rest of the province and the rest of the country and the rest of the continent. There is a long history of struggle relating to the role of Buenos Aires. The creation of La Plata in 1880 to serve as a decentralized capital of the province was meant to address the power imbalance between the city and the province of Buenos Aires, and the designation of Buenos Aires in 1996 as an autonomous federal capital was intended to separate out the responsibility of the city for its own administration, independent from the federal budget off of which it had grown accustomed to living. In 1940 the social essayist Ezequiel Martínez Estrada published *La cabeza de Goliath* (The Head of Goliath), in which he posited a master trope for the relationship between Buenos Aires and the rest of the country, that of the enormous head and the feeble body. This trope became all the more apparent with recent economic processes, because so much of the rest of the country experienced growing impoverishment alongside the overwhelming concentration of capital in Buenos Aires.

The migration of *cabecitas negras*[3] from outlying provinces, mostly to the north, begun during the Peronista period and under very different ideological, social, and economic circumstances nevertheless continued and intensified because there was no work to be had except in Buenos Aires, and it was complemented by the influx of migrants from surrounding Latin American countries. In Valansi's photograph, the all-roads-lead-to-Rome concentration of lights in the Buenos Aires area is an echo of the liberalization of the metaphor, in the sense that it duplicates the very real way in which the railroad system of the nineteenth-century liberal economy worked: It was designed to carry Argentine exports to the port for shipment to Europe and to facilitate the importation of European luxury items to the mansions of the city and the rural estates of the wealthy exploiters/producers of the exports (for the history of this development, see Scobie). These lights are, in turn, complemented by the lights of other urban concentrations in the country, such as the subsidiary cities of Córdoba, Mendoza, and Rosario.

However, the photograph is very effectively dominated by the reflection, in dead center, of the flash of the photographer's camera. This dead-centering of the flash has no function in terms of artistic symmetry. Rather, it is meant to correlate with — and dominate — the lights of Buenos

Aires and other urban, commercial, and financial centers, as the constituting punctum of the photographer's interpretation, by falling on the northern part of the province of La Pampa, partially blotting out the spot on the map Valansi uses where the capital city of La Rosa is located. The province of La Pampa is the Argentine heartland, and its name is the very geographic designation that is most famously associated with the land of Argentina, the vast Pampa that supports its historically most important and prosperous industry, cattle ranching. Interestingly, in the schematic map of Argentina that I have at hand, prepared by the Instituto Geográfico Militar, this area is represented as minimally settled (*Atlas de la República Argentina*). This is true literally, in the sense that it is part of a collection of small towns that network the vast cattle ranches of this and the other provinces of the industry, La Pampa, Córdoba, Santa Fe, and Buenos Aires. In this sense, there is the evocation of the symbiosis linking Buenos Aires and the cattle ranches that is integral to so much of Argentine social and political history.

But there is another way to read this image, and that is in terms of the devastation of the countryside by the neoliberal concentration of the metropolis and its satellite cities. Under the old liberal economy, there was something like a balanced exchange between the countryside and the port city (or port cities, since Rosario, upriver from Buenos Aires, is also a major shipping port): the countryside produces the export wealth, a percentage of which Buenos Aires got as the customs port; the imports this wealth bought was distributed between the wealthy *estancias* (cattle ranches) and the city that served their interests. Indeed, it was customary for the cattle barons to have, in addition to their often quite magnificent country mansions (see the estates featured in *Argentine Ranches*), fancy apartments, or equally magnificent mansions in the city. The large-scale development of industry spurred by Perón in the late 1940s upset this balance, beginning with the transfer of cheap labor from rural areas (which included large numbers from the indigenous north) to the city, which, in the 1990s, was supplemented by the influx of cheap laborers from surrounding countries. It upset the balance because it represented only a minimal transfer for wealth back to the provinces: Buenos Aires became more and more of a universe unto itself, further exacerbating the trend that Martínez Estrada had perceived more than a decade earlier. The consequence has been the unchecked impoverishment of the countryside, so much so that despite any previous perception that Latin America really began outside Argentina's borders, one could now maintain that it begins with the Avenida General Paz that wraps around the southwestern,

western, and northwestern edge of Buenos Aires (the south is bordered by the Riachuelo tributary and ship canal; the north and east, by the Río de la Plata).

A third image continues the transposition of geographic images into photography for the purpose of imagining the centers of symbolic and real control of Argentine society. Just as the train system funnels into and fans out from Buenos Aires as part of the historical control of the entire country by the port city, the subway system, whose origins date to the heyday of Argentine prosperity at the beginning of the twentieth century (the first line was opened in 1910), shows the same sort of pattern as regards the executive and financial center of the city vis-à-vis the outlying neighborhoods (for an interesting series of photographs of the Argentine subway system, see Barreda). Ground zero of the city, on the edge of the old colonial core, is the Casa Rosada, the Argentine Government House; directly to the north extends La City, the financial district. These are the areas served by the original subway system, and the original line (Línea A, which runs under Avenida Rivadavia, the city's principal avenue) ends beneath and behind the Casa Rosada; there are two more lines (D and E) that branch out from a station close to that terminus, and there is a line (B) that runs parallel to A along Avenida Corrientes; it is anchored at Correos, the nineteenth-century palatial main office building of the postal service (Correos is one of the major edifices of the oligarchic liberalism of the late nineteenth century; the Casa Rosada incorporates the previous seat of the postal service and goes back to the colonial period of the eighteenth century). There is also a perpendicular line (E) that links two of the three main railroad stations (Retiro on the north end—actually a cluster of three stations—and Constitución to the south; the third rail station, Miserere—also known as Once—is the western terminus of the A line). Currently, a sixth line (H) is being built west of the city. When completed, it will be the only line outside the center of real and symbolic power.

Thus this image too records the organization of power in the Fatherland. But there is another dimension to this photograph: Valansi has rescued an information board from the Pasteur station of the Corrientes line (Línea C). This was the station in the heart of the old Jewish quarter of Once just blocks from the seat of the Asociación Mutualista Israelí Argentina (AMIA), which was bombed by terrorists in July 1994. The death and destruction caused by the bombing was extensive, and one small trace of the devastation of that blast is the fact that the sign's contacts were frozen at their indication of the Pasteur station; it was years before the sign was repaired.

The three photographs I have discussed so far are related to abstract social interpretations that rely on essentially geometric images of the city. However, the photographs that follow in the exhibition are more immediately personalized: whereas the first images represent overarching questions of economic and political control, the remaining images reflect the actions and circumstances of specific human beings. Though the photographs do not directly record these agents, they do record their actions and circumstances: what we see is the detritus of human lives as they pass through the neoliberal system. I have used the word *detritus* because these images capture metonymically the processes of an economic system that produces waste, garbage, leftovers, material excrescences, and discarded and disposed-of items from daily life. Like an archaeologist reconstructing the nature and dynamics of a society through its garbage — and so much of what archaeologists do dig up is the garbage of the past — Valansi the photographer is analyzing the garbage of present-day Argentina. This detritus appears on the streets at night, as what is replaced each day by the fundamental capitalist principle of programmed obsolescence is discarded to make way for the new, which in this case are the fruits of participation in the global system of imported goods or, at least, goods that are a step up in some way by comparison to what is being discarded. In a crowded modern city, this is garbage that appears on the sidewalks at night, to be carted off by the garbage service — although, with the economic debacle currently gripping the nation and the city of Buenos Aires, there is not only less garbage on the street, but what there is, is exhaustively combed by organized networks of garbage pickers (the *cartoneros*), cousins of those who sift through the metropolitan garbage dumps of the world. Garbage is here a metonymy for the system because it is a byproduct of it, both in terms of the nature of what constitutes garbage and in terms of the way in which garbage is recycled by a society. Finally, since garbage is something that appears at night, in part because much of it is what is generated by human activity and commerce in the course of the "business hours" of the day, it is in the *porteño* night that Valansi must do the analytical work of his photography.[4]

Let us now examine other major images in the exhibition. Among the most obvious faces of the neoliberalist economy are an enormous number of new businesses. Buenos Aires has always been an intensely commercial city, one that prides itself on the number of boutiques, bookstores, restaurants, bars (the city has some of the best bar life in the world, with "bar" being understood here in a far broader sense than the usual American use of the word; perhaps a combination of British pub and French café begins to capture this great *porteño* social institution), along with myriad specialty shops. The opening of new businesses often meant recycling spaces, some with a measure of elegance. This is the case with the bookstore that opened in an old art deco movie house, the Cine Gran Splendid, with the stage area used as a café. Tax credits were available for modernizing and refurbishing older locales, which for some habitués meant, regrettably, the loss of the early-twentieth-century patina that was their most attractive feature.

An interesting detail of this photograph is the disposition of the two mechanical arms that were part of the record player, the stabilizing arm that held the stack of records level and the tone arm that held the stylus that actually read the record's grooves. The arms are crossed in an X, as though suggesting the annulment of the usefulness and usability of the equipment. The tone arm is positioned as though uselessly playing the recordless turntable: there are no more records like this to play.

One of the major items discarded during the periods of *la plata dulce* (the sweet money) and neoliberalism were cars. Those who knew Argentina in the 1960s will recall that the city was filled with ancient cars, many of them venerable Mercedes-Benzes that were bought from Germany after the war. There were cars of somewhat dubious quality made by local subsidiaries of American and European companies, and the tin can–like Citroën, jokingly said to lend itself to disassembly in a matter of minutes with a can opener, was ubiquitous. There were some American imports, but it was generally assumed that they belonged to embassy personnel or other officials. The more than tripling of the number of cars clogging the streets of Buenos Aires in the 1990s meant not just increasing the number of cars geometrically, but getting rid of the old cars as unworthy of the new First World image it was the order of the day to promote.

Valansi's images of a smashed and, apparently, abandoned vehicle figure this dimension of the new economy. One image is of a car seat— one that seems not all that old, because it is possible to discern the female buckle of the seat-belt installation; the seat is covered with smashed-in glass from one of the windows. Another image shows the open trunk, with some sort of garbage dumped into it. Even if the car(s) in question may not be exactly the ancient ones replaced by the influx of new vehicles in the late 1970s and the past decade, they symbolize the "luxury" of the trashing and abandonment of vehicles in a product-replacement/substitution economy. Cars are the quintessential icon of modernity and of personal and collective prosperity, and the greater the complexity of the modern(ized) economy, the more vital cars are as instruments of the mobility that economy requires for both the production and the consumption of goods.

Finally, one last image, that of a discarded painting (likely to be a reproduction); two halves of the piece of art are piled on top of one another, back-to-back, with half of the image exposed. Tucked between the two torn halves is a newspaper. Newspapers are of the day, to be read and discarded; as the saying goes, there is nothing as trite as yesterday's news. By contrast, art, even that art that is preserved in inexpensive and mass-produced reproductions, is supposed to be eternal; yet here both are consigned to the same rubbish heap. It is as though the actuality of First World Argentina, which is what the newspaper would be reporting on (whether favorably or critically), brought down to its own level great works of art, which is the theme of the banalization of culture by neoliberalism and the replacement of the self-reflective nature of art by the superficial newness in which the reporting of mass-society newspapers were all that one needed to know. Both newspaper and artwork are being discarded, but the newspaper is intact, while it is the painting that is torn asunder.

Valansi's photographs in *Fatherland* are highly effective interpretations of the dark side of recent socioeconomic processes in Argentina as viewed through the hardly noticed detritus of the night. Not only does one not customarily scrutinize garbage (except for the highly organized garbage pickers that now make up a booming occupation in Buenos Aires), but it remains essentially unseen: dumped in the street or along the sidewalk at night, the citizen simply assumes that it will be gone by the morning, taken somewhere out of sight, so that no more than passing notice need ever be taken of the machine-produced excrement of modernity.

One closing note: Valansi gives his exposition a title in English. He has claimed, in the interview from which the quote at the beginning of this essay is drawn, that the title is taken from a novel (by Robert Harris) dealing with the triumph of Nazism. But the Nazi inflection would suggest the German *Vaterland*. The use of *Fatherland* in English suggests the resonance of American society, since understanding the complicity of, first, the military dictatorships and, subsequently, the new democratic governments with American financial interests is crucial to an adequate interpretation of the current degradation of Argentine national life.

NOTES

1. "Gabriel Valansi," http://www.leedor.com/fotografia/gabrielvalansi.shtml, accessed July 10, 2002. Translated by Monica Bruno Galmozzi.

2. Valansi has informed me in a personal communication (August 22, 2002) that the arterial is the Avenida 9 de Julio, which crosses the city, perpendicular to Rivadavia, from north to south (it is the one street that does not change name as it crosses Rivadavia). Valansi says that the image was taken from a plane as it approached the downtown Jorge Newberry airport, although he does not re-call whether the segment is north or south of Rivadavia; because of its jagged line, it is probably the southern section, which shifts somewhat east of its basi-cally straight-line path to avoid the Peronist landmark building, Obras Sociales (in its northward march, the Avenida shifts very slightly to avoid an equally im-portant landmark for the Argentine social elite, the palace that houses the French embassy).

3. *Cabecita negra* literally means "black head" and refers to the dark complex-ion (from the point of view of European-like Buenos Aires) of rural Argentines of indigenous origins; by extension, it also refers to Latin Americans from other countries, especially poorer ones. Thus the term, in addition to being a racial slur, has ethnic and socioeconomic overtones.

4. Valansi has shared with me the delightful fact that these photographs were made with a Kyocera camera that he rescued from being thrown in the garbage.

REFERENCES

Argentine Ranches: Cincuenta estancias representativas de la República Argentina. Buenos Aires: Casa Pardo, 1968.

Atlas de la República Argentina; incluye reseñas geográficas y cuadro estadístico. Buenos Aires: Librería "El Ateneo" Editorial, 1992.

Barreda, Fabiana. *La ciudad subterránea.* Buenos Aires: Magna Publicidad, 1998.

Camarasa, Jorge A. *Odessa al sur: La Argentina como refugio de nazis y criminales de guerra.* 2d ed. Buenos Aires: Planeta, 1995.

Davis, Mike. *City of Quartz: Excavating the Future in Los Angeles.* Photographs by Robert Morrow. London: Verso, 1990.

Deutsch, Sandra McGee, and Ronald H. Dolkart, eds. *The Argentine Right: Its His-tory and Intellectual Origins, 1910 to the Present.* Washington, D.C.: Scholarly Resources, 1993.

Duhalde, Eduardo Luis. *El estado terrorista argentino.* 1st ed. Barcelona: Argos Vergara, 1983.

Garber, Pablo. "Gabriel Valansi." *libroarte.com.* http://www.leedor.com/foto grafía/gabrielvalansi.shtml

Goñi, Uki. *The Real Odessa: How Perón Brought the Nazi War Criminals to Argentina.* London: Granata Books, 2002.

Scobie, James R. *Buenos Aires: Plaza to Suburb, 1870–1910.* New York: Oxford University Press, 1974.

Viñas, David. *¿Qué es el fascismo en Latinoamérica?* Barcelona: Editorial de La Gaya Ciencia, 1977.

RUTH BEHAR

While Waiting for the Ferry to Cuba
AFTERTHOUGHTS ABOUT *ADIO KERIDA*

In some ways you might say that my entire life was a kind of preparation for making my documentary, *Adio Kerida* (Goodbye Dear Love). After all, the film is about Cuban Jews and I am a Cuban Jew. Or rather, I'm a Cuban-American Jew or a Jewish Cuban-American. Or, as they say in Miami, I'm a "Juban." I was born a Jew in Cuba and came to the United States as a child. I grew up in New York, where I spoke Spanish at home and learned to speak English in school, and have spent a large part of my life explaining how it is that I am both Cuban and Jewish, since this combination of identities has continually baffled people in the United States, though less so in recent years, thanks to the discovery, at last, of multiculturalism.

Certainly one of my most basic motivations in making *Adio Kerida* was to find my own identity reflected in other Jewish Cubans. I wanted to make visible the way a variety of people negotiate the mix of being Jewish and Cuban. But the story quickly grew more complex than that. In the process of conceiving *Adio Kerida,* I made a strategic political choice. I decided to focus on Cuba's Sephardic Jews, rather than look at the whole Cuban Jewish community, which includes Ashkenazi as well as Sephardic Jews. In other words, rather than look at Jewishness as a single, monolithic category, I chose to call attention to the diversity of the Jewish experience and to challenge the Ashkenazi-centered view of what it means to be a Jew.

In grant proposals I wrote to seek funding for the project, I explained who the Sephardic Jews are in the following way:

Sephardic Jews view themselves as Hispanic people who are connected to both the Arab and African worlds because of their history of cultural and emotional interpenetration with those worlds. They descend from the Jewish populations expelled by the Spanish Inquisition in the fifteenth century. After the expulsion, they settled in the countries of the Ottoman empire and northern Africa, which welcomed them and made it possible for them to live as Jews among Muslims. "Sepharad" means Spain in Hebrew. Sephardic Jews are notable for having clung with a passion to their nostalgia for Spain and their love for the Spanish language, despite having been forced to leave Spain because of their ethnic and religious identity. They are misunderstood and often discriminated against by the mainstream Eastern European Jewish world, which can only imagine Jewish identity in terms of the novels of Philip Roth and the movies of Woody Allen. Beyond the Jewish world, Sephardic Jews are virtually unknown as a community and they are almost invisible in the contemporary world of literature and the arts. The Cuban Sephardic community, both on and off the island, offers so rare a mix of cultural traditions—Spanish, Turkish, African, Jewish, Cuban, and American—that it remains a mystery and has not yet been portrayed in any depth in literature, art, or film.

My own autobiography motivated me to want to learn more about the Sephardic Jews. Although both my parents were born in Cuba, they brought to their marriage quite distinctly different Jewish traditions. To be less diplomatic about it, let's just say they argued a lot when I was growing up. It took me years to understand that their disagreements were rooted in the cultural split between my mother, the daughter of Ashkenazi immigrants from Poland and Byelorussia, and my father, the son of Sephardic immigrants from Turkey. In my mother's family, my father was known as "el turco," and this was not a term of endearment. Instead, it was a way of referring to my father's hot temper, unforgiving soul, and patriarchal dominance. The Ashkenazi side, who thought of themselves as more rational, tolerant, and modern, viewed those character flaws as elements of a primitive Turkish character. I learned this early in life, because whenever my mother got angry at me she'd say I was just like my father. And my mother's family, in which I largely grew up, always reminded me that with my dark, curly hair, my less than good temper, and my own inability to forgive, I too was more like my relatives on the other side, more like the "turcos."

In retrospect, I realize that I was fortunate to have known more than one way of being Jewish. It allowed me to understand from an early age that Jews were a diasporic people and had always had to find ways to creatively mesh their Jewish identity with the culture of the people they lived among. On a more critical note, I learned early on that, for reasons that eluded me, the Ashkenazi Jews had gained the upper hand in defining what it meant to be a Jew. When I was growing up, on the first night of Passover we always held our first Seder at the home of my maternal grandparents and ate gefilte fish, matzo ball soup, and boiled chicken. On the second night, always *the second night,* we went to the home of my paternal grandparents and we ate *haroset* made with raisins and dates, egg lemon soup, stuffed tomatoes, and a holiday almond cake dripping with honey; this cuisine, my mother always reminded me, was very delicious but very bad for our figures, and indeed my father's mother was quite fat. Finally, at the end of the eight days of Passover, as if trying to resolve the contradiction of our doubled Jewishness through gastronomic means, my father would insist on taking my mother, my brother and me to El Rincon Criollo on Junction Boulevard for Cuban black beans and palomilla steak with onions.

In short, the Sephardim were mysterious to me, even though as a "halfie" and an ill-tempered soul I was a part of them. I didn't really know who these people, "my people," were. It all came down to the basic fact that being my father's daughter and being Sephardic were inseparable things for me. Inheriting my Sephardic identity from my father was a vexed issue because for many years he and I were locked in a contest of wills. In our life together, my father had either been absolutely furious with me or not speaking to me at all. As a teenager I'd upset him by going to college against his will, and as a grown women I'd upset him by writing stories about him and my mother that he thought shamed and dishonored them. When I began to travel regularly to Cuba in the 1990s, I further upset him by returning to the country from which he had fled at great risk in the early 1960s, and he viewed my desire to reconnect with Cuba as yet another manifestation of my ingratitude and disrespect.

So naturally, given this history of heartbreak between my Sephardic father and me, I knew I had to make *Adio Kerida* and I had to make it for my father. Although I couldn't convince my father to go to Cuba with me, I would go and make this film for him. I would dedicate it to him, even if I had to do it against his will. I would show him what kind of people we are, we the Sephardic Jews, with our strong tempers and our inability to forgive. For despite the years of conflict with my father, I had never given up my Behar last name, the name I inherited from my father, the Béjar that is still the name of a town in northwestern Spain. And as I embarked on the making of *Adio Kerida,* it is this name that I would find all over Cuba, both among the living Sephardic Jews I met and the many Sephardic

Jews who have departed to the next world and whose tombs abound in the cemeteries of the island.

Once I realized that *Adio Kerida* would be for my father, I hoped that he would appear in the film. But my father vehemently refused. So I proceeded to begin filming in Cuba, until I could convince him to cooperate. One way or another, I was going to get him to be in my film, and this informed the other key strategic political choice I made in the early stages of conceiving *Adio Kerida.* I decided that I would include in my film both Sephardic Jews who remain on the island and Sephardic Jews from Cuba who now reside in the United States. This meant that my film would create a bridge that doesn't yet exist in reality. The Sephardic Jewish community of Cuba is divided by the politics of revolution and exile, and many members of the community who live in the United States are unwilling to return to Cuba or even to be in touch with fellow Sephardic Jews on the island. But at least in my film, these Cuban Sephardic Jews would be shown side by side, embracing their common Sephardic and Cuban heritage.

Adio Kerida was the culmination, for me, of a long process of reconnecting with Cuba and of forging ties with the literary, artistic, and intellectual communities of both the island and the Cuban American left in the United States. I have traveled back and forth to Cuba since 1991, going three times a year for brief but intense visits.

I first returned to Cuba in 1979 as a graduate student, in the hope of gaining permission to carry out my dissertation fieldwork in anthropology on the island. This was during the famous moment of the thaw in U.S.-Cuba relations led by then-President Jimmy Carter, when it appeared that normalization of relations would soon take place. After much internal debate, Cuba both released political prisoners and agreed to the family reunification program, which allowed more than a hundred thousand Cuban Americans who left the island in the 1960s to return to visit their families between 1978 and 1979. But then, in 1980, came the Mariel exodus, which took everyone by surprise, leading to the dramatic departure of 120,000 Cubans to the United States. Blame for the mass exodus was placed on the *gusanos,* the so-called worms of the revolution. The returning immigrants came to be viewed as a contaminating force, who returned to Cuba to flaunt the wealth they had obtained as immigrants in the capitalist U.S.A. Relations between the United States and Cuba returned to their previous freeze and Cuban Americans were again viewed as suspect by the official island sectors. My desire, as a Cuban American, to return to the island to do research was no longer looked upon with favor. Unable to go to Cuba, I embarked on a long detour as an anthropologist, doing research in Spain and then Mexico, before finding myself in Cuba again in the 1990s.

In 1979 it had been impossible to leave the city of Havana without official government permission. Foreign visitors, especially from the United States, were carefully watched. As a Cuban American I was especially suspect and was appointed my own personal spy. At the time I was too innocent to realize that the friendly young man, who always sat next to me on the bus and wanted to know everything about me, was surveying my activities.

When I returned in 1991, I discovered quite another Cuba, a Cuba whose survival now depended on tourists, including those who came from the great enemy to the north, from the same U.S.A. that was maintaining its embargo against the naughty Communist island, and making it illegal, in fact, for Americans to visit Cuba as tourists. This was a Cuba whose survival now also depended on offering a new kind of welcome, including to those Cuban Americans who were not the confident, idealistic Marxists who returned to Cuba with the Antonio Maceo Brigades of the 1970s. By the 1990s the island was extending its welcome even to those wishy-washy Cuban Americans of the left, uncertain liberals who hadn't yet made up their minds about Cuba.

The first years of the 1990s were painful years as Cuba sought to maintain its revolutionary goals while making the transition from being dependent on the former Soviet Union to becoming an independent player in the new global economy. The country was badly in need of hard currency and fell into an economic and moral crisis. On a Cuban television cooking show, Cuban women were shown how to make breaded grapefruit-rind "steaks" for their families to curb the sudden hunger. Contradictions between socialist ideology and everyday social life grew ever more dissonant. By the mid-1990s the U.S. dollar became a legal currency in Cuba. Essential items like soap, detergent, and cooking oil could only be obtained with dollars, yet Cuban salaries were still paid in Cuban pesos. The informal economy expanded as more and more Cubans went hustling for dollars, and tourism, including sex tourism, became a major sector for economic growth.

At the same time, after three decades of suppressing religious observance, the government ceased to penalize any Cubans, including Party members, who openly practiced religion. Increasing numbers of Cubans began to return to Catholicism, Protestantism, Judaism, and Santería, among other religions, in search of spiritual solace. In turn, with the return of God to Cuba, the island became safe again for Americans to visit.

The Americans began to come in record numbers, bolstered by the fact that the embargo permits Americans to travel to Cuba legally if they are traveling as part of a humanitarian mission to deliver religious assistance.

Not only was religion a legally open door for Americans to cross the border into Cuba, but so too was the larger category of cultural exchange. The charm that Cuba holds for so many American visitors has precisely to do with the fact that Cuba represents a form of utopian dreaming carried out in opposition to American political interests. By the late 1990s numerous Americans were traveling to Cuba in search of the unique independence of Cuban music, art, and literature. Ry Cooder's *Buena Vista Social Club* music CD, followed by Wim Wender's documentary about Cooder's heroic discovery of the lost ancient Cuban mariners, gave new nostalgic attention to Cuba and suggested to Americans that their embargo against Cuba was depriving them of the richness of Cuban culture.

The American market is now flooded with CDs of Cuban music (you can hear them in any Starbucks or Borders), new films about Cuba, novels and memoirs about Cuba, ethnographies of Cuban Santería, photography books about Cuba, and architectural studies of the island. A Cuban revolution is happening in the United States, and it has created an insatiable desire for all things Cuban.

My own return journey to Cuba, which began over a decade ago and is still in progress, unfolded in the midst of all these 1990s developments. As the years passed, and I traveled back and forth to Cuba from Michigan for more than thirty visits, I began to recognize that my return journey, even though it was profoundly personal and spiritual and began long before what I call "the Cuba boom," could not be seen as more or less exalted than the Cuba journeys of Ry Cooder, or the sex tourists, or the gallery curators, or Pastors for Peace, or Jewish Solidarity, not to mention the Cuba journeys of all the other Cuban Americans who were embarking on their own personal and spiritual quests.

I found myself unable to think of Cuba as a field site, and in my first emotional reencounters with the island I turned to poetry, one of my youthful passions, which I'd given up when I went to graduate school. Reconnecting with the Afro-Cuban woman who cared for me as a child and returning to the apartment where I'd spent my early childhood were all deeply moving experiences for me, which became sources for my poetry. But the anthropologist in me wanted to know whether my experiences had any social foundation, and so I became involved in creating a collective tapestry of voices and visions of Cubans of the island and Cubans of the Diaspora who were of my generation and likewise seeking a common culture and memory. This project turned into an anthology, *Bridges to Cuba* (1995), which I edited, and also led me to forge ties with Ediciones Vigía in Matanzas, an artisan publishing house that encouraged my efforts as a poet and writer and inspired me to start writing in Spanish as well as English.

During these years of visits to Cuba, I attended Jewish services at the synagogues in Havana and also took trips to the provinces to get to know the synagogues and Jewish communities in Cienfuegos, Camaguey, and Santiago de Cuba. But I wasn't in any way trying to study the Jews of Cuba. I myself was still uncertain about what my Jewishness meant to me. I'd spent years of my life studying Catholic cultures in Spain and Mexico and keeping my Jewish identity well hidden so as not to raise any eyebrows, especially since I was so readily accepted in the communities I studied because I am a native Spanish speaker. Although I took pleasure in meeting Jews in Cuba and found it moving to attend services at the Patronato synagogue in Havana, which is just down the street from where I lived as a child, I rarely snapped any pictures or carried out interviews.

I wanted simply to be a Jew in Cuba and not have to explain my identity to anyone. I found that the combination of Cuban pluralistic tolerance and revolutionary secularism made it easy to be a Jew in Cuba. I could openly say I was Jewish to any and every Cuban. This was immensely liberating after my years of *conversa*-like hiding of my Jewishness in Spain and Mexico. In turn, I felt comfortable among the Jews of the island because they were often as uncertain about their Jewishness as I was about mine. Not that Judaism was foreign to me. After all, I went to Hebrew School and can read liturgical Hebrew, and my family observed the major Jewish holidays. But over the years I'd lost touch with my Jewish identity. I was no longer sure what kind of Jew I wanted to be. I found it reassuring to be among Jews in Cuba who didn't quite know what to say or do at Jewish services, to be among Jews who were learning how to be Jews. If there was hope for them, there was hope for me. Later, as my son Gabriel's Bar Mitzvah approached and I decided to learn how to chant Torah along with him, I took pleasure in seeing that the Jews in Cuba, whom I'd gotten to know over the years, were becoming more confident and knowledgeable about their Jewishness too.

The four synagogues in Havana—Chevet Ahim, Adath Israel, El Patronato, and El Centro Hebreo Sefaradí—had never been shut down (although the fifth, the American synagogue, had been allowed to fall into ruins). Yet older people largely attended Jewish services during the 1960s, 1970s, and 1980s. The Jewish community, once at least fifteen thousand strong, had been decimated by the Cuban revolution, which undertook to nationalize the many small businesses owned by Jewish Cubans, the majority of whom left in the early 1960s and resettled in Miami and New York. With only a few thousand Jews left on the island, a number that eventually declined to around a thousand, it was difficult to maintain a strong Jewish community. In addition, the Cuban revolution frowned on religious observance of any kind. Jews weren't singled out for persecution because of their ethnicity or faith, but they chose like other Cubans to pull away from religion and to suppress any sense of their own ethnic difference in order to fully integrate themselves into the revolutionary process, which was firmly rooted in nationalism and unity.

But by the 1990s, in the new atmosphere of religious tolerance, Jewish families and Jewish young people began to flock to the synagogues. Most of these Jews were of mixed heritage, and many were discovering their Jewishness for the first time. Motivations for coming out as Jews were diverse. Some were attracted by the possibility of exploring their spirituality because it had previously been taboo. Others were glad for the Sabbath meals that were offered after the services. Yet others, learning that the Israeli government would cover the voyage and resettlement of Jewish Cubans who wanted to leave the island, treated the synagogues as travel agencies that could yield a ticket out of Cuba and to a new life in Israel.

Throughout the revolutionary period, Jewish life had been sustained on the island with the assistance of Jewish organizations in Canada and Latin America, which sent matzoh and wine on Passover and provided other modest but essential help. But it wasn't until the 1990s that major support began to arrive through the American Joint Distribution Committee and B'nai Brith. Helping the Jews of Cuba to survive as Jews became a priority of these Jewish American organizations, which set up "missions" to assist the Jews of Cuba through donations of food, medicine, clothes, and books, as well as through Jewish education, which is most desperately needed in a country where there is not even a single rabbi.

These "missions" had a very strong impact, indeed. By the end of the century, Jewish synagogue life in Cuba was beginning to more closely resemble standard Jewish practice in the United States. The Patronato synagogue, which I'd seen in the early 1990s with a leaking roof that let in the doves, had been restored to its former grandeur and updated with computers and a video screening room. Although the Jewish community in Cuba appeared to be shrinking as a result of elderly deaths and recent immigration to Israel, more and more Jewish American visitors continued to arrive on the island on goodwill missions to save the last of the Jews who survived Communism. Jewish American visitors became so ubiquitous that it seemed like every Jew in Cuba had at least ten Jewish Americans who wanted to help him or her continue being a Jew in Cuba.

The Jews of Cuba, by the end of the century, had become an exotic tribe. To outsiders, they had come to seem as rare as the Kung of the Kalahari Desert, and as overstudied, overobserved, overphotographed, over-anthropologized, and elusive.

In the midst of this largely Ashkenazi American "discovery" of Jews on the island, I entered the scene with a video camera wanting to make a documentary called *Adio Kerida* about the Sephardic Jews of Cuba, which would be dedicated to my Sephardic Cuban father. But where was I to place myself as a Cuban American Jew of mixed Ashkenazi-Sephardic heritage? It was December 1999, the century was ending, and I felt an immense urgency to begin telling the story I knew about the Jews of Cuba. I thought of following in the footsteps of the filmmaker Dennis O'Rourke and making a kind of Jewish Cuban version of *Cannibal Tours,* focusing my camera on the Jewish American tourists who came on missions to see the Jews of Cuba. I knew I was, to an extent, complicit in their exoticizing gaze, for in the end I too would be returning to the United States. And yet, though I wanted to incorporate a strong touch of irony in my film, it wasn't a tonality I wanted to sustain for the entire piece. There were too many other sentiments, experiences, and forms of knowing I wanted to examine. So I opted instead to show how my own shifting identity, as a returning Cuban Jew, a cultural anthropologist, and a tourist in my native country, opened a window onto a range of diasporic identities.

With minimal funds and little previous filmmaking experience (I'd studied photography and made a short 16 mm film in graduate school), I jumped into the project of *Adio Kerida,* assisted by Gisela Fosado and Umi Vaughan, graduate students in anthropology at the University of Michigan, who were embarking on their own ethnographic research projects in Cuba, in itself yet another phenomenon of the "Cuba boom." (For Anglo-American ethnography departed the island after the embargo, with the sole exception of Oscar Lewis's trilogy, which brought him much suffering. A new generation of young anthropologists is now doing ethnography in Cuba.)

I didn't have a script, and I had only a rough idea of who would be the main protagonists of the story. One thing I knew from the start: the documentary would be called *Adio Kerida,* which is the title of a popular Sephardic song of nineteenth-century origin. *Adio Kerida* was one of the few Sephardic songs I knew by heart and could actually sing. It was among the few remnants of Sephardic culture that had been passed on to me. And the song spoke of unforgiveness, the quality that my Ashkenazi family had seen as so strongly a Sephardic characteristic. It is, indeed, the bitter lament of a lover who utters an angry good-bye after a beloved's rejection.

I was drawn to the song because I felt it could reference many layers of good-byes, from the bitter good-byes of Sephardic Jews, who were forced to leave their beloved Spain in 1492, to the more recent good-byes of Sephardic Jews who had left Cuba in the 1960s, and yet more poignantly, to the immediate good-byes of those Sephardic Jews who were leaving the island for Israel even as I hurried to interview them for *Adio Kerida*. I also felt the song could reference the desire for return that is so often the other side of exilic departure, and speak to my own desire to find a way to return to Cuba, in contrast to my father's definitive good-bye and unwillingness to look back.

With the lyrics to the "Adio Kerida" song in my head, I went in search of Jewish spaces, the synagogues and Jewish cemeteries where Jews had left traces of their presence on the island. One of the most important epiphanies took place early in the process of filming. As José Levy Tur, the director of the Centro Hebreo Sefaradí, was showing us the nine Torahs brought to Cuba from Turkey by the Sephardic Jews, I could hear live Afro-Cuban music and singing from someplace close by. Interrupting the interview, I asked José Levy where the music was coming from, and he casually told me it was coming from next door, from the space that had once been the main sanctuary of the synagogue. As he explained, the Jewish community was now so small that their religious services had been moved to what had once been the women's meeting room, the room we were in. But what had been the majestic main sanctuary was located next door. Moving to the back of the room, we discovered a peephole through which we could look to the other side and see the musicians, who turned out to be Síntesis, a well-known Afro-Cuban musical group. We then went outside and entered through the main door of the synagogue to the old sanctuary, which was now used as a rehearsal space by Síntesis. They were rehearsing the song "Obbatala," a Santería deity, and I was struck by the way an Afro-Cuban working of spirit now inhabited what had once been a Jewish religious space.

I became fascinated by the idea of Jewish Cuban and Afro-Cuban religiosity existing side by side and realized I could explore this theme in the relationship between José Levy and his daughter, Danayda, who is Afro-Cuban and has been brought up Jewish by him. José Levy's relationship with his daughter, I saw, offered yet another take on the father-daughter theme, from the perspective of the island. And I was drawn to Danayda's strong sense of herself as Jewish and how she'd negotiated being both Jewish Cuban and Afro-Cuban.

Not long after, while observing the children in the Sunday Hebrew school at the Patronato synagogue, I met an Afro-Cuban boy, Miguelito, whose mother told me he liked to drum Afro-Cuban rhythms on the buckets he uses to take his bath. As soon as I saw him drumming passionately on the buckets, a Jewish star dangling from his neck, I knew that Miguelito had to be in my film. What I couldn't have predicted is that on my last filming trip in summer 2001, he would announce on camera his upcoming departure to Israel with his family. Joyful that he would hopefully soon be able to acquire brand-name drums in Israel, the tears came to his eyes as he spoke of having to say good-bye to his friends and classmates.

Alberto Behar, whose name, curiously, is the same as my father's, had already told another differently painful good-bye story to me. Alberto's revolutionary father, who rejected religion throughout his adult life, asked his son on his deathbed to bury him in the Jewish cemetery. Confronted at the cemetery with the need to say the Kaddish, the mourner's prayer, Alberto discovered he didn't know what the Kaddish was. He refused to simply repeat the words senselessly and was haunted for years by his inability to bid his father a proper good-bye. Only by learning to chant Torah was Alberto finally able to bring peace to his heart and say good-bye to his father. Telling this story was such a transformative experience for Alberto that he subsequently pulled together all of his savings and had a tombstone built for his father in the Jewish cemetery outside of Havana.

With these key stories in place, the Cuba section of the documentary began to take shape. In Miami, I looked for other cultural fusions and was immediately attracted to Alberto and Elza Habif, sellers of Turkish good luck charms, whose mirrored store is full of protective eyes. SAMY, a flamboyant gay hairdresser who keeps both a Jewish *hamsa* and a pair of scissors from the Vatican in his salon and whose grandfather, Samuel Cohen, "was like a rabbi," offered some very necessary humor and bold honesty, while the belly dancer Myriam Eli, who merges flamenco, Afro-Cuban, and Turkish traditions, raised key questions about the "boxes" into which identities have to fit in the United States.

My own relatives in Miami offered the closing fragments to the mosaic of Cuban Sephardic identity that has unfolded in the Diaspora. My uncle Enrique, a nouveau street peddler, sells clothes from his truck in the tradition of my grandfather and other Sephardic street peddlers from Turkey.

My aunt Fanny conserves a nightgown that belonged to her grandmother in Turkey and traveled with her mother, my grandmother, from Turkey to Cuba to the United States. And my cousin Isaquito uproariously remembers what it was like to grow up in a Havana tenement on Calle Oficios, where the Sephardic Jews, the *turcos,* lived upstairs and looked out on the sea, above the prostitutes below, and where sometimes even the nicest of Sephardic Jewish boys succumbed to the temptation of visiting the ladies they delicately referred to in Turkish as *oruspu.*

Finally it came time to go to New York to see if my father would agree to be in my film. Although my father said he would only allow us to film him for fifteen minutes, he had clearly been preparing himself for his interview. He'd hunted down the lyrics to "Adio Kerida" and rehearsed his singing with my mother. When Gisela Fosado turned on the camera, he was clearly moved to be able to sing the song for us, and held his hand to his heart, trembling with emotion. Afterward, he surprised me by walking around the house, giving a kind of tour and pointing out the significance of different objects he'd brought home from his journeys over the years, including a Sephardic cookbook from Istanbul. And I was overjoyed when he agreed to allow us to film him in the Rincon Criollo Restaurant. This was the one setting in which I had dreamed of capturing him, because this is his "little Cuba" and he is always in a good mood there.

It was only later, in the last stages of the editing process, that I realized we needed to balance the Cuban part of my father's scene with the Sephardic part. I also wanted to connect the Cuban cemetery clips, where the Behar name hauntingly surfaces on so many of the tombstones, with cemetery clips in the United States. With a bit of fear, I asked my father if we could film him in the Jewish cemetery in New Jersey where both his parents are buried and where he and my mother wish to be buried when their time comes. He willingly agreed, and I went with Marc Drake, my other key cameraperson and editor, to be filmed with my parents in the cemetery in New Jersey. It was, naturally, for me, an eerie moment, one that reinforces the theme of good-bye, because my parents already know that their final resting place will not be in Cuba but in the United States.

From the beginning, I expected to include my brother Mori in the film. He is such a strong counterpoint to me and is one of the few people who can always make me laugh. When asked to think about being Sephardic, the first association that comes to him is that all the women were very fat. This he then connects jokingly to his dedication to playing the bass, "the big old lady." He hates to travel and can't understand what this anthropology thing is all about. And yet he participates in my film by improvising beautiful piano music, most memorably around "Adio Kerida," joining me in my journey through the medium he most adores.

In an early version of *Adio Kerida,* the movie ended with my brother and then cut to the ocean splashing wildly over the Malecón of Havana. But when I showed this version to colleagues and students at Michigan in spring 2001, I was told that I ought to add a scene in Michigan after the scene with my brother in Philadelphia. I decided to create a Michigan scene that would revolve around a poem I'd written called "Prayer," about fears I've experienced often, of getting lost and not finding my way home.

I thought this scene was finished when the Spanish-language version of *Adio Kerida* premiered at the Havana Film Festival in December 2001. But as I watched it several times in Cuba, I realized the scene wasn't yet complete. I came back to a snowy January in Michigan and realized that this snow and the desolation it evoked for me needed to be added to that last section. I also realized that the story of my own "intermarriage" to my husband, David, needed to be told, even if briefly, at the end, so that viewers could see that I too, like the Jews still on the island, had married out, was that kind of Jew who'd crossed the border.

After working on it for more than two years, I tell myself that *Adio Kerida* is done. It has been enthusiastically received by the Jewish Cuban community in Havana and Miami, and most crucially of all, my father likes it. My mother's eating of the mango on camera (my father calls it her "Mango 101") is now part of the folklore of the Jewish Cuban community, as is my father's line about how he'll return to Cuba when the ferry from Key West is operating again.

It's unusual to see a film that is so thoroughly Cuban and Latino and yet focuses on Jewish identity. As a film that is mostly spoken in Spanish, it has a broad appeal for Latinos. The film has been shown already in two important Latino film festivals, in San Antonio and San Diego, and there is continuing interest in the film among Latino viewers. It hasn't been picked up quite so readily yet by Jewish film festivals (though it was shown in the Detroit Jewish film festival and will be shown in the Boston Jewish film festival), and I can only speculate as to whether this has to do with the Sephardic theme (always of lesser interest to Ashkenazi Jewish Americans, who run the festivals, than films about Israel, the Holocaust, and the ultra-Orthodox Lubavitch), or my touch of irony about Jewish American visits to Cuba, or the inclusion of Afro-Cubans and other Jews of mixed heritage in a film about Jews.

Or perhaps my film is Jewish without being quite Jewish enough. It ends on a decidedly Cuban note, with the trio of Cuban musicians on the famous Havana Malecón improvising a song about the split persona of Ruti/Ruth saying good-bye to Cuba but returning every year to visit the island she left behind before she was old enough to remember it. Maybe this desire for Cuba is something only Jewish Cubans can fully understand. The *kerida*, after all, is Cuba, but "beloved" is spelled in Ladino with a *k* rather than the standard Spanish *querida*, to emphasize that the beloved Cuba is always a fiction, always an imaginary homeland. And I expect that will still be true even if the ferry from Key West to Cuba ever starts operating again.

This essay originally appeared in the *Michigan Quarterly Review's*, special issue "Jewish in America," 41.4 (fall 2002): 651–667.

POR MARJORIE AGOSÍN
TRADUCCIÓN POR LAURA NAKAZAWA

La menora de la alegría

PARA JOSEFINA AGOSÍN

Como un llamado de bosques
O presagios entre las brumas,
Regresas a la tierra
Con tus trajes ocres
Y tus pasos que borran huellas.
Eres tú abuela mía,
Ángel de la memoria
Y de la historia.
Regresas en este año nuevo
Para asegurarme de la perdurabilidad
De la ternura.
Tus ojos se han vuelto espesos como la resina
De los árboles,
Como la miel que cada año degustamos en la
Promesa de los tiempos dulces.

Me gusta sentirme confundida ante tu presencia en la
Ambigüedad de lo que es real.
Pero es real esta memoria mía de tu risa,
De tus brazos como un inmenso candelabro de nueve velas,
El candelabro de la alegría.

Cuánto extrañar tu presencia sobre la tierra,
Cuánto extrañar el beso sobre tus ojos que aleteaban
A mi mano sobre tu corazón que era un trazo de sol,
Una ráfaga de un vientecito inquieto.

Y en este nuevo año donde los culpables siempre piden perdón
Y las víctimas los perdonan,
Yo sólo quiero sentir tu mejilla sobre la mía,
Verte recostada entre los espejos
Como una odalisca cometiendo imprudencias,
Hablando de lo que no se debe decir, pero lo dices,
Quejándote de la poca cortesía de los caballeros de ahora.

Entonces, sólo entonces, untas la miel en la Jalah,
Las nueces, las almendras, el cardamomo,
La buena fortuna de todos los comienzos
Que son el origen de la pasión.
Porque a mi lado estás
Abuela maga,
Cristalina,
Habitando la esperanza
En la tierra ocre
Que es una menora de nueve brazos.

Like a call from the forest
Or omens in the mist,
You return to the earth
With your ochre dresses
And your steps erasing footprints.
You are my grandmother,
Angel of memory
And history.
This new year you return
To assure me of the lasting presence
Of tenderness.
Your eyes have become as thick as tree sap
Or the honey that each year
We taste with the promise
Of sweet times.

I love to feel perplexed before you in the
Ambiguity of what is real.
But it is real, my memory of your smile,

Of your arms like an immense candelabra of nine candles,
The candelabra of joy.

How much I miss your presence on this earth,
How much I miss kissing your twinkling eyes,
My hand on your heart like a ray of sun,
A gust of restless wind.

And in this new year when the guilty ask always for forgiveness
And the victims forgive them,
I just want to feel your cheek over mine.
To see you lying among the mirrors
Like an indiscreet odalisque,
Talking about what must not be said, but you say it,
Complaining about the lack of common courtesy among men of today.

Then, only then, I dip in honey the challah,
Nuts, almonds, and cardamom,
The good fortune of all beginnings
That are the source of passion.
Because you are next to me,
Magician grandmother,
Crystalline,
Inhabiting hope
On this ochre earth
That is a nine-branched menorah.

Index